BRADNER LIBRARY
SCHOOLCRAFT COLLEGE
18600 HAGGERTY ROAD
LIVONIA, MICHIGAN 48152

LA 1311.82 .S439 2005
Shibata, Masako, 1961-
Japan and Germany under
‎eU.S. occupation

Japan and Germany under the U.S. Occupation

STUDIES OF MODERN JAPAN

Series Editor: Edward R. Beauchamp, University of Hawaii

Studies of Modern Japan is a multidisciplinary series that consists primarily of original studies on a broad spectrum of topics dealing with Japan since the Meiji restoration of 1868. Additionally, the series aims to bring back into print classic works that shed new light on contemporary Japan. In all cases, the goal is to publish the best scholarship available, by both established and rising scholars in the field, in order to better understand Japan and the Japanese during the modern period and into the future.

Editorial Advisory Board

William K. Cummings, George Washington University
Sin'ichi Kitaoka, Tokyo University
Sharon Minichiello, University of Hawaii
Masato Miyachi, Tokyo University
T. J. Pempel, University of California, Berkeley
Merry White, Boston University

Titles in the Series

Jews in the Japanese Mind: The History and Uses of a Cultural Stereotype, by David G. Goodman and Masanori Miyazawa
Chōshū in the Meiji Restoration, by Albert M. Craig
Japan and the Security of Asia, by Louis D. Hayes
The Web of Power: Japanese and German Development Cooperation Policy, by Kozo Kato
Unhappy Soldier: Hino Ashihei and Japanese World War II Literature, by David M. Rosenfeld
In the Shadow of the Miracle: The Japanese Economy since the End of High-Speed Growth, by Arthur J. Alexander
Spanning Japan's Modern Century: The Memoirs of Hugh Borton, by Hugh Borton
Agony of Choice: Matsuoka Yosuke and the Rise and Fall of the Japanese Empire, 1880–1946, by David J. Lu
A Yankee in Hokkaido: The Life of William Smith Clark, by John M. Maki
Roadblocks on the Information Highway: The IT Revolution in Japanese Education, edited by Jane M. Bachnik
Limits to Power: Asymmetric Dependence and Japanese Foreign Aid Policy, by Akitoshi Miyashita
Constructing Opportunity: American Women Educators in Early Meiji Japan, by Elizabeth Eder
The Return of the Amami Islands: The Reversion Movement and U.S.–Japan Relations, by Robert D. Eldridge
Life and Resources in America, by Mori Arinori; edited, annotated, and introduced by John E. Van Sant
Japan and Germany under the U.S. Occupation: A Comparative Analysis of the Post-War Education Reform, by Masako Shibata

Japan and Germany under the U.S. Occupation

A Comparative Analysis of Post-War Education Reform

Masako Shibata

LEXINGTON BOOKS

A Division of
ROWMAN & LITTLEFIELD PUBLISHERS, INC.
Lanham • Boulder • New York • Toronto • Oxford

LEXINGTON BOOKS

A division of Rowman & Littlefield Publishers, Inc.
A wholly owned subsidiary of The Rowman & Littlefield Publishing Group, Inc.
4501 Forbes Boulevard, Suite 200
Lanham, MD 20706

PO Box 317
Oxford
OX2 9RU, UK

Copyright © 2005 by Lexington Books

All rights reserved. No part of this publication may be reproduced, stored in a retrieval system, or transmitted in any form or by any means, electronic, mechanical, photocopying, recording, or otherwise, without the prior permission of the publisher.

British Library Cataloguing in Publication Information Available

Library of Congress Cataloging-in-Publication Data

Shibata, Masako, 1961–
  Japan and Germany under the U.S. occupation : a comparative analysis of post-war education reform / Masako Shibata.
    p. cm. — (Studies of modern Japan)
  Includes bibliographical references and index.
  ISBN 0-7391-1149-3 (cloth : alk. paper)
  1. Education—Japan—History—20th century. 2. Education—Germany—History—20th century. 3. Reconstruction (1939–1951)—Japan. 4. Reconstruction (1939–1951)—Germany. 5. Comparative education. I. Title. II. Series.
LA1311.82.S439 2005
370'.952'09044—dc   2005006550

Printed in the United States of America

∞™ The paper used in this publication meets the minimum requirements of American National Standard for Information Sciences—Permanence of Paper for Printed Library Materials, ANSI/NISO Z39.48-1992.

I dedicate this book to my parents,
Kisaburo and Yoshiko Shibata,
persons of wisdom and integrity.

Contents

List of Tables and Figure	ix
Foreword	xi
Acknowledgments	xv
List of Abbreviations	xvii
1 Introduction	1

PART I

2 State Formation, the State Education System, and Elite Formation in Meiji Japan	17
3 State Formation, the State Education System, and Elite Formation in the German *Kaiserreich*	35
Conclusion of Part I	55

PART II

4 The Occupation Reform in Japan, 1945-1952	59
5 The Occupation Reform in the US Zone of Germany, 1945-1949	107

PART III

6 Conclusion	161

Appendix A: The Imperial Rescript on Education [1890]	175
Appendix B: Archival Documents	177
German Glossary	179
Japanese Glossary	181
Bibliography	183
Index	203
About the Author	213

List of Tables and Figure

TABLES

Table 2.1	The Enrollment Ratio of Cohorts in Primary, Secondary, and Higher Education in Japan, 1875-1905	21
Table 2.2	The Experience of Overseas Study of Japanese Professors, 1877-1893	25
Table 4.1	The Classification of Purged Persons within the Japanese Ministries, 1945	69
Table 4.2	The Number of Higher-Education Institutions in Japan, 1940-1951	91
Table 5.1	The Trend of Denazification: Percentage Distribution of Special-Branch Findings by Regions in the US Zone, November 1945-February 1946 (%)	115

FIGURE

Figure 2.1	The Structure of Japanese Higher Education in the 1890s	26

Foreword

This book tells a fine story. It is, for an academic book, a good read: the rapid nineteenth-century development of Germany and Japan and later efforts to construct new education systems. The book can be read for these narratives alone. But, in addition, the text slices brilliantly through three strands of work in comparative education, illuminating all three and posing fresh questions for contemporary comparative education.

One of the revitalized areas in comparative education is now the theme of "transfer," that is, the (usually deliberate) movement of educational ideas and practices from one country to another. This is a classic theme in comparative education, started as early as 1817 by Marc Antonie Jullien in Paris who wanted to create a "positive science" of comparative education that would permit the best educational practices in one county (e.g., Prussia) to be moved to another (e.g., France). The theme is captured again powerfully in 1900 in Sir Michael Sadler's famous lecture: How may we learn anything of practical value from the study of foreign educational system? Currently many ministers of education and the international educational agencies are optimistic about the answer, though even they are beginning to pay some attention to Sadler's complex response to his own question.

Currently the theme of transfer is attracting some of the best new writing in comparative education, notably by David Phillips in Oxford, Jürgen Schriewer in Berlin, and Gita Steiner-Khamsi in New York. What are the politics of attraction, the referential education systems, and the legitimations for foreign educational borrowing, and how can we avoid the naiveté of several scholars in the effective and efficient schools movement—that doing comparative education was a pretty simple exercise, really?

Masako Shibata contributes to this literature in a fascinating way. She raises the transfer question in its extreme form: what happens during an "occupation"? Surely here the rules of transfer are simple: the occupiers decide, and the defeated accept. The massive political power which comes not merely with armies but also control of all of the levels of the state means that a rather precise and literal transfer, like a child's transfer sticker, will occur. Place, wet, and peel off. A very close approximation of the original picture will be visible in a new site. Here analyses of why it was not like that in Japan or in parts of occupied Germany after 1945 are offered: there were marked differences in the acceptance and rejection process in the two societies, not least because what was aimed at in both societies was the construction or reconstruction of liberal democratic polities. Given that, there was—even in these extreme conditions of Occupation—room for maneuver.

The second classic theme in comparative education which the work of Dr. Shibata illuminates indirectly is the work on colonialism. Martin Carnoy, Robert Arnove, Gail Kelly, and Phillip Altbach, as well as the dependency theoreticians of Latin America, revitalized this theme in the 1970s, and the work continues most fruitfully on contemporary work in post-colonialism. Carnoy's title for his classic text *Education as Culture Imperialism* captured one of the core themes in the literature: the deliberate construction of different educated identities, new moral maps, and fresh definitions of an imagined future.

Shibata pulls out the implications of this theme in the Occupation periods in her two societies brilliantly. She shows how the American reform and reconstruction efforts were far more strenuous—and far more directly aimed at alteration of a culture—in Japan than in parts of West Germany. The themes of religion, "the University" and notions of *Bildung* permitted remarkable resistance in parts of Germany to the American reform efforts. The temporarily colonized had major cultural and educational capital which was used as isolation devices to block reforms which they did not like. Occasionally there was a remarkable cultural counterattack, less readily available to the Japanese. The aggressive Japanese counterattack had to wait for Japan's economic recovery and the new cultural confidence, which came with that, and the Asian values debate on the 1980s and early 1990s. Perhaps colonists, even temporary colonists, can be classified on the basis of what they judge to be evil in the societies they occupy. What needs eradication? The removal of a few extremists from powerful positions in politics or the bureaucracy–, a regime-change? Or a redefinition of a civilization?

The third theme in the classical canon of comparative education which Shibata revitalizes is the off-and-on debate about the role of the historical work in good comparative studies. This theme has quite a strong corpus of work, notably the use of history by scholars such as Margaret Archer, Andy Green, Hans Muller, Fritz Ringer, and Theda Scokpol. Very recently, Andreas Kazamias has again reasserted the principle of the significance of a historical perspective—as much of comparative education tips into an analysis of contemporary policy (including how to move up international league tables of measured educational achievement).

Shibata does not make an abstract case for a historical discussion in comparative education: she delivers an example of the crucial explanatory power of historical contextualisation. The struggles of the Occupation period, and the way these struggles turned out, make sense only against the long-term modernity project of Germany and Japan with their roots in the changing class structures, religious patterns, political systems, and educational forms of the late nineteeth and early twentieth centuries. Much of the deep coherence of her study—and its place of permanence in the comparative literature—comes from the historical analysis she developed in her Ph.D. on which this book is based.

Overall, this book is a fascinating read and a text which has powerful contemporary implications.

Robert Cowen
Professor of Education
The Institute of Education
University of London

Acknowledgments

This book was made possible by the unfailingly thoughtful support extended to me by David Phillips. He opened a door to my long academic journey, which was started when he introduced me to his fine library on the Allied Occupation. I owe much to his invitation to work within the traditions of the English academic world, fascination with which has laid the basis of my intellectual approach to this study.

I would also like to express my profound gratitude to Robert Cowen. His guidance and personal encouragement have benefited me throughout my academic life in London. Without his incisive criticisms and the breadth of his scholarly approach to comparative education I would have never come to be fascinated by this field of study let alone attempted to complete this work. I feel fortunate to have received such support from my *Doktorvater*.

I can never forget the warm welcome offered during my research in Germany by Professor Jürgen Schriewer, Dr. Karl-Heinz Füssl, and Ms. Martine Tarrieux at Humboldt University and by Professor Gerd Hoff and Professor Peter Drewek at Free University Berlin. There I was also privileged to enjoy a cordial invitation from Professor Jürgen Kocka at the Friedrich Meinecke Institute.

For this work I am also indebted to a number of people in Japan for their insightful advice. All of them responded so favorably to my request for discussion. I am particularly grateful to Professor Ikuo Amano, Professor Masao Terasaki, and Professor Gary Hoichi Tsuchimochi, who generously proffered the results of their previous research to me.

My sincere gratitude goes to all the other people who have helped me with this study by reading the draft and discussing it with intellectual rigor.

List of Abbreviations

ACJ: Allied Council for Japan
AG: Adjutant General
AGTS: Adjutant General Top Secret
BCOF: British Commonwealth Occupation Force
CAC: Civil Administration Committee
CASA: Civil Affairs Staging Area
CATS: Civil Affairs Training School
CC: Control Council
CCG (BE): Control Commission for Germany (British Element)
CI&E: Civil Information & Education Section
CDU: *Christlich-Demokratische Union* [Christian Democratic Union]
CSU: *Christlich-Soziale Union* [Christian Social Union]
E&CR: Education and Cultural Relations Division
E&RA: Education and Religious Affairs Branch (later "Division")
FEC: Far Eastern Commission
G-5: Civil Affairs Section (of the Military Government)
GHQ: General Headquarters (of SCAP)
GS: Government Section (of SCAP)
HICOG: Office of the High Commissioner (US), Germany
IA&C: Internal Affairs and Communications Division
ICD: Information Control Division
JCS: Joint Chiefs of Staff
JEC: Japanese Educators Committee [*Nihongawa Kyoiku-ka Iinkai*]
JERC: Japan Education Reform Committee [*Kyoiku Sasshin Iinkai* (*Kyoiku Sasshin Shingikai*)]

NIER: National Institute for Educational Policy Research [*Kokuritsu Kyoiku (Seisaku) Kenkyusho*]
NSDAP: *Nationalsozialistische Deutsche Arbeiterpartei* [National Socialist German Workers' Party]
NSDStB: *Nationalsozialistischer Deutscher Studentenbund* [National-Socialist German Student Association]
OMGBY: Office of Military Government for Bavaria
OMGHE: Office of Military Government for Hesse
OMGUS: Office of Military Government for Germany of the US
PH&W: Public Health and Welfare Division
POLAD: Political Advisers' Office
PWC: Post-War Programs Committee
SCAP: Supreme Commander for the Allied Powers
SCAPIN: SCAP Instructions
SHAEF: Supreme Headquarters, Allied Expeditionary Forces
SPD: *Sozialdemokratische Partei Deutschlands* [Social Democratic Party]
SWNCC: State-War-Navy Coordinating Committee
UPC: University Planning Committee
USEMG: United States Education Mission to Germany
USEMJ: United States Education Mission to Japan
USEMJ2: Second United States Education Mission to Japan
USFET: US Forces European Theater

Chapter One

Introduction

1. THE MAJOR FRAMEWORK

This book is about the deconstruction and reconstruction of the education system in Japan and Germany during the US Military Occupation after World War Two. The patterns of the reforms of the Occupation period were different in the two countries: in Japan (1945-1952), a large-scale education reform was undertaken. Along with many other political and social reforms, the ideas and the system of pre-1945 Japanese education were largely changed within the period of the Occupation. The US authorities were actually surprised by their "achievements," which were more than they had anticipated before their landing in Japan.[1] In the US-controlled zone of Germany (1945-1949), in contrast, most of the traditional patterns of education were maintained. The US officers in Germany regarded the result of their attempt as a "tragic failure."[2]

This book explores the genesis of these distinct differences. In this book, it is attempted to test that the major deconstruction of the education system in Japan and the retention of much of it in Germany largely resulted from the enthusiasm of Japanese leaders for the absorption of foreign educational models and the strong affirmation of indigenous educational patterns as a model by German leaders. It is also attempted to show that these different reactions during the Occupation need to be understood in a complex sociological, cultural, and historical way. The roots of the reactions stretch back into the period of state formation in Japan and Germany and the ways in which the core political agenda of state formation shaped the role of the university and the pattern of elite formation. Thus, the book analyses developments in Meiji

Japan (1868-1912) and the German *Kaiserreich* (1871-1918), before concentrating on the Occupation period.

I have conducted this research during my graduate studies in comparative education in the Institute of Education. Most of my studies there were historically based and about the relationship between the state and education. I have investigated how education played a political role within the process of state formation. The political role of education seemed to me to be particularly overt in Japan. The formation of a modern state in the *Meiji Ishin*[3] (Meiji Restoration)—the state political project of the modernization and Westernization of Japan from 1868—went hand in hand with the development of the education system. After the defeat of the country in World War Two, this political framework was seriously reconsidered. Japanese education experienced enormous changes, which have been maintained mostly until today. Thus I was drawn to this attempt of a historical positioning of the education reform during the Occupation, not least because of my acknowledgment about the relevance of the study to discussions on educational issues in contemporary Japan.

My preliminary view was that changes during the Occupation stemmed from the pattern of Japan's development since the *Meiji Ishin*. To test this view, the Occupation in Germany seemed to be appropriate as an area for comparison. From 1868, Japan adopted many aspects of the political system and the technology of Germany, as well as of other Western countries. From the last third of the nineteenth century, the pattern of political and economic development in Japan and Germany seemed to be similar.

I conducted research in England, Germany, and Japan. Research in Japan, in particular, re-stimulated my original interest in the historical roots of the changes in the Japanese education system under the Occupation. Especially, the retrospective statements by those Americans and Japanese who were involved in the Occupation reforms brought me back to my initial question: how could the leaders of a nation have so much faith in ideas and values developed in foreign countries? Even some of the Americans raised the same question—they were somewhat puzzled about the ready acceptance of their proposals by Japanese leaders. The wide-ranging powers of the Americans in Japan may be a basis for such absorption. The defeat of the nation in World War Two was shocking to the Japanese, too. East Asia, unlike Europe, had no history of recurrent international wars. Probably the Japanese did not know how to cope with the unprecedented foreign Military Occupation. But were these the reasons which fully explain the "puzzling" reactions of the Japanese during the Occupation? This question started this study.

2. THE SOURCES OF RESEARCH AND THEIR TREATMENT

For this comparative study, research sources were sought in the English, Japanese, and German languages. The analysis of the Occupation is largely based on archival research. Original documents on the Occupation in Japan were sought in the National Diet Library, which had the largest collection of Occupation materials. Among the collections, the SCAP Instruction for the Imperial Japanese Government (SCAPIN) and the microfilm record of the Far Eastern Commissions (FEC) keep the details of the overall allied policies for Japan. The political and economic reconstruction of Japan and Germany are recorded in Post-World War II Foreign Policy Planning: State Department Records of Harley A. Notter, 1939-1945 (Notter File). The Joseph Trainor Collection (Hoover Institute, Stanford University) and the two-volume microfiche of Education Reform in Japan, 1945-1952 (ERJ1 & 2) embrace most of the archives on the education reforms during the Occupation in Japan. The discussions on the education reforms by leading Japanese educators were comprehensively noted in the thirteen-volume minutes of *Kyoiku Sasshin Iinkai, Kyoiku Sasshin Shingikai Kaigiroku*. The audio record of interviews with the Americans and the Japanese who were in charge of the education reform was found in the National Institute for Educational Policy Research (NIER) and Meisei University.

The documents on the Occupation in Germany were predominantly drawn from the Bundesarchiv Koblenz. The archives of the period of the *Kaiserreich* and of the Nazi regime were sought in the Bundesarchiv Berlin. Along with the materials in Koblenz, some documents found in the National Archive Public Record Office in Kew and the British Library in London were also valuable. Several pamphlets collected in the Nazi *Gedenkstätten* in Berlin were also used. *OMGUS-Handbuch* and *Documents on Germany under Occupation 1945-1954* are useful sources of research on the overall American scheme of the Occupation in Germany.

The orthography adopted for Japanese terms and names is the common Hepburn system. The long vowels in Japanese names, pronounced in actual intonation, are drawn without special marks, e.g., Tokyo instead of Tōkyo and Ito instead of Itō. The names of Japanese persons in the main text are given in indigenous order, i.e., surnames first. To keep the liveliness of statements and the specificity of individual terms, many expressions are retained in the original languages. They are translated into English in the main text, with some exceptions which seem to be better dealt with within endnotes. These translations are mine, unless otherwise specified. However, some compromises had to be made for clarity and simplicity. Some names of official institutions are, therefore, translated uniformly. For example, the *Staatsministerium für Unterricht und Kultus* in Bavaria, the *Ministerium für Kultus und Unterricht* in Hesse, the *Kultusministerium* in Württemberg-Baden, the *Senator für Schulen und Erziehung* in Bremen, and the *Monbusho* in Japan are all named the "Ministry of Education."

3. EXISTING STUDIES

Despite the wealth of these primary research sources on the Occupation, there had been no comparative interpretation of the education reforms in the two countries, as Beate Rosenzweig herself points out, before her book *Erziehung zur Demokratie?* was published in 1998. A comparative study of Bernd Martin, *Japan and Germany in the Modern World*, focuses on the similar processes of the national development of Japan and Germany from the nineteenth century which, according to Martin, had acted as a prelude to their military aggressions and their defeats in World War Two. He traces the origin of what he calls "fatal affinities" back to blindly adopting Prussian military structure in the political system of the Meiji regime.[4] Martin, like many other German authors such as Rosenzweig, sees strong continuities in the conservative aspects of pre- and post-1945 Japanese society, compared with the situation of *Stunde Null*, or zero hour, in post-1945 Germany. Although his analysis is concentrated on the political and economic systems in the two countries and, deliberately, the unilateral influence of Germany on Japanese national development, his book offers an important comparative analysis of the two societies.

Separate studies on the Occupation reforms in Japan and Germany are many. The edited work by Robert Wolfe, *Americans as Proconsuls*, offers a collection of individual studies on the Occupation in Japan and Germany submitted as conference proceedings. They, however, propose no comprehensive comparative analysis of the two Occupations. Along with other conference proceedings published in Thomas Burkman's edited collection *The Occupation of Japan: Educational and Social Reform*, these studies are, nonetheless, useful secondary sources.

Gary Hoichi Tsuchimochi offers detailed research on the United States' education mission to Japan in his book *Education Reform in Postwar Japan*. As seen in *6-3 sei kyoiku no tanjo*, most of his work, which is based on archival research, concentrated on testing the ideas that the Americans had only a small commitment to imposing their educational patterns on Japan and that the Japanese offered their own initiatives for education reforms. Based on acute analysis about the administrative aspect of the reform, Eiichi Suzuki also points out in his book *Nihon senryo to kyoiku kaikaku* the strong impact of Japanese initiatives on the major changes during the Occupation. The ten volumes of Tokiomi Kaigo and Masao Terasaki's *Sengo Nihon no kyoiku kaikaku* are also based on extensive archival research, in addition to analysis of the historical development of the modern Japanese education system as an important basis for the education reforms during the Occupation.

A number of accounts, on the other hand, stress the strong political pressure of the Occupation authorities imposed on the Japanese government and the Ministry of Education. Among them, Hitashi Osaki's book, *Daigaku Kaikaku 1945-1999*, and Seishiro Sugihara's work, *Nihon no Shinto/Bukkyo to seikyobnunri soshite shukyo-kyoiku*, argue that the radical changes brought into Japanese education during the Occupation ought to be understood with the impact of American imposition rather than as the product of "Japanese liberalism" developed earlier.

Among the abundant studies on the education reforms in occupied Germany, Manfred Heinemann's edited collection *Umerziehung und Wiederaufbau* also offers individual studies on the education reforms in Germany. The work provides some comparative analyses of the reforms within the four occupied zones.

Rosenzweig's *Erziehung zur Demokratie?*—the first comprehensive comparative study on the education reform in occupied Japan and Germany—illustrates the "authoritarian" patterns of pre-war German and Japanese education and describes how they were or were not changed on the basis of the Deweyan model of American democratic education. In its main argument, her book addresses contradictions between the democratic education system of post-war (West) Germany, where the American democratization had failed, and persistently undemocratic post-war Japanese education, whose system had been largely reconstructed on the American model during the Occupation. She concludes her work with a discussion about the "continuity" and "discontinuity" within the education systems and practices of post-war Japan and West Germany. As she puts it:

Die japanische Nation habe insgesamt keinen Respekt für die Ideale der Humanität und der Individualität entwickelt. Die gegenwärtige Gesellschaft sei infolge dessen noch weitgehend feudalistisch strukturiert. Dies träfe insbesondere auch auf die Verhältnisse in den Schulen zu, in denen die Lehrer oftmals das Verhalten von Feudalfürsten an den Tag legten.[5]

Despite her careful illustration of the development of pre-1945 Japanese education, Rosenzweig has probably misread the educational environments and society of present Japan in discussing the continuity between the pre- and post-1945 Japanese education systems. Contradictions brought about by what

John Montgomery called the "Artificial Revolution" have a more complex form in the actual Japanese school in the post-war period. In the new education system which Japanese leaders had willingly reconstructed with or without understanding the ideas of American democracy, "democracy" has been implemented in a post-war Japanese society within which, as Rosenzweig indicates, traditional social values are still prevalent especially among the older generations. Her phrase about "feudal lords" in the Japanese school is an obsolete idea. The following figures released in 1998 are no longer striking for many Japanese: over 80% of lower-secondary schools have students with a record of school delinquency; 36,396 cases of bullying in schools were reported; 90% of suspensions from school were due to some sort of student violence, of which about 40% were toward teachers; and 40% of the school teachers on sick leave were affected by nervous depression.[6]

Indeed, all these studies of the Occupation reforms and debates which stressed "continuity" and "discontinuity" or "imposed" or "non-imposed" arguments were stimulating. Yet, the argument about the crucial impact of the democratic "traditions" from the inter-war period or even earlier on the reforms in occupied Germany and Japan is not fully explicable, especially if one looks back upon the period of pre-Nazi Germany. As was well known, Germany had made various attempts to reform its educational system before the Occupation and continued to seek a more democratic educational system after the withdrawal of the Allies. From the 1950s, the American influence on education began to take a firm hold in West Germany and, as Hansfried Kellner and Hans-Georg Soeffner rightly claim, it became Americanized more than any other Western society, as one can see startling resemblance between the US and Germany in their political, economic, and social systems and cultures, including in education.[7] But the period between 1945 and 1949 was, for German leaders, complete interregnum as a sovereign state, and the occupiers had to be detached from the laws of the occupying territory as articulated in international law.

Thus my thinking moved toward a different interpretation from existing studies. This book discusses the continuous ambivalence between indigenous and exogenous aspects which have both been important in Japan as influences on the development of Japanese society and education. The radical transitions in the last third of the nineteenth century and the middle of the twentieth century have a historical link. There is a continuity, but of a different sort, which draws most attention of the book: the tension between indigenous socio-cultural values and exogenous ideas held by leaders who guided Japan to radical transformation. To begin opening up this theme, it is possible to offer a number of arguments which are developed and tested throughout the book.

4. THE CENTRAL ARGUMENTS

There are two central arguments which will be tested. First, during the Occupation the reactions of the educational leaders in occupied Japan and Germany had a decisive impact on reforms proposed by the Americans. In Japan, the major changes were largely based on the acceptance of American reform schemes by the Japanese. In Germany, the retention of the pre-1945 system resulted from the rejection of foreign educational patterns by the Germans. Differences in the political power structure among the Occupation authorities in Japan and Germany, as well as differences in the views of these two countries held by the Americans, also had significant implications. However, these political and cultural power struggles were affected by the ideas about the adoption of the American educational patterns by Japanese and German leaders.

The second argument is that these different reactions of the Japanese and German leaders had long-standing historical and sociological causes. These causes are investigated through a comparison of selected aspects of the historical experience of the two societies. That is, it will be argued, the role of the university and the pattern of elite formation, traceable back to the period of the formation of Meiji Japan and the *Kaiserreich*, created the conditions for the different approaches of the Japanese and German leaders to the adoption of foreign educational patterns during the Occupation. In other words, the way in which elites were formed in the university within the process of state formation in Japan and Germany in the nineteenth century played an important role in the disputes about education reform in the middle of the twentieth century, after World War Two.

To test these arguments the book has the following structure.

5. THE STRUCTURE AND THE LINES OF ANALYSIS

The book has six chapters. Chapters 2 to 5 are analytical and narrative chapters, and chapter 6 is a conclusion. Chapters 2 and 3, on nineteenth-century Japan and Germany, make up part I. The purpose of part I is to investigate the patterns of elite formation and the role of the university, both of which were shaped by the process of state formation in the two countries. Chapter 2 begins with an analysis of the political framework of state formation in Japan. It then explores the development of the university and elites within the state education system in Meiji Japan. Chapter 3 offers an account of the *Kaiserreich*, following the same themes as chapter 2. Chapters 4 and 5, making up part II, describe the characteristics of the Occupation as a whole in Japan and

Germany, respectively. Chapter 6 discusses the differences in education reforms in occupied Japan and Germany and the relationships between these differences and the earlier processes of the formation of the modern state and elite in the two countries. What holds these chapters together is a number of lines of analysis.

The investigations of the book are historical because of the focus on the slow genesis of the reasons for the different reactions to proposed reforms by the Japanese and the Germans. The investigations are also sociological, because they analyze some powerful relationships between major social agents—the state, the university, and culture—and the typical modes of action of a specific social group.[8] The argument thus has a number of complex layers. This section sets out these layers, first, by giving a synoptic account of state formation in Japan and Germany, a theme which is fully revisited in the following chapters. Second, the possible causalities of the relationship of the process of state formation, the role of the university, and elite formation are sketched.

State Formation

The basis of a state is autonomous power.[9] This power is concentrated in central political machinery and is exerted in social institutions within a given geographic territory. The state forms and transmits an ideology, as the central value system of the state, to legitimize its autonomous power. Overall, a high level of monopolization of political power marks the modern state. It is possible to illustrate these themes in the cases of Japan and Germany.

In the last third of the nineteenth century after the Western threat to the territorial integrity of the country, the Meiji regime established a central state bureaucracy for the first time in Japanese history. The vision of the Meiji regime was most clearly articulated in the national ideology of *Fukoku-Kyohei* (to enrich the nation and strengthen the military) and *Sonno-Joi* (to expel barbarians and revere the *Tenno* [Emperor]). Immediately after its seizure of power, the new Meiji regime took control of education as a means of disseminating the new national ideology.

The German cultural domains were finally brought together as a political realm under the Prussian king in 1871. The victory of the Prussian policy of *Kleindeutsch* and the consequent expulsion of Austria made it clear where "Germany" was. The Prussian hegemony derived its legitimacy from its powerful military, which had defeated neighboring countries, and from the clarification of the German political boundary. Prussian hegemony was also legitimized by its policy of retaining much of the traditional social order in German society and an emphasis on German cultural identity as the fulcrum of the political unity of the German states.

In this book, the phenomenon of state formation is looked at sociologically. Specifically, the processes of state formation in Japan and Germany are analyzed by concentrating on the following aspects of state formation: the source of the legitimacy of the state; the impact of economic action, in particular industrialization, social transformation, and the development of social institutions—inter alia, education.[10]

State Formation, the Role of the University, and Elite Formation

First, in trying to understand the different reactions of the Japanese and Germans to the US Occupation, the historical relationship between the process of state formation and the political framing of the "underpinning" agenda of the two states is explored. In Japan, the Western threat to national sovereignty and economic backwardness provided the starting point for the formation of a modern state. The central political agenda was to catch up with the Western powers, while maintaining national sovereignty. The Meiji government aimed at political consolidation through the establishment of a modern state bureaucracy and the strengthening of the national economy through industrialization. Thus the goals of the Meiji regime were pragmatic ones. These double goals were pursued deliberately by absorbing Western knowledge. Thus a "powerful modern Japan" was sought within a state political project of modernization and Westernization. Moreover, the intensity of the national crisis inclined the government to adopt meritocratic principles. This loosened social stratification. The Meiji government derived its legitimacy from the destruction of what may be loosely called the ancien régime and the construction of modern society.

In Germany, the long-desired political unification of the German states was the incentive for the national unification. The formation of a modern state in Germany was realized under Prussian hegemony. Prussia stressed the retention of its traditional social order: "God, king, aristocracy, army, and bureaucracy"—a conservative policy for the retention of Christianity, the monarchy, and a class society. This conservative policy of the *Kaiserreich* was legitimized by its power to maintain the unification of Germany. Late industrial development led Germany to state-driven industrialization, as in Japan. However, the backwardness of the German economy was not so pronounced, and meritocratic principles did not gain much ground in German society. An increase in social mobility based on meritocratic principles was not desired by the state. An important consequence of the German pattern of late industrialization was the almost simultaneous occurrence of the social ascendance of the middle class and the rise of socialist labor movements at the turn of the twentieth century. This resulted in the political and social inclination of the German middle class toward conservative policies. The core political agenda of the *Kaiserreich* centered on the maintenance of the German-speaking domains as a political and economic unit within the existing social stratification system.

Second, it is suggested that the political agenda of each state framed the role of the university. In Japan, the university was established during the process of state formation. The establishment of the university was an important state project to achieve political and economic goals: the provision of capable bureaucrats for the state and technical experts for industry. Regardless of their future occupations, most students were to pursue their learning through the absorption of Western knowledge in the university. Moreover, due to meritocratic principles and the still weak national economy, the state gave priority to an apex institution, Tokyo Imperial University, which predominantly produced state bureaucrats. The state also gave privileges to other universities and controlled them, according to the political priorities of the state. This policy of differentiation brought about academic demarcations among institutions which were positioned within a hierarchy of higher education. In Japan, the intellectual development of institutions was therefore uneven, unlike universities in Germany. Within this structure, intellectual interaction between institutions was severely hindered. The Japanese concept of academic freedom worked within a higher education system which was stratified by this state policy of differentiation.

In contrast, the German university had developed prior to the formation of a modern state and industrialization. The traditional role of producing capable bureaucrats was continued. Along with the development of the state bureaucracy and the national economy in the *Kaiserreich*, the state increasingly controlled the university. The conservative policy of the *Kaiserreich* shaped the role of the university in generating political loyalty to the state. Culturally as well, the university acted as a guardian of the traditional social order and indigenous German cultural traditions. A conservative socio-political atmosphere in the *Kaiserreich* created a basis for the assimilation of the political ideas and socio-cultural values of the aristocracy by middle-class students in the university. Thus, the universities in Germany shared a similar role as well as similar academic standards throughout the nation. The long-established principle of *Lehrfreiheit und Lernfreiheit* and the tradition of *Kulturhoheit* encouraged the vigorous intellectual interactions of academics and students. This promoted open and fair competition among institutions relatively free of state intervention.

Third, the relationship between the pattern of elite formation and the role of the university is analyzed. In general, both in Japan and Germany, those who were educated in the university were extremely small in number. Before university education became open to a wide range of the population, a university degree was an important benchmark as the highest educational qualification. Such persons shared a number of the aspects of "an elite."

An elite, by definition, is identified as a minority group with a number of common characteristics. Elites form groups within society on the grounds of similar and "allegedly" superior capacities.[11] Their collective claim to such superior capacities brings about—in principle—a shared sense of esprit de corps and consequent group cohesion. Because of their alleged capacities and group cohesion, they exert political power or social influence.

However, this social group, whose concept is drawn from Weber's "status group" in this book, can be distinguished from a "class," though some of the earliest theoreticians of elites failed to do this.[12] By status group, Weber meant a plurality of persons who, within a larger group, successfully claim a special social esteem and possibly also status monopolies.[13] Moreover, the members of a status group share "a common style of life" created by upbringing and education, independently of wealth. With the rise of modern capitalism, the concept of status group has been played down—vis-à-vis that of class—in theories about social stratification systems. Nonetheless, status groups as a form of social organization still affect the distribution of political power and social influence in a society. An elite based on the allegations of intellectual superiority derived from high levels of educational attainment is also self-conscious. Often such an educated elite is seen as "the intellectuals" in a society and on that basis make claims to power and influence within it.[14] Zygmunt Bauman said that "Definitions of the intellectual are many and diverse. They have, however, one trait in common, which makes them also different from all other definitions: they are all self-definitions." This type of elite—which Bauman identifies in diverse professions in French society but generally in Germany only among university academics and state bureaucrats—in theory draws a boundary around its own identity as "the same rare species."[15]

However, in practice in Japan, the cohesion of university-educated people as a status group was—it will be argued—relatively weak. The academic hierarchy of the Japanese university and restricted academic mobility hampered the overall development of the esprit de corps of university-educated people across institutions. Furthermore, the emphasis on the principles of meritocracy in university education and a strong inclination toward Western ideas among the educated people lessened their valuation of the traditional social order and socio-cultural traditions. Consequently, there was an ideological gap between the elite and the rest of the Japanese.

In contrast and also in practice—it will be argued—the German *Bildungsbürgertum* was recognised as a status group, as an elite, within German society.

The group enjoyed a sense of esprit de corps which was broadly shared across institutions. Shaped by the conservative policy of the *Kaiserreich*, university-educated people, including an increasing number of middle-class students, came to share traditional socio-cultural values with the aristocracy.

Given these backgrounds, the historical and sociological causes of the reactions of these Japanese and German elites are, therefore, sought within three different characteristics of those elites—group cohesion, views about indigenous socio-cultural values, and the ideological consistency of the elite—as these were shaped by the process of state formation and the role of the university. During the Occupation, Japanese leaders showed a more receptive approach to foreign ideas or at least did not offer powerful counter-arguments. In contrast, the Germans showed strong resistance toward American proposals and strongly reaffirmed indigenous educational patterns. Their arguments were consistent throughout the US zone, notwithstanding some differences in the *Länder* of the Western zone. How, in detail, did this happen? What were the processes at work in these two societies? These themes are addressed in the following investigation about the patterns of the formation of the modern state in Japan and Germany in the last third of the nineteenth century.

NOTES

1. Joseph Trainor, *Educational Reform in Occupied Japan: Trainor's Memoir* (Tokyo: Meiji University Press, 1983), 119.
2. G. Ziemer, "Our Educational Failure in Germany," *American Mercury* (June, 1946), 726.
3. After the *Meiji Ishin*, Japan adopted the system of chronological divisions based the reign of the *Tenno* [Emperor]. The period of Meiji (which means "Enlightened Rule") was during the reign of the Meiji *Tenno* (1868-1912), followed by the thrones of the Taisho (1912-1926), Showa (1926-1989), and present Heisei (1989-) *Tenno*s. From the Meiji period, the throne was taken over by the first son of the *Tenno* after his death.
4. Bernd Martin, *Japan and Germany in the Modern World* (Oxford: Berghahn Books, 1995), 40. For the account of Meiji Japan's adoption in education, see: Masako Shibata, "Educational Borrowing in Japan in the Meiji and Post-War Eras," in *Educational Borrowing: Historical perspectives*, ed. David Phillips and Kimberly Ochs (Oxford: Symposium Books, 2005).
5. "On the whole, the Japanese nation has developed no respect for the ideals of humanity and individualism. Because of this, the present society is still structured largely in a feudalistic way. This situation would especially be the case in the area of relationships in schools within which teachers often display the behavior of feudal lords." Beate Rosenzweig, *Erziehung zur Demokratie?* (Stuttgart: Franz Steiner, 1998), 202.
6. Ministry of Education, Japan, *Waga-kuni no bunkyo seisaku: Susumu 'kyoiku kaikaku'* (Tokyo: Ministry of Education, 1999), 83, 254-58; "Koritsu chugakko no 80% ni fu-toko-sei," *Naigai Kyoiku*, 28 December 1999.

7. Hansfried Kellner and Hans-Georg Soeffner, "Cultural Globalization in Germany," in *Many Globalizations: Cultural Diversity in the Contemporary World*, ed. Peter Berger and Samuel Huntington (Oxford: Oxford University Press, 2002), 119-45.

8. Max Weber, *Economy and Society: An Outline of Interpretive Sociology* (Berkeley: University of California Press, 1978), 4-5, 24.

9. Michael Mann, *The Sources of Social Power: The Rise of Classes and Nation-States, 1760-1914* (Cambridge: Cambridge University Press, 1993), 6, 37-38, 44-49, 55.

10. Mann, *The Sources of Social Power*, 8-10, 13-14, 18-20; Weber, *Economy and Society*, 13-14.

11. "Superiority" was claimed to be central to the characteristics of an elite: "The outstanding idea in the term '*élite*' is 'superiority.' That is the only one I keep. . . . In a broad sense I mean by the *élite* in a society people who possess in marked degree qualities of intelligence, character, skill, capacity of whatever kind." (Marie Kobabinska, in: Vilfredo Pareto, *The Mind and Society: Theory of Residues* (London: Jonathan Cape, 1935), §2026. Similar definitions of elite: Raymond Aron, *Main Currents in Sociological Thought 2: Pareto, Weber, Durkheim* (Harmondsworth: Penguin Books Ltd., 1967); Gaetano Mosca, *The Ruling Class* (New York: McGraw-Hill Book Company, 1939); Rupert Wilkinson, "Elites and Effectiveness," in *Governing Elites*, ed. Rupert Wilkinson (New York: Oxford University Press, 1969), 215-24.

12. Initially, Pareto and Mosca called the group of elite a "class" without the economic connotation of the term in Marxist accounts. Pareto saw no significance in the selection of the term. In fact, Mosca loosely identifies the elite as the *classe politica*, commonly translated as "ruling class," "governing class," "the ruling clique" or occasionally "organized minority." While using the term randomly, both Pareto and Mosca concentrate on exploring the "governing" functions of elite within society. Vilfredo Pareto, *The Mind and Society: Non-Logical Conduct* (London: Jonathan Cape, 1935a), §119; Norberto Bobbio, *On Mosca and Pareto* (Genève: Librairie Doz SA, 1972), 14; Tom Bottomore, *Elites and Society* (London: C. A. Watts & Co. Ltd., 1964), 9, 20-27.

13. Weber, *Economy and Society*, 306.

14. On intellectual power as the source of political and social influence, see: Raymond Aron, *Opium of the Intellectuals* (New York: WW Norton & Company Inc., 1962); Ron Eyerman, Lennart Svensson, and Thomas Söderqvist, eds., *Intellectuals, Universities, and the State in Western Modern Societies* (Berkeley: University of California Press, 1987); Aleksander Gella, ed., *The Intelligentsia and the Intellectuals: Theory, methods and case study* (Beverly Hills: SAGE Publications Inc., 1976); Alvin Gouldner, *The Future of Intellectuals and the Rise of the New Class: A frame of Reference, Theses, Conjectures, Arguments, and an Historical Perspective on the Role of Intellectuals and Intelligentsia in the International Class Contest of the Modern Era* (London: Macmillan, 1979); Antonio Gramsci, *The Modern Prince and Other Writing* (London: Lawrence and Wishart Ltd., 1957), 123-24; Karl Mannheim, *Ideology and Utopia: An Introduction to the Sociology of Knowledge* (London: Routledge & Kegan Paul Ltd., 1936); Philip Rieff, ed., *On Intellectuals: Theoretical Studies Case Studies* (Garden City: Doubleday & Company, Inc., 1969); Edward Said, *Representations of the Intellectual: The 1993 Reith Lectures* (London: Vintage, 1995); Edward Shils, "The Intellectuals and the Powers: Some perspectives for comparative analysis," in *On Intellectuals: Theoretical studies case studies*, ed. Rieff). Mann regards the social influence of intellectual power as significant, since it is often represented by the particularly vital role of the university as one of the "principal media" of state ideology for social control. Mann, *The Sources of Social Power*, 36, 40. Hans Gerth and C. Wright Mills stress that the concept of "intellectual capacities" is precarious. Thus the superiority of the intellectual elite on the ground of intellectual capacities is only recognizable by their own claim of such capacities. One of the clearest examples is the Chinese literati which enjoyed

status privileges on the grounds of success in examinations. However, an elite which derived its legitimacy from their high level of educational attainment, often from university education, is identifiable only when this education is open to a minority of people. Hans Gerth and C. Wright Mills, eds., *From Max Weber: Essays in Sociology* (London: Routledge & Kegan Paul Ltd., 1970 [1948]), 422-36.

15. Zygmunt Bauman, *Legislators and Interpreters: On Modernity, Post-Modernity, and Intellectuals* (Cambridge: Polity Press, 1987), 8, 25, 35. Conventionally, the social group which claims its superiority in intellectual capacity is categorically identified with a number of vocations, e.g., high-ranking public officials, academic professionals, such as university professors, and those who are engaged in the so-called "liberal professions," e.g., lawyers, doctors, and writers. Dmitri Mirsky, *The Intelligentsia of Great Britain* (London: Victor Gollancz Ltd., 1935), 9-10; Fritz Ringer, *Fields of Knowledge: French Academic Culture in Comparative Perspective, 1890-1920* (Cambridge: Cambridge University Press, 1992), 27.

Part I

Chapter Two

State Formation, the State Education System, and Elite Formation in Meiji Japan

1. THE FORMATION OF A MODERN STATE

The Political Framework of State Formation

The direct cause of the formation of a modern state in Japan was the national crisis of the Western threat to Japan's national sovereignty, marked by the Blackship Turmoil in 1853.[1] The collapse of the Tokugawa *Bakufu* [shogunate] (1603-1867) and the establishment of the Meiji regime were the consequence of this threat rather than the results of the inexorable downfall of Tokugawa feudalism.[2] During the second half of the nineteenth century, Western technology had gradually been introduced in some *hans* [Tokugawa fiefs], despite the belief about Japan's centuries-long closure to the outside world.[3] After 1853, Japan was forced to sign a sequence of unequal treaties with the US, Britain, France, and Russia. This brought about a strong sense of national dishonor held by the *Daimyo* [Tokugawa feudal lord] and the *Samurai* [warrior]. The *Bakufu* quickly lost the authority to govern the country, and political power was gradually seized by a number of the lower-ranking, anti-Tokugawa *Samurai*s. In 1867, these *Samurai*s overthrew the Tokugawa *Bakufu* and resuscitated the sovereign power of the *Tenno* after 260 years of Tokugawa rule. About 300 former *han*s were seized by the new regime in the form of reverential return to the Imperial Household. The abolition of the feudal right of the *Daimyo* and *Samurai* to a stipend marked the end of the Tokugawa socio-political hereditary system in name and deed. Meiji Japan imposed political, economic, and social transformation on itself. For the government, the achievement of these goals would make Japan into a modern state comparable to, and recognized as such by, Western states.

Institutional transformation in the political system took place deliberately through the adoption of Western models. Despite initially adopting ideas randomly, the state bureaucracy of Meiji Japan developed using a combination of the tradition of the Tokugawa bureaucracy and the influence of the Prussian political system and ideas. The German political idea of state organism, which stresses the organic unity of the state and society, became a useful political instrument of the Meiji government for social consolidation of the family state—a people with common ancestry headed by the *Tenno*. The notions of the *Omnipotentz des Staates* [supreme power of the State] were adopted and worked effectively. This strong ideological inclination toward Prusso-German political ideas was lampooned by the British as "German measles" and satirized by the French as the "*Liaison Allemande*." What Bernd Martin calls the "fatal affinity" between German idealism and the Japanese version of Confucianism created a basis of the *Tenno* State.[4]

The deliberate adoption of the principle of meritocracy was another driving force for the development of the Meiji bureaucracy. This principle worked well also for the legitimization of the overthrow of the Tokugawa *Bakufu* by lower-ranking *Samurai*s and their establishment of the new regime. Among upper civil servants within the central bureaucracy, the ratio of the upper social echelons declined (from the average of 1867-1873 to 1875): i.e., the imperial household from 1.5% to 0%; the court aristocracy from 28.0% to 11.4%; the *Daimyo* from 8.3% to 2.8%; and the upper *Samurai* from 19.8% to 15.7%.[5] During the same period, on the other hand, the ratio of the lower *Samurai* substantially increased from 35.5% to 70.0%. These figures show considerable social mobility and the emergence of a new structure of the political and administrative elite in the *Meiji Ishin*. Although the *Samurai* was still dominant in the bureaucracy in the 1870s, most of the members were lower-ranking *Samurai*s and had actually never been rulers within the Tokugawa *Bakufu*. After the introduction of the Western cabinet system in 1885, the preferential policy for civil service recruitment from court nobles disappeared. Thus the *Meiji Ishin* did not show the consequences of the enjoyment of the "advantages of the ruling class in the ancien régime" in Barrington Moore's *Dictatorship* thesis.[6]

Industrial development in Meiji Japan also affected the stratification of its society. The Japanese pattern of an industrial revolution exemplified the state-guided industrialisation adopted by many catch-up countries.[7] While maintaining its general control over the industrial sector, the government began to privatize industry except for the production of munitions. The politically and economically strong relationship between the state and private industries became a direct vehicle of Japanese industrialization. In the Japanese context, the development of industry, including in the private sector, was regarded as a great contribution to the state project of industrialization. The nationalist thrust in Japanese industrialization framed a new social positioning of business people, who, despite their wealth and because of the Confucian tradition of disdain for commerce, had been classified in the lowest echelon within the Tokugawa social hierarchy. Because of Japan's great industrial backwardness, the economic role of social institutions was pronounced.

Thus, the *Meiji Ishin* was not an aristocratic revolution, comparable to the Prusso-German unification in the *Kaiserreich* or the Kemalist modernization project in Turkey.[8] The "Meiji Restoration," a loosely coined English term, actually involved more than restorations and entailed extensive innovations which the original Japanese characters for *"Ishin"* imply. Witnessing the colonization of neighboring countries by the Western powers, the Meiji government saw no alternative to strengthening the national economy and the military through the adoption of advanced Western technology. Robert Bellah captures the political aspirations of Meiji leaders:

> Behind the Meiji Restoration stood no Locke or Rousseau, no Marx or Lenin, no Gandhi or Mao Tsu-tung, but only a group of open-minded young men, ready to learn, committed to Japan, but with no determinate vision of the future.[9]

The universal value of Western civilization claimed by the Western powers had gained great validity in world politics and in cultural discourses in the later part of the century.[10] The sudden rise of threats to the sovereignty of the country, and the consequent abrupt formation of the modern Japanese state, necessitated the political as well as ideological consolidation of the state.

The Abrupt Formation of National Ideology

Given the context of the formation of the modern Japanese state, the national ideology of Meiji Japan developed within a synthesis of a belief in indigenous ideas and a partial but strong faith in Western thought. The basis of the national ideology of Meiji Japan was an abrupt creation of a sense of national identity by the state, unlike the pattern of the development of German identity in the long process of state formation as national unification.

In the Tokugawa period, territorial insecurity and a sense of nationhood were not the concern of the majority of the Japanese in their day-to-day life.[11] The Meiji regime used the indigenous religion, *Shinto*, to awaken nationalist sentiment among all the Japanese. Essentially, *Shinto* is not a dogmatic religion. The word *Shinto*, as such, is generally defined as the way of *kami*, gods or supernatural forces. This polytheistic religion has no doctrine to teach the code of morals, but has permeated the ways of people's thinking through the indigenous religious practices of the people and the worldview, based on their concept of *kami*.[12] The government politicized *Shinto* as *Kokka Shinto* by instilling the deification of the *Tenno*'s throne in the theology of *Shinto*'s ancestor worship. The *Tenno* assumed divine right as a direct descendant in the unbroken imperial lineage of the Sun Goddess. Moreover, to systematize *Shinto* theology as a political device, the government embedded the ethics of Confucianism, in particular neo-Confucianism, into *Shinto*.[13] The processes of ideological consolidation and the building of key institutions by the Meiji regime were parallel with each other. By the time of the promulgation of the Imperial Constitution in 1889 and the establishment of the National Diet in 1890, the political system of Meiji Japan was in place. Within the Constitution, the political status of the *Tenno* was enshrined and fully legitimized. Now, he *was* the state.

In the process of the absorption of Western ideas and the emphasis on the national ideology, cultural contradictions experienced by Meiji leaders were overt. According to Martin, the Japanese assimilation of Western ideas signalled its "inability to critically integrate Western thinking" and created ideological ambiguity among the leaders.[14] Ito Hirobumi, the main author of the Constitution and the first Prime Minister, recognized ambivalence about indigenous and exogenous values among Meiji leaders. "We were," said Ito, "just then in an age of transition. The opinions prevailing in the country were extremely heterogeneous and often diametrically opposed to each other."[15]

From the 1880s, economic and military development had taken firm hold in Japan. Its victories over China (1895) and Russia (1904) were symbolic of this development. The Western powers were gradually recognizing the political power of Japan, as its industrialization and military expansion progressed. In the face of such rapid national development, Meiji leaders saw no reason for arresting the state political project of Westernization. The political resistance of Japanese conservatives was only minor. The cultural contradictions and ideological ambiguity of national leaders were the side effects of Japanese state formation in the context of world politics and economy in the late nineteenth century.[16]

While shaping the leadership of the nation along Western lines, the government reinforced national identity and indigenous socio-cultural values among all the Japanese. For this purpose, the Meiji regime devoted itself to the establishment and development of a modern education system, identifying that as the best means for the ideological consolidation of the new state.

2. THE ESTABLISHMENT OF THE STATE EDUCATION SYSTEM

The Political and Cultural Framework of the Education System in Meiji Japan

The government quickly established the Ministry of Education in 1871. In the next year, a state education system was introduced by the promulgation of the Fundamental Code of Education. Mori Arinori, the first Japanese minister of education, believed that all Japanese should share the same sense of patriotism and see themselves as Japanese citizens. Mori as well as other leaders in the early Meiji period recognized the development of a national education system as a driving force to realize their political aspiration:

> Our country must move from its third-class position to second class, and from second class to first, and ultimately to the leading position among all countries of the world. The best way to do this is [by laying] the foundations of elementary education.[17]

The universalization of primary education was the state political project of the Meiji government. After Mori's assassination in 1889, the government maintained his policy. The tuition fees for four-year compulsory education were abolished by the Elementary School Ordinance of 1890. The government was steadily reaching its goal of the universalization of primary education.

However, the wide dissemination of education was not new to the Meiji education system. There was a strong tradition of respect for, and practice of, learning in Japanese society, as in Germany. The literacy rate in the late Tokugawa period, for example, was already high even in the lower strata of Tokugawa society. It is estimated that almost all *Samurai*s, 50-70% of merchants, and 20-60% of peasants could read and write.[18] Confucian learning was available in the *Samurai* school as well as in the *Terakoya* [commoners' school]. In the Tokugawa period, 97.3% of the *Terakoya*s taught children the cartography of Confucian books as the prime subject.[19] The development of the

Table 2.1. The Enrollment Ratio of Cohorts in Primary, Secondary, and Higher Education in Japan, 1875–1905

	1875	1885	1895	1905
Primary Education	35.2	49.6	61.2	95.6
Secondary Education	0.7	0.8	1.1	4.3
Higher Education	0.4	0.4	0.3	0.9

Source: Ministry of Education, Japan, *Education in Japan 1971: A graphic presentation* (Tokyo: Ministry of Education, 1971), 16.

Japanese modern education system was laid on a solid basis of *Education in Tokugawa Japan*, as Ronald Dore has shown.

Yet, as seen in his study, Tokugawa education was provided for individuals of various social strata in diverse forms, contents, and standards. The occasional opportunities for *Samurai* education which were given to commoners were exceptional. The innovative aspect of the Meiji state education system was the provision of uniform educational content for the children of all social strata and all regions. This was a great leap forward from Tokugawa education to a modern education under a state education system. The government understood that education could act as the monolithic, ideological channel which would make all Japanese contribute to the achievement of the national goals.

The Role of the School

Initially, as shown, the underlying idea of Mori and other early Meiji leaders was the cultivation of a sense of citizenship among all Japanese through education. Mori believed that the cohesive national identity in some Western countries derived from a strong sense of citizenship based on the ideas of individualism and egalitarianism. Fukuzawa Yukichi, who like Mori had developed his liberal ideas during his studies in America, shared Mori's idea. Fukuzawa argued in his widely read book *Encouragement of Learning* that "all nations are equal. But when the people of a nation do not have the spirit of individual independence, the corresponding right of national independence cannot be realized."[20] Early Meiji leaders, such as Mori, Fukuzawa, and Tanaka Fujimaro, the vice minister of education, strongly admired American liberalism. Mori and Tanaka attempted to limit state intervention in educational administration and to transfer it to the local school boards by adopting the principles of the American common school.[21]

However, the ideas of Mori and Tanaka were regarded as too radical and were not accepted by the other government officials. Fukuzawa's views did not influence governmental policy for education either, since he had never taken an official position within the government. Along with the development of the state bureaucracy, staffed by graduates of the Imperial University, such liberal ideas faded out within the governmental policy for education. Given the clear signs of development in the national economy and politics, criticisms of this governmental policy came neither from inside the government nor from the Japanese people.

In 1880, the government re-emphasised Confucian learning by upgrading *Shushin*, moral education largely based on Confucianism, to the prime subject within the curriculum of the primary school. In 1889, the government announced that *Kokka Shinto* was not a religion but the national ideology.[22] This measure legitimized instruction in *Kokka Shinto* as non-religious education. At the same time, instruction in all the other religions was ruled out in public schools, in the name of freedom of religion. In 1890, the *Tenno* promulgated the *Kyoiku Chokugo* [Imperial Rescript on Education] as the defining educational principles of the state. As the statement of *Tenno*'s will, it asserted that the people as the subjects of the *Tenno* ought to maintain the virtues of the state as well as filial piety to parents and benevolence to others (see the full text in appendix). Rituals, such as the recitation of the script and obeisance to the imperial portrait, were enforced. By this time, the government's initial preference for Anglo-American educational ideas had been replaced by Herbartian pedagogy, which combined moral training and knowledge attainment. As a consequence of the establishment of the state education system, Japan was equipped with a reliable and solid network for the dissemination of the national ideology to all the citizens.

3. THE STATE, THE UNIVERSITY, AND ELITE FORMATION

The Role of the University

At the same time it was indoctrinating all children in the national ideology shaped by *Kokka Shinto*, the government created national leaders in the university. In 1877, the Meiji government founded Tokyo University with full state funding, on the basis of a number of shogunal schools of the Tokugawa *Bakufu*. After the preliminary phase of about a decade, the university was endowed with the title of Tokyo Imperial University upon the promulgation of the Ordinance of the Imperial University in 1886. The ordinance indicated that the purpose of the university was to provide instruction in accordance with the needs of the state. Tokyo Imperial University was the only university in the country from its foundation in 1877 until the establishment of Kyoto (1897), Tohoku (1907), and Kyushu (1910) Imperial Universities. The Meiji government granted the title of "university" exclusively to these four institutions.

Within its limited budget, the state granted university education only to a small number of selected future national leaders. The government positioned Tokyo Imperial University as the apex university. The state bureaucracy was predominantly staffed by graduates of Tokyo. Between 1894 and 1947, 62.4% of the successful candidates of the higher civil service examination (administrative sections) were graduates of Tokyo Imperial University—that is, 5,969 were Tokyo's graduates out of a total number of 9,565.[23] Among the graduates of Tokyo, 5,653 belonged to the faculty of law. In this examination, Kyoto Imperial University had only 795 successful candidates (8.3%).

Another role of the university was to provide leading technical experts for industry. For this purpose, despite the opposition of academics, the government set up "non-academic" fields of study, namely agriculture and engineering, at Tokyo in 1890. Based on this pragmatic policy, the Imperial College of Engineering was modeled after the Polytechnic in Zurich, but staffed with a number of experts from Scotland. Within the university curriculum, the amount of time given to classical Japanese and Chinese literature was far less than that given to Western learning.

Heavy emphasis on Western learning was evident also in the government's investment in the university. The government hired a large number of foreign teachers at Tokyo. Between 1871 and 1898, a total of 1,664 foreign experts was employed by the government.[24] In 1877, the ratio of Japanese professors and associate professors to foreign professors at Tokyo was 4:3:17 in the faculties of law, science and letters. The salaries of foreign teachers were extremely high, compared with those of Japanese professors and even of some ministers in the Japanese Cabinet. The government deliberately bore such a financial burden, considering it as a necessary operational cost for the formation of the modern Japanese state. State investment was also made in offering scholarships for study in Western countries to Japanese academics.

Between 1868 and 1874, the government spent nearly one-sixth of the annual national education budget in dispatching over 500 students to Western countries: 209 students to the US, 168 to Britain, 82 to Germany, and 60 to France.[25] Tokyo Imperial University, equipped with expensive foreign tutors and opportunities for study abroad, was always the window to the West.

As well as pragmatic principles, the government followed meritocratic principles in the organization of the university. The policy of meritocracy was institutionalized within the academic track. In principle, all students could enter this track as long as they succeeded in a series of highly competitive entrance examinations. Before the competitive entrance examination to the Imperial University, students had followed the so-called elite route of the "*Koto Gakko* [higher middle school]—Imperial University line." The *Koto Gakko* actually became the gateway to the university.

In taking up these political and economic roles, the Imperial University enjoyed a number of privileges. The government recognized the academic autonomy of the university, compared with other state higher education institutions. The idea of university autonomy was laid down during the administration of Mori and Inoue Kowashi, the minister of education (1893-1894). They believed that the independent thinking of academics would shape the academic culture of the university, as it had in the West.

Table 2.2. The Experience of Overseas Study of Japanese Professors, 1877-1893

Faculty	Overseas Experience						No Experience	TOTAL
	UK	USA	Germany	France	Others	Subtotal		
Law	3	1	5	4	—	13	3	16
Medicine	—	—	23	1	1	25	3	28
Engineering	11	5	3	2	—	21	6	27
Letters	1	4	3	—	—	8	15	23
Science	8	6	9	2	—	25	1	26
Agriculture	—	2	5	—	1	8	2	10
TOTAL	23	18	48	9	2	100	30	130

Source: Ikuo Amano, *Kyoiku to kindai-ka: Nihon no keiken* (Tokyo: Tamagawa University Press, 1997), 264.

	PRIVATE SECTOR		PUBLIC SECTOR	
UPPER LAYER				Imperial University
LOWER LAYER	Senmon Gakko [Vocational School]		Senmon Gakko and Others	Koto Gakko
	Special Course	Regular Course		
		Secondary School		

Figure 2.1. The Structure of Japanese Higher Education in the 1890s
Source: Ikuo Amano and William Cummings. "The Changing of the Japanese Professor." In *Changes in the Japanese University: A Comparative Perspective*, eds. William Cummings, Ikuo Amano, and Kazuyuki Kitamura (New York: Praeger, 1979), 18.

The Imperial University was privileged, not least financially. In contrast to the advantaged conditions of the university, private higher-education institutions received neither financial support nor legal recognition from the state. The government's laissez-faire policy for private institutions was overt. In 1928, only 8.3% of the total budget of the Imperial Universities relied on tuition fees, whereas the equivalent figure for private institutions was 60.5%.[26]

Institutionally as well, the Meiji government had neither a legal definition of, nor regulations for, private higher-education institutions until 1903 when the government finally gave them the legal status of a *Senmon Gakko*.[27] Until 1918, the government did not permit private institutions to label themselves as "universities." Those institutions were diverse in size and academic standards, which were by no means comparable to those of the Imperial University. This policy of differentiation within higher education created a sense of academic insularity in the university system within which the intellectual standards of individual institutions were greatly uneven. Moreover, the way the government set up the system of the Imperial University insulated it from these other institutions. Inoue set up the *Koza* [professorial chair] system in 1893 exclusively in the Imperial University. At the first implementation, the fields of study were divided into 123 units. Despite the government's initial intention to establish a collective professional ethos among academics in each *Koza*, the consequence brought about by this system was rather academic demarcations and the prevention of the Japanese university from enjoying dynamic intellectual interaction and open competition within and among institutions. As broadly accepted, neither the Meiji government nor academics developed the idea of the university as an intellectual community, as it had been developed in Germany.[28]

Politically, as well, the Imperial University was insulated—to its own advantage—from the other higher-education institutions. The academics of the Imperial University not only enjoyed academic autonomy in relation to the state, but also participation in the actual governmental decision-making process. For example, in 1896 in the Council of Education within the Ministry of Education, seven out of the whole twenty-seven seats, the largest single bloc, were reserved for the president and the faculty chairmen of Tokyo. Four seats were reserved for the academics of Kyoto who were former professors of Tokyo. They were even allowed to suggest modifications in state policies prior to their promulgation.[29] As Byron Marshall has noted, Tokyo Imperial University "was conceived of as a government agency standing at the apex of this integrated educational pyramid with its faculty an integral part of the larger officialdom of civil servants."[30] The university enjoyed its autonomy and privileges until the government was gradually dominated by militarist propaganda from the middle of the 1920s. Even during the military regime, the actual cases of the breach of university autonomy by the state were relatively few, compared with not only the university under the Nazis but also other military regimes in modern history.[31] Occasionally there were ideological confrontations between the state and university academics, in particular Marxist scholars. Nevertheless, the Japanese university remained relatively immune to criticisms from outside the university.[32]

In sum, university autonomy per se was initiated by the state. Its leaders believed that the modernization of Japan should incorporate Western ideas and knowledge useful to the Japanese. The aim of the state was to achieve the core national goals, developed within a state policy of differentiation for making new national leaders. The consequence of this was the creation of an academic hierarchy in Japanese higher education, within the broader principles of an emphasis on meritocracy and Western learning.

Elite Formation in the University of Meiji Japan

Another important implication of the university policy of the Meiji regime was the decomposition of the traditional social order among the university-educated people. In the *Meiji Ishin*, the political privileges and financial sources of the *Daimyo* and the *Samurai* were lost or severely damaged. Within the reconstruction of the political system in the *Meiji Ishin*, the majority of lower-ranking *Samurai*s sought the replacement of these losses by becoming high-ranking state officials. A university degree was, as indicated, an important means for social ascent. The proportion of the former *Samurai* was high among graduates of Tokyo Imperial University: 63.3% in 1890, 59.0% in 1895, and 50.8% in 1900.[33]

There was a potential for the sharing of a sense of esprit de corps and the formation of a social group of the intellectual aristocracy by former *Samurai*s in the university.[34] However, this potential was wasted because of the academic segregation in the hierarchy of higher-education institutions. The esprit de corps of university students and graduates in Meiji Japan developed within this state policy for differentiation and its product of academic demarcations. As stated earlier, the vast majority of them outside the Imperial University were not even recognized as universities by either the state or the academics and students of the Imperial University. In Meiji Japan, universities neither developed evenly throughout the nation, nor could form a group of people within a solid social stratum, as universities in Germany cultivated the *Bildungsbürgertum*.

Moreover, the strong emphasis on meritocratic principles discouraged the group solidarity of students around the rankings of the traditional social order. Because of this social aspiration, the large quota of the former *Samurai* among university students did not support the restoration of the Tokugawa social order. The strong disagreement in Japan between higher-ranking civil bureaucrats, mostly consisting of graduates of the Imperial University, and the leading military bureaucrats, of relatively humble social origin with lower educational qualifications, illustrates the fact that social re-organization and academic demarcations resulted in the failure of the consolidation of new elites. This was in sharp contrast with the harmonious relationship between the civil-service elite and the military elite in Germany based on a shared, and high, social origin and the similar academic experiences in the university of both elites.[35] The constant political and moral dissension between the civil-service elite and the military elite brought about the fatal disintegration of national politics in pre-1945 Japan.[36]

Among leading Meiji educators, Fukuzawa probably had the most foresight on the theme of the formation of the middle-class intelligentsia. He believed that the consolidation of educated young men within the middle stratum of Japanese society and the cultivation of their sense of respect for high bourgeois culture would lead Japan to build a modern and enlightened society, comparable to a civil society in the West.[37] However, most of the Meiji bureaucrats failed to share the ideas of Fukuzawa, an outsider from the point of view of the officialdom.

Another implication of the governmental emphasis on meritocratic principles was the partial destruction of the value system of the educated elite in Meiji Japan. The powerful governmental promotion of, and the consequent intellectual inclination toward, Western learning further discouraged the re-affirmation of conservative political ideas and older socio-cultural values among university-educated Japanese. No organized political and socio-cultural movement which could arrest Westernization was created by national leaders in Japan, as witnessed in Russia, Latin America, and Islamic nations. The ideological struggle of Japanese leaders was far more complex than a simple dichotomy between liberal and statist views or between Western and Japanese values.³⁸

There was no such social group which formed its own social stratum in a society and acted as a guardian of indigenous high culture of their own society comparable to the German *Bildungsbürgertum*, the Russian intelligentsia, and the French *intellectuels*. The ambiguity of the identity of the university-educated elite in Japan derived from their strong faith in Western ideas and the inspiration they drew from the national ideology in their earlier education.

Westernized Meiji thinkers, such as Fukuzawa, even advocated that a modern Japan should detach itself from its "old Asian ill-fated friends," such as China and Korea.³⁹ Robert Bellah identified succinctly the ambiguity of the cultural identity of the Japanese educated elite by suggesting that "Compounding the aloofness of the intellectuals is the fact that they have been far more profoundly penetrated by Western culture than any group in Japan and suffer disequilibrium from this exposure."⁴⁰ Similarly, Andrew Barshay captured the theme of the cultural contradictions of Meiji Japan:

> Japan's spectacularly successful entry into the stream of universal development also produced recurring fears that someday the bubble would burst, that the nation would forever be forced to play catch up with the West. This complex has given Japan's modern history an urgent, and sometimes violent and frenetic, quality. And it has, in most periods, fostered a preoccupation with national identity, with being "understood" by the outside world. In its efforts to "stand shoulder to shoulder with the West," Japan met great success at the turn of the twentieth century, only to find its "special relationship" to East Asia a source of friction, hostility, and frustration vis-à-vis its fellow colonial powers (not to mention those actually subject to Japanese rule). Such experiences have in their turn produced spates of compensatory truculence and encouraged explanations for the actions of the state that look directly to cultural predisposition and the national character.⁴¹

The clear vision of the formation of a modern state, held by the Meiji regime, shaped the role of the university and the characteristics of the university-educated elite. The government's deliberate intention to establish the university for the state and the consequent privileged status of the Imperial University set up the academic hierarchy of the university system. Academic demarcations also curtailed the development of a shared sense of esprit de corps among university-educated people across institutions. Furthermore, the Meiji government did not recognize a social stratum of the university-educated elite—a potentially cohesive status group—as a basis of the ideological consolidation of the Meiji new society. This governmental vision for the university and elite formation was present in Japan until the end of World War Two.

4. CONCLUSION

As argued, the Meiji regime derived its legitimacy from its political power to safeguard the country from the Western threat. The legitimacy also derived from the deconstruction of the ancien régime and the loosening of Tokugawa social stratification to overcome the national crisis. In this context, the state policy was deliberately dual. Thus, while importing some Western ideas, the government expressed a sense of repulsion toward Western countries and strengthened a sense of nationalism.

This vision of the Meiji government was clearly shown in the state education system. The strong historical basis for the development of the modern education system in Japan was laid down by the well developed but differentiated education of the Tokugawa period. While both the school and the university served the state to make Japan modern, each of them was given a specific role defined by the political frame of the state. At the lower level, centrally controlled universal primary education provided a firm ideological basis for solidarity.

Elitist university education was linked to the political and economic modernization of the country. University-educated people were recognized as an elite group, important because of their significance in the state bureaucracy and important because of the traditional respect for learning. The simultaneous development of the state bureaucracy and industry influenced the social positioning of this educated elite vis-à-vis the economic elite in Japan. Moreover, the university-educated elite was formed in the process of radical transformation of Japanese society in the *Meiji Ishin*. As this transformation was carried out predominantly through the introduction of Western ideas, there could be seen a partial destruction of the ideas and values of indigenous traditions in tension with Western ideas among the university-educated elite. Furthermore, the state's emphasis on meritocracy and practical knowledge—the key principles of Meiji state formation—created academic demarcations and a hierarchy within the university system. This affected the group cohesion of this elite in Japan. All these themes, as will be shown later, had an effect on what happened in the reform of Japanese education after 1945: the roots of those reactions are traceable back to the Meiji period.

In sum, Japan's pattern of modernization in the form of Westernization and an emphasis on meritocratic principles shook the faith of the Japanese elite in indigenous socio-cultural values and a traditional social order. The practical idea of the university held by the state also hampered the development of the university as a cultural community. High social mobility in the Meiji society did not create a sufficient condition for the university-educated elite to form a new social stratum, either. In addition, the academic demarcations, a creation of the governmental emphasis on meritocratic principles, also became a barrier for the elite to share an esprit de corps. These characteristics were the basis of the adoption of Western ideas and the condition for the further absorption of the Western patterns of political, economic, and social development in the modern Japanese state.

NOTES

1. This incident arose when the American Commodore Perry came to Japan in the battleship to demand Japan's opening.
2. Politically and economically, the *Bakufu* was still sustaining its unique rule of centralized feudalism in the middle of the nineteenth century. Herbert Norman, ed., *Origins of the Modern Japanese State: Selected Writings of E. H. Norman* (New York: Pantheon Books, 1975); Bernard Silberman, *Cages of Reason: The rise of the Rational State in France, Japan, the United States, and Great Britain* (Chicago: The University of Chicago Press, 1993). Cf. Barrington Moore, Jr., *Social Origins of Dictatorship and Democracy: Lord and Peasant in the Making of the Modern World* (London: Allen Lane the Penguin Press, 1966).
3. For example, foundries, iron furnaces, and shipyards had been set up in the Satsuma, Saga, Mito, and Nagasaki *han*s. Occasionally, they had received the technical assistance of Western experts.
4. Martin, *Japan and Germany*, 33, 44-47. In the 1930s, not only politically but also culturally, there were vigorous interactions between Germany and Japan: Kurt Meißner, *Grundlagen der nationalen Erziehung in Japan* (Tokyo: Deutsche Gesellschaft für Natur- und Völkerkunde Ostasiens, 1934); Carl von Weegmann, *Die Vaterländische Erziehung in der Japanischen Volksschule: Tokuhon und Shushinsho* (Tokyo: Deutsche Gesellschaft für Natur- und Völkerkunde Ostasiens, 1935); "*Deutsche Kinderzeichungen nach Japan!*," *Rundschreiben von NS-Lehrerbund*, 25 July 1939 [NS12/15]. Cf. Perry Anderson, "The Prussia of the East?," in *Japan in the World*, ed. Masao Miyoshi and Harry Harootunian (Durham: Duke University Press, 1993).
5. Bernard Silberman, "Elite Transformation in the Meiji Restoration: The Upper Civil Service 1868-1873," in *Modern Japanese Leadership: Transition and Change*, ed. Bernard Silberman and Harry Harootunian (Tucson: The University of Arizona Press, 1966), 235, 237.
6. Cf. Moore, *Social Origin of Dictatorship*. Trimberger also points out Moore's failure in perceiving the revolutionary aspects of the *Meiji Ishin*. Ellen Trimberger, "A Theory of Elite Revolution," *Studies in Comparative International Development* 7 (Fall 1972), 201.
7. Alexander Gerschenkron, *Economic Backwardness in Historical Perspective: A Book of Essays* (Cambridge: Harvard University Press, 1962), 6-7. Per capita industrialization in 1900 (UK=100): 69 in US, 52 in Germany, 39 in France, 23 in Austria-Hungary, 15 in Russia, 12 in Japan, and 3 in China. Mann, *The Sources of Social Power*, 263.
8. Johann Arnason, *Social Theory and Japanese Experience: The Dual Civilization* (London: Kegan Paul International, 1997); Reinhard Bendix, *Kings or People: Power and the Mandate to*

Rule (Berkeley: University of California Press, 1978); Masako Shibata, "Controlling National Identity and the Role of Education: The Vision of State Formation in Meiji Japan and the German *Kaiserreich*," *History of Education* 33, no. 1 (2004): 75-85. Cf. Perry Anderson, *Lineages of the Absolutist State* (London: Verso, 1974); Theda Skocpol, *States and Social Revolutions: A Comparative Analysis of France, Russia, and China* (Cambridge: Cambridge University Press, 1979), 100-110; Thomas Smith, "Japan's Aristocratic Revolution," in *Class, Status, and Power*, ed. Reinhard Bendix and Seymour Lipset (London: Routledge & Kegan Paul Ltd., 1967), 135-40; Ellen Trimberger, *Revolution From Above: Military Bureaucrats and Development in Japan, Turkey, Egypt, and Peru* (New Brunswick: Transaction Books, 1978); Robert Ward and Dankwart Rustow, eds., *Political Modernization in Japan and Turkey* (Princeton: Princeton University Press, 1964).

    9. Robert Bellah, "Intellectual and Society in Japan," *Daedalus* 101, no. 2 (1972), 101.

    10. Eric Hobsbawm, *The Age of Extremes: The Short Twentieth Century 1914-1991* (London: Abacus, 1994); Mann, *The Sources of Social Power*; Shigeki Toyama, *Meiji Ishin* (Tokyo: Iwanami, 1951).

    11. Hugh Borton, *Japan's Modern Century* (New York: The Ronald Press Company, 1955); Delmer Brown, *Nationalism in Japan: An Introductory Historical Analysis* (Berkeley: University of California Press, 1955); Janet Hunter, *The Emergence of Modern Japan: An introductory history since 1853* (London: Longman, 1989); Byron Marshall, *Learning to Be Modern: Japanese Political Discourse on Education* (Boulder: Westview Press, Inc., 1994). Cf. William de Bary, Ryusaku Tsunoda, and Donald Keene, *Sources of Japanese Tradition* (New York: Columbia University Press, 1958).

    12. Mircea Eliade, ed., *The Encyclopedia of Religion*, vol. 13 (New York: Macmillan Publishing Company, 1987), 280-94; Richard Ince, *A Dictionary of Religion and Religions, Including Theological and Ecclesiastical Terms* (London: Arthur Barker Limited, 1935), 144.

    13. de Bary, *Sources of Japanese Tradition*; Marshall, *Learning To Be Modern*. Neo-Confucianism was developed by Chu His in the twelfth century in China. This philosophy was transmitted to Japan through *Zen* Buddhists and influenced the development of *Bushido* [warrior ethics] in the Tokugawa period. Bellah argued that *Bushido* virtues were intact not only among *Samurai*s in the Tokugawa period but also throughout modern times in Japan. Robert Bellah, *Tokugawa Religion: The Values of Pre-Industrial Japan* (Glencoe: Free Press, 1957), 98. For similar accounts, see: Shmuel Eisenstadt, *Japanese Civilization: A Comparative View* (Chicago: University of Chicago Press, 1996); Shmuel Eisenstadt, "Some Observations on the Transformation of Confucianism (and Buddhism) in Japan," in *Confucian Traditions in East Asian Modernity*, ed. Wei-ming Tu (Cambridge: Harvard University Press, 1996), 173-85.

    14. Martin, *Japan and Germany*, 55-56. Similar arguments: Benjamin Duke, ed., *Ten Great Educators of Modern Japan: A Japanese Perspective* (Tokyo: University of Tokyo Press, 1989); John Hall and Richard Beardsley, *Twelve Doors to Japan* (New York: McGraw-Hill Inc., 1965); Josef Kreiner, *Deutschland-Japan Historische Kontakte* (Bonn: Bouvier Verlag Herbert Grundmann, 1984).

    15. Quoted from Mann, *The Sources of Social Power*, 40.

    16. A minor voice of criticism was raised by Okakura Kakuzo, one of the few Japanese among Meiji leading figures who attempted to introduce Japanese cultural traditions to the West rather than vice versa. He wrote that the average Westerner "was wont to regard Japan as barbarous when she indulged in the gentle arts of peace; he calls her civilized since she began to commit wholesale slaughter on Manchurian battlefields. . . . Fain would we remain barbarians, if our claim to civilization were to be based on the gruesome glory of war. Fain would we await the time when due respect shall be paid to our art and ideals." Kazuo Okakura, *The Book of Tea* (New York: Dover Publications, Inc., 1964 [1906]), 2-3.

17. The English translation of Mori's speech to a Saitama normal school in February 1885: Herbert Passin, *Society and Education in Japan* (Tokyo: Kodansha International Ltd., 1965), 68. Mori studied in the University of London as one of the first Japanese who studied abroad in the late Tokugawa period. He served the government also as the deputy minister to the United States in 1870 at the age of twenty-three. Like Mori, the Meiji new leaders were remarkably young, in their twenties and early forties, when the *Meiji Ishin* started.

18. Passin, *Society and Education*, 11-12, 47-48, 56-60; Ronald Dore, *Education in Tokugawa Japan* (London: The Athlone Press Ltd., 1992 [1965]), 291.

19. Shoji Fujita, "Shushin no seiritsu katei," *The Bulletin of Tokyo University, Department of Education* 8 (1965): 191-224.

20. English translation from Bellah, "Intellectual and Society," 107.

21. Cowen argues that the basic idea of this American egalitarian education was laid down by Horace Mann on "mandatory inclusionary principles" which identified compulsory education as "a social duty and a political necessity" of and for citizens. Robert Cowen, "Nigel Grant and Plato: A question of democratic education," *Comparative Education* 36, no. 2 (2000): 135-41.

22. Horio argues that bureaucratic control in education and the indoctrination of *Kokka Shinto* ideology by the state was a "natural consequence" of the pre-war education of the "para-religious *Tenno*-State." Teruhisa Horio, *Tenno-sei kokka to kyoiku* (Tokyo: Aoki Shoten, 1987). Coulby also identifies this process of making a nation through the formation of a state in Japan as the state's "disguise as a nation" in order "to create and reproduce loyalty to and acceptance of the state." David Coulby, "Educational Responses to Diversity within the State," in *World Yearbook of Education: Intercultural Education*, ed. David Coulby, Jagdish Gundara, and Crispin Jones (London: Kogan Page, 1997), 7-17; David Coulby, *Beyond the National Curriculum: Curricular Centralism and Cultural Diversity in Europe and the USA* (London: Routledge/Falmer, 2000).

23. Ikuhiko Hata, *Kanryo no kenkyu: Fumetsuno Power 1868-1983* (Tokyo: Kodansha, 1983), 17.

24. Ikuo Amano, *Kyoiku to kindai-ka: Nihon no keiken* (Tokyo: Tamagawa University Press, 1997), 259; Robert Schwantes, "Foreign Employees in the Development of Japan," in *The Modernizers: Overseas Students, Foreign Employees, and Meiji Japan*, ed. Ardath Burks (Boulder: Westview Press, 1985), 209.

25. Roger Goodman, "Japan: Pupil turned teacher?," in *Lessons of Cross-National Comparison in Education*, ed. David Phillips (Oxford: Triangle Books Ltd., 1992), 156.

26. Ikuo Amano, "Continuity and Change in the Structure of Japanese Higher Education," in *Changes in the Japanese University: A Comparative Perspective*, ed. William Cummings, Ikuo Amano, and Kazuyuki Kitamura (New York: Praeger, 1979), 27.

27. At the end of the nineteenth century, Tokyo Imperial University had about 1,300 students, compared with 8,700 students in *Senmon Gakko*s of which only three were publicly funded. Ikuo Amano, *Koto-kyoiku no nihon-teki kozo* (Tokyo: Tamagawa University Press, 1986), 32-33.

28. Ikuo Amano, *Nihon-teki daigaku-zo wo motomete* (Tokyo: Tamagawa University Press, 1991); Shigeru Nakayama, *Rekishi to shite no gakumon* (Tokyo: Chuo Koronsha, 1974); Masao Terasaki, *Daigaku kyoiku no sozo: Rekishi, system, curriculum* (Tokyo: Toshindo, 1999).

29. Masao Terasaki, *Daigaku no Jiko-henkaku to Autonomy* (Tokyo: Toshindo, 1998), 163-64.

30. Byron Marshall, "The Tradition of Conflict in the Governance of Japan's Imperial Universities," *History of Education Quarterly* 17, no. 4 (1977), 386. See also: Byron Marshall, "Professors and Politics: The Meiji Academic Elite," *Journal of Japanese Studies* 3 (1977): 71-97.

31. According to Hartshorne, "faculty losses" under the Nazi regime in 1933: Düsseldorf (only Medicine) 50.0 (%); Berlin 32.4; Frankfurt/M 32.3; Heidelberg 24.3; Braunsberg 22.2,

etc. Edward Yarnall Hartshorne, *The German universities and National Socialism* (London: Allen & Unwin, 1937), 94. In Argentina, too, about 1,250 academics were forced out of universities after Peron's victory in the 1946 presidential election. Mónica Rein, *Politics and Education in Argentina 1946-1962* (New York: M. E. Sharpe, 1998), 92-94. The Chilean coup d'état in 1973 also brought about the dismissal, detention, torture, or murder of 18,000 academics and students. Felicity Edholm, *Education and Repression: Chile* (London: WUS, 1982), 59-62.

32. William Cummings, "The Conservative Reform of Higher Education," *Japan Interpreter* 8, no. 4 (1974): 421-31; Saburo Ienaga, *Daigaku no jichi* (Tokyo: Hanawa Shobo, 1962); Marshall, "The Tradition of Conflict." Terasaki argues that the governmental control in university administration became rather tighter after 1945. Terasaki, *Daigaku no Jiko-henkaku*, 164.

33. Amano, *Koto-kyoiku*, 374.

34. Masamichi Inoki, "The Civil Bureaucracy: Japan," in *Political Modernization in Japan and Turkey*, ed. Robert Ward and Dankwart Rustow (Princeton: Princeton University Press, 1964), 283-301.

35. Samuel Finer, *The Man on Horseback: The Role of the Military in Politics* (Harmondsworth: Penguin, 1976); Samuel Huntington, *The Soldier and the State: The Theory and Politics of Civil-Military Relations* (Cambridge: Belknap Press of Harvard University Press, 1957). Cf. Hermann Beck, *The Origins of the Authoritarian Welfare State in Prussia: Conservatives, Bureaucracy, and the Social Question, 1815-70* (Ann Arbor: The University of Michigan Press, 1995), 238.

36. Arnason, *Social Theory*, 452-53; James Fulcher, "The Bureaucratization of the State and the Rise of Japan," *British Journal of Sociology* 39, no. 2 (1988), 229, 239-41.

37. Ikuo Amano, *Gakureki no shakai-shi: Kyoiku to Nihon no kindai* (Tokyo: Shincho Sensho, 1992), 100.

38. Hall and Beardsley, *Twelve Doors*, 396-97; Chomin Nakae, *San suijin keirin mondo* (New York: Weatherhill, 1984 [1887]).

39. Fukuzawa's essay in *Jiji Shimpo* on 16 March 1895 is quoted from Tomoji Fujita, "Fukuzawa Yukichi no Tenno-kan," in *Chishikijin no Tenno-kan*, ed. Gendai Shiso Kenkyukai (Tokyo: San'itsu Shobo, 1995), 51. Occasionally, Fukuzawa showed that he was not a blind follower of Western ideas.

40. Bellah, "Intellectual and Society," 104, 110.

41. Andrew Barshay, *State and Intellectual in Imperial Japan: The Public Man in Crisis* (Berkeley: University of California Press, 1988), 2-3.

Chapter Three

State Formation, the State Education System, and Elite Formation in the German *Kaiserreich*

1. THE FORMATION OF A MODERN STATE

The Political Framework of State Formation

Before 1871, the development of political ideas in Germany was uneven. In the southern and Rhine-Westfalia areas, liberalism developed well and the idea of the *Rechtsstaat*—the state ruled by law—had begun to take shape from the early nineteenth century. In contrast, Prussia had maintained a feudal political system. The Eastern Elbe was backward economically as well, compared with the areas along the Rhine. After the victory of Prussia over France and Austria, the German states were finally unified in the reign of the Prussian king Wilhelm I as the *Kaiser* of the empire. The policy of the *Kaiserreich* derived its legitimacy from Prussian political as well as military power to maintain this political unification. Long-standing territorial insecurity in the German cultural domains and their political aspirations to create a unified Germany resulted in the state's emphasis on the retention of the traditional social order and socio-cultural values in Germany.[1] At the inception of the *Kaiserreich*, Otto von Bismarck, a Prussian *Junker*, took the office of the chancellor. Bismarck treasured the traditions of the Prussian socio-political institutions—the king, the aristocracy, the army, and the bureaucracy. He stated that "I am no democrat . . . and cannot be one. I was born and raised as [an] aristocrat. I am a *Junker*, and I mean to profit from it."[2]

The aristocracy benefited from the system of the constitutional monarchy of the *Kaiserreich*. Despite its economic weaknesses after industrialization, the aristocracy, the *Junker* in particular, maintained this political and social hegemony within German society. On average, 64.5% of the cabinets in the *Kaiserreich* consisted of the aristocracy, whereas 35.5% were from the middle class and none from the working class.[3] Under the constitution, election to the *Reichstag* was based on the principle of the *Dreiklassenwahlrecht*. That is to say, electorates were organized in three layers on the basis of tax payments.[4] Disproportionately large voting rights were given to the upper social strata. This "thorough politicization of society without parliamentalization" provided the unfavorable conditions for the development of liberalism in the German context.[5]

In military and civil administration as well, the aristocracy remained powerful. In contrast to Japanese military bureaucrats, as shown earlier, the well-educated military officers of noble social origin—"the most caste-bound and privileged officer corps in Europe"—had little conflict with the civil bureaucracy over state affairs. "In no other modern western society," said Samuel Huntington, "for such an extended peacetime period have the military career and the military officer had the popular prestige which they had in Wilhelmine Germany."[6] The civil bureaucracy exerted strong political influence by frequently taking over the power of the legislature in the *Kaiserreich*. In 1888, bureaucrats dominated 23% of seats in the *Reichstag*. As Max Weber has observed, the parliamentary political system developed weakly within the political institutions and processes of the Wilhelmine-Bismarckian bureaucratic state:

> He [Bismarck] left behind him a nation *without any political sophistication*. . . . Above all, he left behind him a nation *without any political will of its own*, accustomed to the idea that the great statesman at the helm would make the necessary political decisions. . . . A *completely powerless parliament* was the purely negative result of his tremendous prestige. . . . The naïve moralizing legend of our unpolitical literati reverses the causal relationship and maintains that parliament remained deservedly powerless *because* of the low level of parliamentary life. . . . The level of parliament depends on whether it does not merely discuss great issues but decisively influences them; in other words, its quality depends on whether what happens there matters, or whether parliament is nothing but the unwillingly tolerated rubber stamp of a ruling bureaucracy. [italics in the original text][7]

The German pattern of industrialization also showed the conservative aspects of German society. Industrial development was driven by the political power of the state, and the middle class developed limited political aspirations and a conformist political stance.[8] The German middle class was empowered in the late nineteenth century, when socialist movements were prevalent in Western Europe, and the German working class became politically powerful within these movements. Unlike its counterparts in France and England, the middle class in Germany was unable to challenge the upper class, as the working class had already begun to threaten their increasing political privileges and social status. Faced with this "simultaneous double burden" from above and below, the German middle class chose to associate itself with the conservative political ideas of the upper class for survival.[9]

These conservative implications of late industrialization in Germany derived also from the general trends of political ideas in the late nineteenth century in Europe. During this period, intellectual scepticism about the theory of natural law and the social contract was gaining ground. With the rise of socialist movements, the Rousseauistic political philosophies of popular sovereignty were severely criticized as myth and fiction.[10] The association of the aristocracy and the middle class was marked by the so-called "alliance of rye and steel." The politically and socially influential East Elbian *Junker* and the economically powerful Ruhr industrialists collaborated to maintain the traditional social order and to block political privileges for the German working class. With these constraints, the newly developed middle class in Germany remained politically docile and socially conservative. Thus German industrialization progressed without radical change in the social stratification system or political challenge by the middle class to the still powerful aristocracy.[11]

In sum, the state succeeded in maintaining the political unity of Germany by strengthening social cohesion. The preservation of the traditional social order was the key to holding the German cultural domains within a political unit. Social transformation in Germany toward the end of the nineteenth century mainly changed the distribution of economic power within the society. This so-called *Strukturwandel* of German society did not lead to the demise of the landed aristocracy, as had occurred during the *Meiji Ishin*. Radical social transformation, which the Meiji regime deliberately adopted, was neither the intention nor the reality of the *Kaiserreich*. In contrast, the modern German state could be sustained by defending the status quo ante. The social stratification system of German society was maintained even in the Weimar Republic.

The Gradual Development of National Ideology

Strong historical continuity was also present in the *Kaiserreich* within the notions of national ideology. Its basis had a profound cultural frame and was closely related with the long process of the fixing of the political border of Germany. The insecurity of German-speaking people about the fragile political border of their country resulted in the development of cultural identity as a "German," despite the political fragmentation of the German-speaking domains before 1871. In other words, before the political settlement of a German border, the nation of Germany existed within the consciousness of the people in the German cultural domains. George Mosse captured the theme of Germany's national destiny, i.e. the effect of the prolonged quest of the German people for national unity upon their adherence to indigenous culture: "those Germans who wanted unity looked increasingly to the formation of a cultural cohesion among their people, rather than to a political unity which seemed far distant."[12] Before the formation of the German state, the language was a crucial and workable definition of German nationality. It is important to note that German cultural identity first developed among those who were educated and had a good command of German. Ernest Gellner further elucidates that:

> The term 'culture' on its own is never used in this discussion in its other sense, as *Kultur*, high culture or great tradition, a style of conduct and communication endorsed by the speaker as superior, as setting a norm which should be, but alas often is not, satisfied in real life, and the rules of which are usually codified by a set of respected, norm-giving specialists within the society. 'Culture' without qualification means culture in the anthropological, non-normative sense; *Kultur* appears as high culture.[13]

The German language had then spread widely with a great impact on people's lives as the means of their communication with the government and church.[14]

After the formation of the *Kaiserreich*, the Prussian-guided regime reinforced the consciousness of German *Volk* and deliberately added extra meanings to the idea of the German national identity. This *Volk*-nationalism framed by the people's consciousness of "*Volk*" was the essence of the *Obrigkeitsstaat* [authoritarian state], the rule of the *Kaiserreich*.[15] The notion of political citizenship rested on racial and cultural conceptions. The *Kaiser* proclaimed that "I no longer recognize parties: I only recognize Germans."[16] In the *Kaiserreich*, *Volk* was a powerful political metaphor.

Furthermore, Bismarck strove to locate Protestantism at the core of the German national identity, paradoxically through political secularization. The state attempted to remove the undesirable influence of Catholic dogma and the "Papal dictatorship" in the national politics of the *Kaiserreich*. From the late eighteenth century, Prussia had adopted a policy of strict censorship over freedom of thought in favor of Protestantism. This tradition was deliberately followed in the *Kaiserreich*. From 1871, arguably until the end of World War Two, Protestants enjoyed a higher social status than Catholics in German society, and being a Protestant became something of an elite factor.[17]

Thus, the national ideology of the *Kaiserreich* was consolidated around indigenous elements of *Kultur*, *Volk*, and Christianity, in particular Protestantism. Within this political framework of the formation of the unified German state, the national ideology was synonymous with German cultural

2. THE DEVELOPMENT OF THE STATE EDUCATION SYSTEM

The Political and Cultural Framework of the School System in the *Kaiserreich*

The development of the education system in the German states has a long history. The consolidation of the powerful state bureaucracy in the absolutist state in Prussia laid down a basis for the early development of the state education system.[18] As early as 1794, it was pronounced in the *Peußischen Allgemeinen Landrecht* that "Schools and universities are the organizations of the state." This Prussian education system developed also along with the intensification of nationalism from the early nineteenth century. The military defeat by Napoleon led Prussia to its reform era and became an incentive for strengthening the state. Friedrich Wilhelm III, the king of Prussia, pronounced that *"der Staat muß durch geistige Kräfte ersetzen, was er an physischen verloren hat."*[19] This inaugurated what Hans-Ulrich Wehler coined the "defensive modernization" of Germany.[20] Johann G. Fichte spelled out the significance of education in strengthening German identity by saying that "By means of the new education *we want to mould the Germans into a corporate body*, which shall be stimulated and animated in all its individual members by the same interest."[21] By the middle of the nineteenth century, primary schooling at the *Volksschule* in Prussia became practically universal for children between six and thirteen years of age.[22] The Prussian education system influenced, for example, the French Guizot's School Bill of 1833 and Horace Mann's ideas of the education system of Massachusetts in the United States.

The basis for the development of the education system in Germany was cultural. Edward Reisner noted that "Germany was a land of schools before it was a land of factories."[23] This situation was seen not only in the absolutist state of Prussia but also in the other liberal German states in the south and along the Rhine under similar educational administration to that of Prussia. Calvin Stowe celebrated Bavarian education as the "second best to Prussia."[24] In the German context, the strong presence of state guidance was not the only basis for educational advance. Educational expansion in Prussia as well as in the other German states is to be explained also by the traditionally high respect for *Bildung*. From the days of Kant through the epoch of Humboldt, *Bildung* was meant in Germany to be a life-long *Aufgabe* in the process of *Selbstbildung*, independent of the provision of education by political authorities.[25]

In German, the notion of *Bildung* implied a cumulative process of the cultivation of the inner self of individuals. Bethold Auerbach noted in 1843: "*Nichts vermag Selbstbildung zu ersetzen, aber Schule und Erziehung sind bedeutsame Hilfsmittel derselben.*"[26]

The policy of the *Kaiserreich* fit in with this long-established respect for *Bildung*—education and personal cultivation—in Germany. Within a combination of the effects of socio-cultural traditions and the political framing of education, the state education system in the *Kaiserreich* developed as a reliable political instrument for the retention of the traditional social order and socio-cultural values. The state deliberately used the education system as a means of political consolidation before the 1890s when the state bureaucracy became powerful in Germany.

The Role of the School

The inclination to nationalism could be seen in school curricula, teaching methods, and public rhetoric which centered on an emphasis on pride in German nationality. At the same time the state recognized the system of education as an important cultural asset to strengthen the cultural unity of the German states. Thus, in the *Kaiserreich*, a shared faith in indigenous socio-cultural values among the German people was identified as an important basis of their collective sense of political citizenship. School instruction was conceptually framed as *Staatsbürgererziehung*, education for the cultivation of state citizenship.

The simple curriculum of the *Volksschule* reflected the concept. Instruction in German language, traditional moral disciplines, and Christian religion predominated. In the early stage of the *Volksschule*, more than half of all school hours were spent in learning the German language.[27] During the *Kaiserreich*, the aim of instruction was extended to the creation of "culturally German" people out of those who were ethnically non-Germans, the Poles in particular. Konrad von Studt, the Prussian minister of education (1899-1907), enacted a law which made religious instruction in the German language compulsory.

With a strong framing of Kantian pedagogy, moral education also reinforced the traditional cultural values of German society. Despite Dewey's later criticisms, Kant actually discouraged children's blind obedience to teachers.[28] In fact, he was initially influenced by Rousseau's educational theories in *Émile*, before he became critical about the heavy emphasis on psychology in Rousseauian pedagogy. What Kant valued was children's learning of *Zucht*, which can be called "discipline" in English. The Kantian notion of *Zucht* was an important component of German *Kultur*. This traditional value of *Zucht* was particularly strong in Prussia, Kant's homeland. This Prussian tradition provided a solid basis on which the *Volksschule* could function in the *Kaiserreich* as an important means of the socialization of all the people in the German cultural domains.

Christian education in the *Volksschule* was an additional key means to teach uniform moral discipline. The *Preußische Allgemeine Landrecht* stated that pupils "may be intelligent in regard to all matters within the narrow sphere to which God has called them."[29] The additional importance of Christian religion can be found in its role as part of political education in Germany, as in many other European countries. Europe has been "a normative, ideological community" of a single Christian *ecumene* for a millennium.[30] The Germans have shared such values as being Christian, white, Europe and Western with other Europeans.[31]

However, in the context of Prussian hegemony, Protestantism was strongly emphasised among diverse Christian dogmas. Among university-educated Germans, being a Protestant was important, whereas Catholics were positioned as a marginal group in German society. During this period, the superiority of the Protestants was not only part of their consciousness, it was sanctioned by law. The interpretation of the dogma was intertwined with the political interests of the secular and religious authorities. Under Bismarck and Adalbert Falk, the Prussian minister of education (1872-1879), the state monopolized religious education. In 1876, the fundamental principle of religious instruction and requirements for teacher certificates were defined. Moreover, the state safeguarded a small number of Protestants and founded interconfessional schools in areas dominated by Catholics. This policy eventually triggered a harsh political conflict with the Catholic church, marked by *Kulturkampf*.

The *Volksschule* developed in the *Kaiserreich* as a means of the fulfilment of state political purposes: to form culturally the German people as political citizens of the *Kaiserreich* and to equip non-German people with a German cultural identity. This idea of the education system was applied by the state to all levels of education, including the university.

3. THE STATE, THE UNIVERSITY, AND ELITE FORMATION

The Formation of an Educated Elite in Germany

In the German university, the traditional socio-cultural values of German society had long been maintained, and the university created a social stratum recognized as an elite in German society. Among a flurry of claims about the powerful presence of the social position of educated people in German society, Friedrich Paulsen pinpointed their characteristics:

> In Germany those who have a university education form a kind of intellectual aristocracy.... As a whole they constitute a kind of official nobility, and as a matter of fact, they all really take part in the government and administration.... On the whole, those who follow these callings constitute a homogeneous social stratum; they recognize each other, because of their academic training, as social equals, although this does not, of course, exclude differences of rank within a profession nor gradations of respectability among the professions.[32]

Far earlier than the establishment of a state education system, educated Germans as a social group claimed their common identity based on university education. Although the precise timing of the emergence of this group is unclear, it can be traced back as long ago as the period of Martin Luther, when those who received university education enjoyed their *status scholasticus* in German society.[33] Having won social recognition, the *Gelehrtenstand* separated itself from the majority of the unlearned Germans. In the epoch of *Sturm und Drang*, largely due to the work of Johann G. Herder, *Bildung* was conceptualized as an outstanding quality which would verify the social prestige and the elite status of educated people. They, despite some heterogeneity, shared common characteristics. Under the influence of the French salon culture, they enjoyed intellectual discussions and aristocratic behavior as a social group. Although the term *Bildungsbürgertum* came into actual use in the early twentieth century, *Gebildete* started making a clearer distinction between *Ungebildete* and themselves approximately from the time of Fichte.[34] Humboldt further idealized the notion of *Bildung*. In Germany, particularly in Prussia, Humboldt and his contemporaries formed a tradition in which the aim of university education was identified as the pursuit of purpose-free *Wissenschaft*. The German term indicates not only the English notions of knowledge and science, but also, by extension, the idea of academe or scholarship.[35] While Humboldt undermined the traditional university dominated by snobbish nobles, nepotism, and a pedantic atmosphere, he re-shaped the German university into an intellectual community for philosophers. Humboldtian university culture created a basis for the formation of a new elite marked by *Wissenschaft*, who began to replace the old elite based on noble blood.

In addition to this historically developed esteem for university education, the increasing demand for it by the state bureaucracy elevated the social position of the *Bildungsbürgertum*.[36] As the bureaucracy grew, the educated middle class increasingly filled high-ranking positions, by superseding the previously dominant aristocracy. Max Weber argued that the attainment of

Bildung was an important element of the formation of *Stände* in German society, while economic factors created the division of *Klassen*. Weber spelled out that:

> *Unterschiede der „Bildung" sind heute, gegenüber dem klassenbildenden Element der Besitz- und ökonomischen Funktionsgliederung, zweifellos der wichtigste eigentlich ständebildende Unterschied. . . . Unterschiede der „Bildung" sind—man mag das noch so sehr bedauern—eine der allerstärksten rein innerlich wirkenden sozialen Schranken. Vor allem in Deutschland, wo fast die sämtlichen privilegierten Stellungen innerhalb und außerhalb des Staatsdienstes nicht nur an eine Qualifikation von Fachwissen, sondern außerdem vor „allgemeiner Bildung" geknüpft [sind] und das ganze Schul- und Hochschulsystem in deren Dienst gestellt ist.*[37]

Indeed, the principles of tenure and seniority were present in the civil administration in the nineteenth century in Germany. At the same time, however, the access of the middle class to the bureaucracy had gradually grown. This paralleled the expansion of the university. University education attracted the middle class also because of the wider career opportunities for university graduates in the private sector after industrialization.

Within this expansion process, the sons of the aristocracy and the *Bürgertum* began to share a sympathetic kinship through academic experience despite the barriers of social origins. Although the number of students from the middle class exceeded those from the aristocracy in the nineteenth century, middle-class students were absorbed by the aristocracy in terms of its political stance and social values. Both the old ruling groups and the new leading *Bürgertum* acted as the fortress of German society and its tradition. It was a distinct German social phenomenon which Hans Rosenberg termed "social neo-feudalisation."[38] By absorbing aristocratic political ideas and socio-cultural values, the *Bildungsbürgertum* gained further social recognition.

Another condition for the eminence of the *Bildungsbürgertum* rested on delayed industrialization and the tardy structural change of German society. Late industrial revolution and its consequence of slow urbanization in German cities led to the political underdevelopment of the urban middle class.[39] This slow progress in urbanization made the group solidarity of the *Wirtschaftsbürgertum* weak. In contrast, the well-developed system of the *Gymnasium* and the university formed the *Bildungsbürgertum* as a solid social group. Even before the unification, the students of the German university moved across *Länder* and often enjoyed intellectual interaction in more than one university. By the time the *Wirtschaftsbürgertum* began to be recognized in German society, the *Bildungsbürgertum* had already grown as a solid social group with high intellectual standards and similar academic culture in each *Land* or region almost throughout the nation.

Indeed, Prussian hegemony in the *Kaiserreich* affected the state policy of differentiation for the universities and made their development uneven. Nonetheless, the principle of *Kulturhoheit* has been maintained in German education policy after the *Preußische Allgemeine Landrecht* of 1794, and universities in each region developed well according to their own political, economic, and social circumstances. Universities were scattered in cities and towns. Germany had a greater number of universities throughout the nation than many other countries in Europe. By the first half of the nineteenth century, for instance, England had possessed only three universities.[40] The academics and students of German universities shared similar academic standards of learning as well as intellectual competition based on inter-state academic mobility.[41] In Germany, despite differences in size and preference for some fields of study among universities, institutions were not organized within a vertical structuring of the university system.

In these processes of the development of the *Bildungsbürgertum*, traditional socio-cultural values were continually reproduced by the members of the status group which solidly resided in the upper-middle echelon of German society. The assertion of *Kultur* and the strong academic inclination in the university toward German philosophies, in particular romanticism and idealism, reinforced this reproduction of traditional cultural values. Through their attainment in the *Wissenschaften* and in philosophical idealism, the German intellectual elites maintained their self-consciousness as the "guardians of *Kultur*," as well as of the traditional social order.[42] As Norbert Elias has argued, the idea of French civilization and that of *die deutsche Kultur* were the clear articulation of an insistence upon national quality, the specific values of the individual nations. Moreover, as Elias has suggested, the notion of *Kultur* embraced not only a sense of national identity, but also specific class values.[43] The *Bildungsbürgertum* continued to maintain its traditional characteristics during the *Kaiserreich* with some adjustments to changes in German society at the turn of the century.

The Role of the University

Traditionally in Prussia where many of the German universities were located, the sovereignty of the university was in the hands of the state according to the *Preußische Allgemeine Landrecht*. Despite this legal sanction, however, state intervention in university affairs was actually not strong until the first half of the nineteenth century. Until the middle of the nineteenth century, society in Germany was on the whole quite rebellious.[44] In fact, during the so-called early Biedermeier period, Germany enjoyed bourgeois culture and bourgeois liberalism more than after the German middle class became economically strong.

However, the failure of the 1848 revolution marked a significant turning point in the development of liberalism in Germany as well as in Western Europe. The cleansing of liberal professors after 1848 had a significant impact on this tendency of the German university and led to a change in its political and social role. Actual freedom was limited to purely academic matters. For example, university administration, including the appointment and dismissal of personnel, was under state control. Professors, who were approved by the state, had the authority to appoint junior professors. According to Paulsen, about 20 to 30% of university academics were appointed by the state against or without the consent of the faculties.[45] Lecturers were customarily required to have an authorization from professors for their teaching certification. Given the tighter state control, the university in the *Kaiserreich* maintained aloofness and quietism. As many German professors stated, academics were personally intimidated by the Ministry of Education or its ministers. Max Dessoir, philosophy professor in Berlin, noted the fear of Friedrich Althoff—a "modest czar"—among professors even after his death and blamed this harmful legacy for the continued political obedience of German university academics.[46]

The role of German academics in the *Kaiserreich* is well captured by Bernd Martin:

> German "mandarins," whose political and social outlook had been shaped by Wilhelmian Germany, saw themselves as an apolitical and impartial elite whose main task was to protect the monarchical order and its class distinctions from subversive or foreign influences.[47]

As declared by the minister of education, J. R. Bosse, in 1898, university education was to fill youth with loyalty to God, king, and the monarchy. Weber put it bluntly: "The 'freedom of science' exists in Germany within the limits of ecclesiastical and political acceptability. Outside these limits there is none."[48] Max Weber and Werner Sombart were among the few university academics who contested the threat to scholarly autonomy by bureaucratic control and the inflation of the self-esteem of academics in the *Kaiserreich*. Weber's magnum opus drew much attention in his lifetime in the United States—but not in Germany.[49]

The political compliance of the educated middle-class elite was a part of its adjustment to structural changes in German society in the late nineteenth century. After industrialization, the German middle class grew steadily. An increasing number of middle-class people began to attend university. The traditional elite accused the newly developing *Kleinbürger*, or petit bourgeoisie, of being the cause of the decline of the traditions of German *Kultur* and *Bildung*. Toward the turn of the century, cultural pessimism was prevalent among the educated elite.[50] Within this cultural crisis of the German middle class in the *Kaiserreich*, the ideas of *Kultur* and *Bildung* became less aesthetic and were increasingly shaped by provincialism and narrow nationalism, as the former *Kleinbürger* were absorbed as part of the *Bildungsbürgertum*.

The nationalistic sentiment of the educated German elite can also be traced to the epoch of Humboldt. Although Humboldt did not advocate the political obedience of the university to the state, his contribution to the establishment of Berlin University had much to do with his official status as a top-ranking bureaucrat of Prussia. He was also indebted to eminent colleagues, such as Fichte and Friedrich Schleiermacher, for framing the idea of the university and university reform in Prussia. Humboldt valued the role of the university as the guarantor of the moral and cultural quality of the state. Intellectual humiliation through the destruction of German universities under the French Occupation stimulated a sense of statehood and cultural pride among Germans in academic circles.[51] Neo-humanism as well as idealism was an expression by German intellectuals of their antagonism to French rationalism and English pragmatism.[52]

Based on this intellectual tradition established by Humboldt and his contemporaries, the cultivation of *Kultur* through *Bildung* rather than empirical knowledge became an important role of the German university. Friedrich Paulsen and many other German scholars insisted that the university should not become a mere professional state school for the production of bureaucrats, like the French university. In addition, Paulsen believed that the concentration of academic institutions in the capital of the state would bring too much political influence on the university and science.[53] He asserted that "the centralization of scientific life" in Paris, an example followed by Japan, would ruin the aesthetic pursuit of the high notion of *Bildung* and *Wissenschaft* and bring about the "intellectual impoverishment of the provinces," as actually befell Meiji Japan.

The political dedication of the German university to the state exhibited the legacy of the Humboldtian traditions, what Konrad Jarausch termed "the Humboldt syndrome" of apoliticism.[54] The idea of *Einsamkeit und Freiheit* exhibited Humboldt's ideal of educated elites of independent mind. The ideas of the Humboldtian university as a public and moral entity as well as the guardian of German *Kultur* fit within the political framework of the *Kaiserreich*. What the German elite had suffered from the synthesis of the burden of traditions and a particular pattern of the transition of German society during the *Kaiserreich* is epitomised by Fritz Stern:

> German elites were under all kinds of pressure: the Junker class was under economic pressure; the middle classes under pressure from below; and the country, they both felt, was threatened from abroad. Grace under pressure ... was not a notable trait of an illiberal society. ... The German elite were so prone to surrender to illusions, to a kind of negative utopianism, that for this reason alone it would be hard to call them conservative.[55]

The political power and social influence of the bureaucracy and the underdeveloped sense of the *bürgerliche Gesellschaft* in the *Kaiserreich* had an impact on the development of the German university and the university-educated elite. In addition to the traditional role of the university in affirming the values of German *Kultur*, the conservative policy of the *Kaiserreich* reinforced a nationalistic stance.

4. CONCLUSION

Prussian conservative policy was legitimized by its strong political and military power in combining the German states in the *Kaiserreich*. The retention of the traditional social order was the core of the national ideology of the *Kaiserreich*. The state education system developed within this political framework. The role of education—both for the school and the university—centered on the reinforcement of German cultural identity. At the lower level, broadly expanded primary education provided the state with a useful channel for the dissemination of the national ideology to the German-speaking people.

Neither was the university system immune to the political and social contexts of the creation of the *Kaiserreich*. The characteristics of the university-educated elite in Germany are related to specific patterns in the development of German society. This relationship can be located in two historical dimensions.

First, the development of university-educated people as an elite was related to the powerful role of the state bureaucracy, late industrialization, and the tradition of high esteem for *Bildung*. Delayed industrial revolution was a favorable condition for the earlier development of the *Bildungsbürgertum* and the late rise of the *Wirtschaftsbürgertum*. The consequence of this was the high social positioning of the former vis-à-vis the latter.

Second, the political framing of the creation of the *Kaiserreich* reinforced this pattern of the formation of the university-educated elite. The conservative policy of the *Kaiserreich* shaped the traditionalist ideas and socio-cultural values of this elite. With the low social mobility of nineteenth-century Germany, an increasing number of students from middle-class families associated themselves politically and socially with students from aristocratic families. The *Bildungsbürgertum* came to share many assumptions with the aristocracy. They took up the conservative political views and socio-cultural values of the aristocracy and developed a sense of themselves as a group. This reinforced the social recognition of the *Bildungsbürgertum*.

In addition, based on the traditional principle of *Kulturhoheit*, universities enjoyed high standards of *Wissenschaft* and a common sense of academic culture throughout the nation. The equal development of the intellectual standards of universities throughout Germany also created a broad basis for the formation of the esprit de corps of university-educated people. For this cohesive social group in Germany, the traditional values of their own society were not only deeply ingrained in their thinking, but also exhibited the essence of their existence per se within German society.

NOTES

1. William Carr, *A History of Germany 1815-1945* (London: Arnold, 1969); Reinhard Kühnl, "The German *Sonderweg* Reconsidered: Continuities and discontinuities in modern German history," in *Rewriting the German Past*, ed. Reinhard Alter and Peter Monteath (Atlantic Highlands: Humanities Press, 1997), 115-58; Bill Jordan, *The State: Authority and Autonomy* (Oxford: Basil Blackwell, 1985); Wolfgang Mommsen, *Imperial Germany 1867-1918: Politics, Culture, and Society in an Authoritarian State* (New York: Arnold, 1995).

2. Quoted from: Louis Snyder, *Roots of German Nationalism* (London: Bloomington, 1978), 67.

3. Maxwell Night, *The German Executive, 1890-1933* (Stanford: Stanford University Press, 1952), 33. Eisenstadt argues that the aristocracy in Germany was to be grouped among the "politically powerful" nobilities in European countries—such as Poland, Sweden, Hungary, and England—compared with the French, Danish, and Spanish aristocracies. Samuel Eisenstadt, *The Political Systems of Empires* (New York: The Free Press, 1963), 78. See also: Werner Mosse, "Nobility and Bourgeoisie in Nineteenth-Century Europe: A comparative view," in *Bourgeois Society in Nineteenth-Century Europe*, ed. Jürgen Kocka and Allen Mitchell (Oxford: Berg Publishers Limited, 1993), 70-102; Hans-Ulrich Wehler, *The German Empire 1871-1918* (Leamington Spa: Berg Publishers, 1985).

4. Although class I and class II consisted of the people of the upper social strata, which comprised only 4.7% and 12.6% of the whole populations respectively, they contained two-thirds of the electors. On the other hand, though class III, the people of the poorest stratum, had 82.7% of the voters, they could claim only one-third of the electors. Bendix, *Kings or People*, 429.

5. Dieter Langewiesche, "Liberalism and the Middle Classes in Europe," in *Bourgeois Society in Nineteenth-Century Europe*, ed. Jürgen Kocka and Allen Mitchell (Oxford: Berg Publishers Limited, 1993), 50.

6. Huntington, *The Soldiers and the State*, 104-105. See also: Correlli Barnett, "The Education of Military Elites," in *Governing Elites*, ed. Rupert Wilkinson (New York: Oxford University Press, 1969), 193-214.

7. Weber, *Economy and Society*, 1,392. Kocka argues that the bureaucratic tradition of German society explains the "specific continuity" of authoritarian rule in Germany from the period of the *Kaiserreich* through to the 1930s. Jürgen Kocka, "Capitalism and Bureaucracy in German Industrialization before 1914," *The Economic History Review* 34, no. 3 (1981): 453-68. See also: Beck, *The Origin of the Authoritarian Welfare State*; Carl Friedrich, "The Failure of a One-Party System: Hitler Germany," in *Authoritarian Politics in Modern Society: The Dynamics of Established One-Party Systems*, ed. Samuel Huntington and Clement Moore (New York: Basic Books, Inc., Publishers, 1971), 239-60; Mommsen, *Imperial Germany*; Franz Neumann, ed., *The Democratic and the Authoritarian State: Essays in Political and Legal Theory* (New York: Free Press of Glencoe, 1957); Fritz Stern, *The Politics of Cultural Despair: A Study in the Rise of German Ideology* (Berkeley: University of California Press, 1974); Hans-Ulrich Wehler, *Deutsche Gesellschaftsgeschichte: Von der "Deutschen Doppelrevolution" bis zum Beginn des Ersten Weltkrieges 1849-1914*, vol. 3 (München: Verlag CH Beck, 1987). Cf. David Blackbourn and Geoff Eley, *The Peculiarities of German History: Bourgeois Society and Politics in Nineteenth-Century Germany* (Oxford: Oxford University Press, 1984); Geoff Eley, *From Unification to Nazism: Reinterpreting the German Past* (Boston: Allen & Unwin, 1986); Thomas Nipperdey, "Wehlers 'Kaiserreich': Eine kritische Auseinandersetzung," *Geschichte und Gesellschaft* 1 (1975): 539-60; Thomas Nipperdey, *Deutsche Geschichte 1866-1918*, vol. 1 (Munich: Verlag CH Beck, 1990).

8. Ralf Dahrendorf, *Society and Democracy in Germany* (London: Weidenfeld and Nicolson, 1967). A number of prominent academics supported state-guided industrialization, except for a small number of opponents such as Lujo Brentano, Adolf Wagner, and Gustav Schmoller.

9. Jürgen Kocka, "German History before Hitler: The debate about the German *Sonderweg*," *Journal of Contemporary History* 23 (1988): 3-16. Similar accounts: Hermann Glaser, *Bildungsbürgertum und Nationalismus: Politik und Kultur im Wilhelminische Deutschland* (Munich: Deutscher Taschenbuch Verlag, 1993); Harmut Kaelble, "French Bourgeoisie and German Bürgertum, 1870-1914," in *Bourgeois Society in Nineteenth-Century Europe*, ed. Jürgen Kocka and Allen Mitchell (Oxford: Berg Publishers Limited, 1993), 273-301.

10. Reinhard Bendix, *Max Weber: An intellectual portrait* (London: Methuen & Co., Ltd., 1966), 432-33; Guy Dodge, ed., *Jean-Jacques Rousseau: Authoritarian Libertarian?* (London: DC Heath and Company, 1971), 42-43; Mosca, *The Ruling Class*, 51-53.

11. Karl Bracher, *Turning Points in Modern Times: Essays on German and European History* (Cambridge: Harvard University Press, 1995), 125. Struve suggests that the "social dislocation" of this middle class after the collapse of the *Kaiserreich* brought about the political and social insecurity of Germany from the 1920s which caused the rise of the Nazis. Walter Struve, *Elites against Democracy: Leadership Ideals in Bourgeois Political Thought in Germany, 1890-1933* (Princeton: Princeton University Press, 1973). See also: Hannah Arendt, *The Origins of Totalitarianism* (London: Allen and Unwin, 1967 [1951]); Jacob Talmon, *Myth of the Nation and Vision of Revolution: Ideological Polarization in the Twentieth Century* (New Brunswick: Transaction Publishers, 1991).

12. George Mosse, *The Crisis of German Ideology: Intellectual Origins of the Third Reich* (London: Weidenfeld and Nicolson, 1966), 2-3. Similar accounts: John Breuilly, *The Formation of the First German Nation-State, 1800-1871* (London: Macmillan Press Ltd., 1996); Glaser, *Bildungsbürgertum*; Mann, *The Sources of Social Power*, 250, 301-302.

13. Ernest Gellner, *Nations and Nationalism* (Oxford: Blackwell, 1983), 92.

14. Breuilly, *The Formation of the First German Nation-State*, 101-102, 112.

15. Christina Berg, ed., *Handbuch der deutschen Bildungsgeschichte: Von der Reichsgründung bis zum Ende des Ersten Weltkriegs,* vol. IV (Munich: CH Beck, 1991), 183. Similar arguments: Mosse, *The Crisis of German Ideology,* 15; Edward Reisner, *Nationalism and Education since 1789: A Social and Political History of Modern Education* (New York: The Macmillan Company, 1922), 199.

16. Quoted from Karl Bracher, *The Age of Ideologies: A History of Political Thought in the Twentieth Century* (London: Weidenfeld and Nicolson, 1984), 92.

17. Kurt Nowak, "Protetantische Eliten. Aspekte eines Vergleichs zwischen Deutschland und Frankreich (1870/71-1918)," in *Eliten in Deutschland und Frankreich im 19. und 20. Jahrhundert: Strukturen und Beziehungen,* ed. Rainer Hudemann and Georges-Henri Soutou (Munich: R. Oldenbourg Verlag, 1994), 156-73; Ringer, *Fields of Knowledge*; Helmut Smith, *German Nationalism and Religious Conflict: Culture, Ideology, Politics, 1870-1914* (Princeton: Princeton University Press, 1995), 41-42; Klaus Vondung, "Zur Lage der Gebildeten in der wilhelminischen Zeit," in *Das wilhelmische Bildungsbürgertum: Zur Sozialgeschichte seiner Ideen,* ed. Klaus Vondung (Göttingen: Bandenhoeck & Ruprecht, 1976), 20-33. Spranger argued that German Protestantism substantially influenced Humboldt's idea of the university as well. Eduard Spranger, *Wilhelm von Humboldt und die Humanitatsidee* (Berlin: Verlag von Reuther & Reichard, 1909). The academic institutions in the *Kaiserreich,* especially those with high intellectual standards, were also strongly influenced by the ideas of Protestant scholars. Rainer Hudemann and Georges-Henri Soutou, eds., *Eliten in Deutschland und Frankreich im 19. und 20. Jahrhundert: Strukturen und Beziehungen,* vol. 2 (Munich: R. Oldenbourg Verlag, 1994).

18. Andy Green, *Education and State Formation: The Rise of Education Systems in England, France and the USA* (London: Macmillan, 1990).

19. "The state must replace its physical loss with spiritual strength." The quotation from: Hans-Ulrich Wehler, *Deutsche Gesellschaftsgeschichte: Vom Feudalismus des Alten Reiches bis zur Defensiven Modernisierung der Reformära 1700-1815,* vol. 1 (Munich: Verlag CH Beck, 1987), 473.

20. Wehler, *Deutsche Gesellschaftsgeschichte,* vol. 1, 472-74.

21. *The Third Address to the German Nation,* quoted from: James Bowen, *A History of Western Education: The Modern West: Europe and the New World,* vol. 3 (London: Methuen & Co. Ltd., 1981), 259 (italics in Bowen's text). The address was a strong call for an *antiständische, nationalbewußte, allgemeine Nationalerziehung.* That is to say, Fichte believed that social divisions into estates would weaken the political consolidation of the country. For the same reason, Fichte believed that the separation of education for boys and girls would hinder the development of perfect manhood, which consequently would impair the moral consolidation of the nation. Johann Fichte, *On the Nature of the Scholar, and Its Manifestations* (London: John Chapman, 1845); George Turnbull, *The Educational Theory of J. G. Fichte: A Critical Account, together with Translations* (London: The University Press of Liverpool Limited, 1926); Wehler, *Deutsche Gesellschaftsgeschichte,* vol. 1, 481.

22. Fritz Ringer, *Education and Society in Modern Europe* (Bloomington: Indiana University Press, 1979), 33.

23. Reisner, *Nationalism and Education,* 181.

24. From the report of Stowe, a leader of the common school movement in the US, in March 1836, quoted from: Karl Schleunes, *Schooling and Society: The Politics of Education in Prussia and Bavaria 1750-1900* (Oxford: Berg Publishers Limited, 1989), 1-2.

25. Immanuel Kant, *On History* (New York: The Bobbs-Merill Company, Inc., 1963), 3; Wilhelm von Humboldt, *The Sphere and Duties of Government* (London: John Chapman, 1954 [1852]), 66.

26. "Nothing can be a substitute for (the process of) self-cultivation, but the school and education are its meaningful aid." From his essay, *Vom gebildeten Deutschen*, in the appendix of Glaser, *Bildungsbürgertum*, 225-27.

27. Gerhardt Giese, ed., *Quellen zur deutschen Schulgeschichte seit 1800*, vol. 15 (Göttingen: Musterschmidt-Verlag, 1961), 170-71.

28. Imanuel Kant, *Kant on Education (Über Pädagogik)* (London: Kegan Paul, Trench, Trübner & Co. Ltd., 1992 [1899]).

29. Quoted from: Reisner, *Nationalism and Education*, 144-45.

30. Mann, *The Sources of Social Power*, 35-36.

31. David Coulby and Crispin Jones, *Postmodernity and European Education Systems: Cultural Diversity and Centralist Knowledge* (Stoke-on-Trent: Trentham, 1995), 41-42; David Coulby and Crispin Jones, "Post-modernity, Education and European Identities," *Comparative Education* 32, no. 2 (1996), 176-77.

32. Friedrich Paulsen, *The German Universities and University Study* (New York: Longmans, Green, and Co., 1906), 119-21.

33. Berg, *Handbuch*, 18; Ulrich Engelhardt, *Bildungsbürgertum: Begriffs- und Dogmengeschichte eines Etikett* (Stuttgart: Klett-Cotta, 1986), 33-53.

34. Alexander Busch, *Die Geschichte des Privatdozenten: Eine soziologische Studie zur großbetrieblichen Entwicklung der deutschen Universitäten* (Stuttgart: Ferdinand Enke Verlag, 1959), 9-10; Werner Conze and Jürgen Kocka, "Einleitung," in *Bildungsbürgertum im 19. Jahrhundert: Bildungssystem und Professionalisierung in internationalen Vergleichen*, ed. Werner Conze and Jürgen Kocka (Stuttgart: Klett-Cotta, 1985), 9-26; Engelhardt, *Bildungsbürgertum*, 53-84, 117-15, 180; Glaser, *Bildungsbürgertum*, 30; Hans Weil, *Die Entstehung des deutschen Bildungsprinzips* (Bonn: Friedrich Cohen, 1930), 150-51, 219-20.

35. Rosalind Pritchard, "Academic Freedom and Autonomy in the United Kingdom and Germany," *Minerva* 36 (1998), 104-105; Fritz Ringer, *The Decline of the German Mandarins: The German Academic Community 1890-1933* (Hanover and London: University Press of New England, 1990 [1969]), 102-103.

36. Engelhardt, *Bildungsbürgertum*, 20-33, 84; Jürgen Kocka, "The European Pattern and the German Case," in *Bourgeois Society in Nineteenth-Century Europe*, ed. Jürgen Kocka and Alan Mitchell (Oxford: Berg Publishers Limited, 1993), 15-16; Peter Lundgreen, "Zur Konstituierung des „Bildungsbürgertums": Berufs- und Bildungsauslese der Akademiker in Preußen," in *Bildungsbürgertum im 19. Jahrhundert: Bildungssystem und Professionalisierung in internationalen Vergleichen*, ed. Werner Conze and Jürgen Kocka (Stuttgart: Klett-Cotta, 1985), 78; Ringer, *The Decline of the German Mandarins*, 7-8.

37. "Today differences in attained 'education' are without doubt the most important element of the virtual formation of status group instead of the element of property and economic power which had defined a class. . . . The differences of 'education,' unfortunately, create one of the most rigid social barriers embedded within society. This is especially so in Germany, where almost all the privileged positions inside and outside state service are closely linked not only with the qualification in a specific faculty but also with 'general education' and with the whole school and university systems." Max Weber, *Gesammelte Politische Schriften* (Tübingen: JCB Mohr (Paul Siebeck), 235-36.

38. Hans Rosenberg, "The Pseudo-Democratisation of the Junker Class," in *The Social History of Politics: Critical Perspectives in West German Historical Writing since 1945*, ed. Georg Iggers (Heidelberg: Berg Publishers Ltd., 1985), 99.

39. Herbert Marcuse, *Reason and Revolution: Hegel and the Rise of Social Theory* (New York: Humanity Books, 1999 [1941]), 3.

40. Phillips suggests that not only the number, but also the academic atmosphere of the German university were worshipped by young Englishmen who were dissatisfied with "the duller halls of Oxford and Cambridge." David Phillips, "Beyond Travellers' Tales: Some nineteenth-century British commentators on education in Germany," *Oxford Review of Education* 26, no. 1 (2000), 51. In 1894 in Germany, there were eleven universities in Prussia, three in Baden, and two in Bavaria, and the rest of six universities were scattered in Saxony Kingdom, Württemberg, Reichslande, Saxon Duches, Hesse, and Mecklenburg-Schwerin. Friedrich Paulsen, *Geschichte des Gelehrten Unterrichts: Auf den deutschen Schulen und Universitäten. Vom Ausgang des Mittelalters bis zur Gegenwart. Mit besonderer Rücksicht auf den klassischen Unterricht* (Leipzig: Verlag von Veit & Comp., 1896), 248-49.

41. Joseph Ben-David and Awraham Zloczower, "Universities and Academic Systems in Modern Societies," *European Journal of Sociology* 3 (1962), 50-51.

42. Konrad Jarausch, *Students, Society, and Politics in Imperial Germany: The Rise of Academic Illiberalism* (Princeton: Princeton University Press, 1982); Charles McClelland, *State, Society, and University in Germany 1700-1914* (Cambridge: Cambridge University Press, 1980).

43. Norbert Elias, *The Civilizing Process: The History of Manners* (Oxford: Basil Blackwell, 1994 [1939]), 21-22; Norbert Elias, *Studien über die Deutschen: Machtkämpfe und Habitusentwicklung im 19. Und 20. Jahrhundert* (Frankfurt am Main: Suhrkamp, 1998), 176.

44. Charles Tilly, Louise Tilly, and Richard Tilly, *The Rebellious Century 1830-1930* (London: JM Dent & Sons Ltd., 1975), 230; Wolfgang Kaschuba, "German Bürgerlichkeit after 1800: Culture as symbolic practice," in *Bourgeois Society in Nineteenth-Century Europe*, ed. Jürgen Kocka and Allen Mitchell (Oxford: Berg Publishers Limited, 1993), 392-422.

45. Friedrich Paulsen, *Die deutschen Universitäten und das Universitätsstudium* (Berlin: 1902), 101-102.

46. Althoff was the Prussian minister of education (1882-1908). Dessoir claimed that this political obedience of university academics laid down a basis for their surrender to National-Socialism. Max Dessoir, *Buch der Erinnerung* (Stuttgart: Ferdinand Enke Verlag, 1947), 207-208. See also: Daniel Lerner, Ithiel de Sola Pool, and George Schueller, "The Nazi Elite," in *World Revolutionary Elites: Studies in coercive ideological movements*, ed. Harold Lasswell and Daniel Lerner (Cambridge: MIT Press, 1965), 194-318; Friedrich Meinecke, *Erlebtes 1862-1901* (Leipzig: Koehler & Amelang, 1941).

47. Martin, *Japan and Germany*, 44.

48. Quoted from: McClelland, *State, Society*, 315. Cf. Iggers and Hampe (1976) argue that Weber himself was no democrat. Iggers goes further "All except Mommsen supported Bismarck's break with his liberal allies in 1878." Georg Iggers, "Introduction," in *The Social History of Politics: Critical Perspectives in West German Historical Writing since 1945*, ed. Georg Iggers (Leamington Spa: Berg Publishers Ltd., 1985), 1-48; Peter Hampe, "Sozioökonomische und psychische Hintergründe der bildungsbürgerlichen Imperialbegeisterung," in *Das Wilhelmische Bildungsbürgertum: Zur Sozialgeschichte seiner Ideen*, ed. Klaus Vondung (Göttingen: Bandenhoeck & Ruprecht, 1976), 67-79.

49. Peter Gay, *Weimar Culture: The Outsider as Insider* (London: Secker & Warburg, 1968), 38.

50. Paulsen contemptuously said that "*Halbbildung keinen 'inneren Wert' besitz[t].*" Quoted from: Wehler, *Deutsche Gesellschaftsgeschichte,* vol. 3, 733. Nietzsche was no less harsh by complaining about the "destruction of the natural order of ranks in the kingdom of the intellect" His lecture, "On the Future of Our Educational Institutions," in 1872, in: Gordon Alexander Craig, *Germany 1866-1945* (Oxford: Clarendon Press, 1978).

51. Bowen, *A History of Western Education*, 259; David Phillips, "Learning from Elsewhere in Education: Some perennial problems revisited with reference to British interest in Germany,"

Comparative Education 36, no. 3 (2000): 297-307. An example was the reconstruction of Halle University by the king in 1807 after the destruction of the University by Napoleon in 1806.

52. Humboldt, *The Sphere and Duties of Government*; Paulsen, *Geschichte des Gelehrten Unterrichts*; Ringer, *The Decline of the German Mandarins*; Spranger, *Wilhelm von Humboldt*.

53. Paulsen, *The German Universities*.

54. Konrad Jarausch, "The Humboldt Syndrome: West German universities, 1945-1989: An Academic *Sonderweg*?," in *German Universities Past and Future: Crisis or Renewal?*, ed. Mitchell Ash (Providence: Berghahn Books, 1997), 33-49. Similar accounts: Rüdiger vom Bruch, "A Slow Farewell to Humboldt?: Stages in the History of German Universities, 1810-1945," in *German Universities Past and Future: Crisis or Renewal?*, ed. Mitchell Ash (Oxford: Berghahn Books, 1997), 3-27; Peter Lundgreen, "Mythos Humboldt Today: Teaching, Research, and Administration," in *German Universities Past and Future: Crisis or Renewal?*, ed. Mitchell Ash (Oxford: Berghahn Books, 1997), 127-148.

55. Fritz Stern, *The Failure of Illiberalism* (London: George Allen & Unwin Ltd., 1972), xx-xxi.

Conclusion of Part I

Thus the different and particular *raisons d'état* of Meiji Japan and the *Kaiserreich* shaped the notions of Japanese and German national identity and the patterns of elite formation. The university-educated elites in Japan and Germany developed from different traditions in the different contexts of state formation. These elites were formed within the specific political framing of the role of the university by the state.

In Meiji Japan, the absorption of Western knowledge was the key means to achieve the double goals of the formation of the modern Japanese state. The prime political agenda of state formation was directly reflected in the development of the university. Within this state policy, the Japanese university pursued its pragmatic tasks. For this purpose, the state had to undermine the imported idea of the university—particularly the German idea of the cultivation of a common academic culture possessed by a university-educated elite. The consequence was that there developed no cohesive social group of university-educated people. In addition, they remained ambivalent in their valuations of indigenous socio-cultural values and exogenous ideas.

Compared with the case of Japan, the economic role of the university was less salient within the process of state formation in Germany. In the *Kaiserreich*, the core aim of the state was the political consolidation of the German states. The retention of traditional social order and the emphasis on socio-cultural values were major means to fulfil the aim. The political framing of the role of the university by the *Kaiserreich* fitted with the older academic culture of the German university. The university undertook the guardianship of indigenous *Kultur* within the political objectives of the *Kaiserreich*. Within the traditional social order, the national ideology based on German cultural identity was judged by the state to have validity for all social groups and shaped the role of education as a whole from the *Volksschule* throughout the university in the *Kaiserreich*. The high esteem for *Bildung* as a lifelong *Aufgabe* also influenced the social attitudes of most Germans, who had been exposed to the differentiated education provided by the multi-track school system.

This system survived the attempt at the large-scale reform of education in Germany after World War Two. A similar system in Japan was completely replaced by a single-track school system. Overall extensive changes were made in Japanese education, while many proposed reforms resulted in failure in Germany. In other words, Japanese and German leaders reacted differently to American proposals for the education reforms. From the start of the Occupation, Japanese leaders showed willingness to adopt American proposals and change the pre-1945 Japanese education system after the American model. In contrast, in the American zone of Germany, German leaders remained generally opposed to the American proposals and deliberately attempted to retain indigenous educational patterns. Some differences in the individual *Länder* notwithstanding, this reaction of the Germans was consistent.

It is to the details of these processes that our attention now turns in part II.

Part II

Chapter Four

The Occupation Reform in Japan, 1945-1952

1. THE CHARACTERISTICS OF THE OCCUPATION IN JAPAN

The Dominance of the United States

Technically, World War Two in the Pacific theatre ended with the acceptance of the Potsdam Declaration by the Showa *Tenno* and his government on 15 August 1945. Upon the arrival of General Douglas MacArthur, appointed as the Supreme Commander for the Allied Powers (SCAP) in Japan, the Japanese media indicated that the people had already tried to show their full compliance with the victors.[1] On 2 September, Japan signed the Instrument of Surrender in Tokyo Bay, and the actual Occupation started.

From the outset of the Occupation, the Allies failed to organize co-ordination among themselves for the Occupation in Japan. On 26 December 1945, the eleven Allied countries finally agreed to form the Far Eastern Commission (FEC) as an official policy-making body for the Occupation in Japan. The power distribution within the FEC was, however, uneven. The Allied Council for Japan (ACJ), consisting of the US, the UK, the USSR, and China, became exclusively in charge of the Occupation. In the process of the establishment of the ACJ, the US government insisted on, and actually gained, its supreme authority among the Allies.

American supremacy in post-War Japan derived from a number of conditions. First, the Americans were well prepared for the Occupation in Japan compared with the other Allies. In 1939, the US government formed the Advisory Committee on Problems of Foreign Relations under Cordell Hull, the US secretary of state (1933-1944), aiming to gain a leading position for the United States among the allied powers. Strategically, the United States claimed that the integrated power of the Allies, supported by strong leadership, would be necessary for the effective Occupation in Japan. As Positive Policy for the Reorientation of the Japanese stated, the chaos which had occurred in Italy and Germany had to be avoided.[2] Morally, the Americans claimed supremacy in Japan because of their large contribution to the defeat of Japan. MacArthur stressed that "When we desperately needed armed forces for the war in the Pacific, none of the Allies supplied such forces."[3] Realistically, the United States was the only country which possessed the economic and military power to occupy Japan in addition to the Allied operation in Europe. The British sent some troops to an area in southeast Japan, which was physically small in size, politically insignificant, and subject to MacArthur's command.[4] With the agreement of the FEC, American dominance in Japan was affirmed in the Initial Post-Surrender Policy for Japan of 22 September 1945.

This American power was reinforced by the supreme authority of MacArthur endorsed by President Franklin Roosevelt. MacArthur's authority remained unaffected by Roosevelt's death. All through the Occupation, the political authority of General MacArthur was far more powerful in name and deed than that of General Lucius Clay in Germany. Harry Truman delivered the following message to MacArthur in Tokyo on 6 September 1945:

> (1) The authority of the Emperor and the Japanese Government to rule the state is subordinate to you as Supreme Commander for the Allied Powers. . . . Since your authority is supreme, you will not entertain any question on the part of the Japanese as to its scope. (2) Control of Japan shall be exercised through the Japanese Government to the extent that such an arrangement produces satisfactory results. This does not prejudice your right to act directly if required. You may enforce the orders issued by you by the employment of such measures as you deem necessary, including the use of force.[5]

It has been claimed that the idolatry of "Emperor MacArthur" was partly eclipsed especially after the gradual release of more documents of the Occupation from the 1970s.[6] However—apart from the question of MacArthur's personal charisma—judicial, legislative, and administrative powers were in the hands of the Supreme Commander. The fact was that the ACJ was subject to MacArthur's decisions and executive power. The countries of the ACJ actually reported to MacArthur and his American staff, who reported directly to Washington. William Sebald, MacArthur's political advisor at SCAP, noted later that "Never before in the history of the United States had such enormous and absolute power been placed in the hands of a single individual."[7]

The American Views of Japan

Japan was a country whose society and culture had been unknown to the vast majority of the Americans. In their cultures, Japan and Germany were regarded as fundamentally different. For many Americans, Japan was essentially a nation in the Far East and was "still centuries behind the rest of the civilized world."[8] In discussions on the cause of Japanese military aggressions, the political system of the *Tenno* state and *Kokka Shinto* as its ideological basis drew the major attention of the US officials. Robert Ballou's *Shinto* reads that:

> In the war against Japan the United Nations were fighting not only against an army, a navy, and an air force, but also against an ideological force which was more than a thousand years old when Pan-Germanism was born, which, through many vicissitudes, has never been supplanted in Japan by vigorously opposing ideas and which is more powerful in conditioning a people than Nazism could ever be, because it has behind it the strength of an ancient and undying religious reverence.[9]

Similar views of the Germans, held by, among others, Robert Vansittart and Alan J. P. Taylor, were argued in Europe.[10] Nevertheless Japanese ultra-nationalism was regarded as more deep rooted, because of its ideological connection to the metaphysical worldview of the Japanese.

Prior to the Occupation, the US government considered the treatment of the Japanese people to be a key to the success of Allied operations in this enigmatic country. The Americans were concerned about Japanese collective obedience, which MacArthur called the cause of "human enslavement."[11] At the same time, as the Positive Policy had suggested, the Japanese "habit of obedience to authority and uncritical acceptance of the teachings of their leaders" were thought to be useful.[12] An "obedient herd" was a "standard phrase" in describing the Japanese.[13] Henry Stimson, US secretary of war (1940-1945), advised Roosevelt on 2 July 1945 that:

> I think she [Japan] has within her population enough liberal leaders (although now submerged by the terrorists) to be depended upon for her reconstruction as a responsible member of the family of nations. I think she is better in this last respect than Germany was. Her liberals yielded only at the point of the pistol and, so far as I am aware, their liberal attitude has not been personally subverted in the way which was so general in Germany.[14]

As Stimson had rightly assumed, Japanese liberals accepted and actually propelled the US-sponsored reforms during the Occupation.[15]

The other ideas collected inside and outside the US government helped it outline policy for the Occupation of Japan. In making Occupation policy, Daniel Holtom's *Modern Japan and Shinto Nationalism* was heavily used among the books referred to by the US government. His influence was particularly strong on Harold Henderson, who drafted the statement on

Tenno's demystification in January 1946.[16] *The Invention of a New Religion* by Basil Chamberlain also contributed to the demolition of the principles of the *Tenno* State, *Kokutai* ideology [the cardinal principles of the national entity]. Ruth Benedict provided extensive anthropological analyses of Japanese society in what later became the book *The Chrysanthemum and the Sword*. Before the Occupation, Benedict actually played a leading role in designing the Occupation policy of the State Department. Edwin Reischauer, who was born, brought up, and partly educated in Japan, also offered scholarly suggestions and political advice for the government.[17] On the other hand, the favorable views of Japan and the *Tenno* held by Joseph Grew, the US ambassador to Japan (1932-1941), were often regarded as too offensive to Americans by many officials in the State Department.[18] Helen Mears's *Mirror for Americans* also provoked controversies. Washington was strongly opposed to her ideas, which claimed that the Japanese act of aggression in Asia had little connection to indigenous philosophies or culture, but only mirrored what the Western powers had done in former centuries in the world. The US government imposed censorship on this book.[19]

In Washington, there were two opposing groups in discussions on the treatment of post-War Japan as a whole. A group of so-called "Japanophobic" individuals, such as Hamilton Armstrong and Stanley Hornbeck, regarded Japanese society as authoritarian and asserted that the complete deconstruction of pre-1945 Japan, including the imperial household, would be essential. Some authors claim that the so-called Morgenthau debate was absent in Japan.[20] But a call for the punitive measure of quarantining Japan from the international community was not insignificant within the State Department. Hornbeck claimed that Japan was hopelessly isolated from the Western world and too pathetic to be democratized. The group claimed that isolating Japan would affect the allied countries neither politically nor economically, unlike the case of Germany whose economy could not be detached from the world economy. Similar views were found in Britain as well.

The opposing "Japanophilistic" group, which included Hugh Borton and George Blakeslee, argued that a complete deconstruction of the political, economic, and social systems of pre-War Japan would not be necessary. Although they recognized that liberalism in Japan had never "been sparked by Christian idealism," unlike that in Germany, Borton and Blakeslee saw some liberal aspects in Japanese political and social development.[21] Moreover, Borton realized that the *Tenno*'s actual political base rested on "a flimsy foundation." As will be shown later, suggestions given by this group played an important role in deciding the political status of the *Tenno* in post-War Japan.

The Basic Principles of the Occupation in Japan

The core of the major reform policy had already been drawn up in Washington during the war. Hull stated that a post-War world order had to be created by "throwing the weight of our country's moral and material influence" on the defeated countries.[22] The ultimate objective of a post-War military occupation was not merely to disarm the defeated, but also to foster the conditions of a democratic nation and society through the re-education of the people by the Allies. The United Nations began to work for the re-education program for the Axis countries, holding meetings in New York from the fall of 1944.

According to international law, however, certain reforms were not permitted in military occupations. Interference in political affairs in defeated countries had been forbidden since the pre-World War One period. This agreement, articulated in Article 43 of the Hague Rules on Land Warfare of 1907, was reaffirmed after World War One in international law, which states that "the occupant is totally independent of the constitution and the laws of the territory.... As he is not the sovereign of the territory he has no right to make changes in the laws."[23] In the light of US army law as well, measures for political and social transformation were illegal.

Nevertheless, the radical reform of Japanese society brought serious disputes within the policy-making process of the US government, not least because of views about the *Tenno*'s involvement in the war and his position as the highest spiritual authority in pre-1945 Japan. In addition, American leaders, unlike European ones, believed that non-Western people could also understand the principle of democracy and benefit from it.[24] The Asian specialists of the Royal Institute of International Affairs informed the British Foreign Office that the Japanese were "as little fitted for self-government in a modern world as any African tribe, though much more dangerous."[25]

While emphasizing the necessity of re-educating the Japanese, the Americans had to learn lessons from their bitter experience in Germany. It was noted that "The result of the futile and senseless German resistance to the might of the aroused free peoples of the world stands forth in awful clarity as an example to the people of Japan."[26] The US Occupation authorities also suffered from enormous administrative burdens brought by their direct rule of Germany. Thus SCAP decided the effective use of the existing governmental machinery, except for certain bodies, such as the Privy Council. A crucial suggestion was made in the United States' Post-Surrender Policy:

> In view of the present character of Japanese society and the desire of the United States to attain its objectives with a minimum commitment of its forces and resources, the Supreme Commander will exercise his authority through Japanese

governmental machinery and agencies, including the Emperor, to the extent that this satisfactorily furthers United States objectives.[27]

Moreover, Reischauer suggested that the retention of the *Tenno* system work effectively to subdue Japanese communists who had already shown their opposition to the system from the pre-War period. In fact, Japanese communists, who were released from prison immediately after the war, stated that the Japanese people would bring the *Tenno* to the court even if SCAP would not prosecute him for war crimes.[28] As early as December 1945, Reischauer further stressed that the *Tenno* system would also benefit the United States by preventing the Russians and Chinese from attaining hegemony in Asia.[29]

Major Political and Social Reforms

The Change of the Sovereignty of the State

Yet, voices for *Tenno*'s abdication and criminal prosecution were strong among the Allies. The FEC stated that the partial detachment of the militaristic, feudalistic Imperial system "would be neither successful nor possible."[30] In the Gallup survey too, 53% of the Americans questioned in June 1945 responded that Hirohito, the *Tenno*, should be executed, imprisoned for life, or exiled.[31] The Japanophobes in the State Department also said that his abdication was essential to root out the potential political use of the *Tenno* by the remaining ultra-nationalists.

Nonetheless, Hugh Borton and other Japanophilistic members of the State Department insisted that the abolition of the *Tenno* system would be neither necessary nor desirable for an efficient occupation of Japan. They also suggested that the "imperial mystique" should not be fearfully overestimated. Borton and others claimed that most Japanese had not actually believed in the divinity of the *Tenno*, considering that a story about the mental retardation of the Taisho *Tenno*, Hirohito's father, was an "open secret."[32] Although those who had Japanophilistic views were not politically powerful within the State Department, the idea of the retention of the *Tenno* system was adopted as the policy of the US government.

The decision reflected a number of wise suggestions raised by those who had first-hand experience in pre-1945 Japan. Like Grew, Reischauer maintained his belief that the divinity of the *Tenno* could be attacked frontally. His suggestions were given to the subcommittee of the State-War-Navy Coordinating Committee (SWNCC) for the Far East in December 1945:

> The United States could exert strong pressure to influence the Japanese to abandon the imperial institution, but even this would be unwise. Such a course would

probably so antagonize the vast majority of Japanese as to necessitate far greater commitments of American forces and resources than is now contemplated, would probably endanger the spirit of cooperation now being shown by the Japanese government and people.

Reischauer concluded by proposing that:

> The Supreme Commander should exert every effort to influence the emperor voluntarily to demonstrate by word and deed to his people that he is an ordinary human being not different from other Japanese or from foreigners, that he himself does not believe in the divine origin of the imperial line or the mystical superiority of Japan over other lands, and that there is no such thing as the "imperial will" as distinct from government policy. . . . Any attempt to persuade the emperor to participate in his own "debunking" should be made in such a manner as to be unknown to the Japanese people and should be handled with such diplomacy as to give no suggestion of compulsion.[33]

Hull noted that the United States had been convinced that the retention of the *Tenno* system would be "desirable politically."[34]

On 1 January 1946, the *Tenno* offered the Imperial Rescript, which was drafted by SCAP with British cooperation:

> [People] do not depend upon mere legends and myths. They are not predicated on the false conception that the Emperor is divine and that the Japanese people are superior to other races and destined to rule the world.[35]

On 3 April 1946, after strenuously negotiating with the Russians and Australians, the Far Eastern Commission approved the exemption of the *Tenno* from indictment as a war criminal by the following votes: in favor 6 (Australia, France, India, New Zealand, the UK and the US); opposed 1 (the Philippines); and abstained 4 (Canada, China, the Netherlands, and the Soviet Union).[36] Consequently, the *Tenno* remained on the throne and the imperial household survived with a reduction of its size.[37] The status of the *Tenno* was changed in the new constitution, drafted by SCAP, from that in the Meiji constitution:

> Article 1: The Empire of Japan shall be reigned over and governed by a line of Emperors unbroken for ages eternal. (The Constitution of the Empire of Japan of 1890)

> Article 1: The Emperor shall be the symbol of the State and of the unity of the people, deriving his position from the will of the people with whom resides sovereign power. (The Constitution of Japan of 1946)

The new constitution was SCAP's core project which would effectively prove the American democratization of Japan. In fact, SCAP took decisive actions to overhaul the Meiji constitution. While the *Grundgesetz* [Basic Law] of the Federal Republic of Germany of 1949 was promulgated at the dawn of its political independence after long discussions with the German and allied representatives, the process of writing the Japanese constitution, promulgated fourteen months after Japan's surrender, was clandestine for the Japanese, including most of their leaders. Under the constitution, the *Tenno* was made politically impotent but became literally the "national symbol." Thus, in a sense, while depriving him of sovereign status, the Occupation authorities now became the "protectors and mythologizers" of the Japanese *Tenno*.[38] This decision was crucial for the United States, as the retention of the *Tenno* system not only soothed the Japanese people during the Occupation, but also laid down a basis for a cordial alliance between the US and the Japanese conservative governments in the following decades. Because of the decision, as Blakeslee has suggested, the United States could persuade itself that "Japan [would] harbor no lasting resentment" toward the Americans.[39] This decision was, for this reason, of "national importance" to the United States.

The Separation of the State and Religion

The Occupation authorities regarded a peaceful democratic Japan as contingent on the demolition of *Kokka Shinto*. The report prepared by the Religions and Cultural Resources Division of the CI&E (Civil Information & Education Section) noted that:

> In pre-surrender discussions of the postwar world, no principle, save the basic principle of democracy itself, was more frequently cited that that of religious freedom as essential to the establishment of a permanently peaceful world.[40]

The reform process in Japan started very early with a pronouncement on the freedom of religion, assembly, speech, and the press in the Initial Post-Surrender Policy for Japan of 6 September 1945. On 15 December 1945, SCAP issued the Directive of the Abolition of Governmental Sponsorship, Support, Perpetuation, Control, and dissemination of State Shinto (Kokka Shinto, Jinja Shinto), the so-called *Shinto* directive. The content of the directive was not confined to the disestablishment of *Kokka Shinto*. Reform measures were extended to the enactment of a military order for the separation of the state and religion. SCAP stated that the purpose of the directive was "to separate religion from the state, to prevent misuse of religion for political ends, and to put all religions, faiths, and creeds upon exactly the same legal basis, entitled to precisely the same opportunities and protection."[41]

While declaring the principle, SCAP promoted Christian activities in occupied Japan. In doing so, SCAP admitted that they had tried to devise a policy which would resolve the contradiction of their effort to promote Christianity in Japan and to advocate the principle of the separation of state and religion.[42] MacArthur requested that American churches send a large number of Bibles to Japan to distribute to "every hamlet in the country."[43] The Occupation authorities issued an entrance visa for Japan to Christian missionaries one and a half years ahead of all other US civilians.[44] In May 1947, MacArthur was jubilant at the formation of the cabinet led by Katayama Tetsu, a Presbyterian:

> It bespeaks the steady advance of this sacred concept, establishes with clarity and conviction that the peoples of the East and West can find common agreement in the spirituality of the human mind, and offers hope for the ultimate erection of an invincible spiritual barrier against the infiltration of ideologies which seek by suppression the way to power and advancement. This is human progress.[45]

On 25 May in 1949, MacArthur celebrated the 400th anniversary of Christian propagation in Japan started by St. Francis Xavier, and extolled his mission:

> The missionary service is based upon the noblest of all human traits—sacrifice—that trait which outlines man's spiritual image to its closest resemblance of divinity. And it was in such humble spirit this man with his soul of serenity brought to the Far East the greatest concept the world has ever known.[46]

SCAP termed the year 1949 "the Church Year" to increase the number of churches and their members in Japan.

To the disappointment of US Occupation authorities and, inter alia, MacArthur, the result of this reform did not go as far as the Christianization of Japan.[47] Nonetheless, the implementation of the reform was thorough, and the principle has been maintained by the Japanese to this day. William Woodard, an officer in the religious subsection of the CI&E, noted the abnormality of the stress by SCAP on religious issues:

> The concern of the American military with Japanese religions was definitely out of the ordinary. Respect for local customs, including religion, as a basic principle of military government and involvement, not to say interference, in the religious affairs of an occupied country is clearly ruled out by army regulations. Nevertheless from almost the day landings began the Armed Forces found themselves confronted with problems in the field of religion and this situation continued to exist until the termination of the Occupation in April 1952.[48]

As will be described, this politico-religious reform had a significant implication in post-War Japanese education.

The Purge of Militarists

In contrast to the American zeal for uprooting the religious foundation of Japanese militarism and ultra-nationalism, their conduct of purging actual militarists was anodyne. It was more so if compared with their operation of denazification in Germany. From the beginning, the US Occupation authorities narrowed down the target of the purge and examined selected Japanese individuals, instead of trying to screen all adults as in Germany. Out of the population of 71,995,477, SCAP screened 2,308,863 people (equivalent to 3.2% of the population) in Japan. In contrast, in Germany 3,623,112 (equivalent to 21.7% of the zonal population of 16,682,573) people were screened in the US zone alone, which had only one-fourth of the Japanese population.[49] Moreover, the questionnaire for identifying Japanese militarists had only 23 items, instead of 150 queries in the *Fragebogen* [questionnaire] for the Germans. About 770 Japanese were screened by each Occupation official, whereas the US staff in Germany concentrated on meticulous examination by questioning only 16.5 Germans per officer on average.

Altogether, about 210,000 Japanese were removed from their positions: 167,035 military officers (79.6%); 34,892 parliament members (16.6%); 3,438 ultra-nationalists (1.6%); 1,898 industrialists (0.9%); and 1,216 journalists (0.5%).[50] The number of purged civil administrators was 1,809, only 0.8% out of all the cases. The purge of the Ministry of Education was even smaller, although the figures show only the result as of 1945.

Further Reforms

Many other changes took place in Japanese society during the Occupation. After a long struggle for suffrage, women gained the right to vote. Facing the anxiety of Japanese men, Japanese women assumed the right to vote—with SCAP's strong support—for the first time in the general election of October 1946. Ichikawa Fusae, a prominent activist of the women's movement from the pre-War period, acknowledged a great impact of SCAP's power in realizing women's suffrage in Japan.[51]

In addition to the liberation of Japanese women, the depressed conditions of the agricultural and industrial workers were relieved for the "cultural advancement" of Japanese society.[52] The sluggish progress in pre-War land reforms was accelerated with a leap. Measures were taken in two steps by the Land Reform Bill in 1945 and the Law for the Special Establishment of In-

Table 4.1. The Classification of Purged Persons within the Japanese Ministries, 1945

Screening Group	Screened	Removed	Removal Ratio (%)
Imperial Household	128	118	92.2
House of Peers	529	173	32.7
Home Affairs	564	340	60.3
Privy Council	28	9	32.1
Foreign Affairs	153	46	30.1
Welfare	120	23	19.2
Justice	252	37	14.7
Commerce & Industry	69	10	14.5
Agriculture & Forestry	120	15	12.5
Transportation	170	18	10.6
Education	1,805	78	4.3
Cabinet	144	6	4.2
Electors of Highest taxpayers of House of Peers	1,730	39	2.3
Finance	223	5	2.2
House of Representatives	476	9	1.9
Communication	13	0	0.0
Others	2,396	141	5.9
TOTAL	8,920	1,067	12.0

Source: Government Section, Supreme Commander for the Allied Powers, *Political Reorientation of Japan: September 1945 to September 1948* (Washington: United States Government Printing Office, 1948), 29.

dependent Cultivators in 1946. In this rural land reform, all the land owned by absentee landlords became subject to purchase by the government. The government sold these lands to tenant farmers. Given the low purchase prices and the generous installment scheme, it was for landowners, in practice, an act of confiscation. Since the purchase prices of the government were set at a pre-War valuation, the hyperinflation in the immediate post-War period made the valuation worse. The government reduced the ratio of tenanted farming approximately from 50 to 10%.[53] A consequence of this was the decline of a landlord's status within the social hierarchy among rural farmers. For the United States, this land reform was an important political measure to prevent Japanese farmers from being inspired by communist ideas, a phenomenon which had already emerged at the beginning of the century in Japan.[54]

The labor union movement was also reactivated by the creation of the Ministry of Labor and the Trade Union Law of 1946. Union membership dramatically increased from less than half a million during the War period to over seven million in 1949.[55] Theodore Cohen, the "father of the labor movement of post-War Japan," said that the ultimate consequences of the reform during the Occupation "went far beyond those intended or foreseen."[56]

Concluding Remarks

Hardly any sector of Japanese society was left untouched during the Occupation. The US Occupation in Japan was redirection of socio-political values, social behavior, and institutions in Japan. Through the Occupation, the United States established strong and reliable, political, economic, and ideological ties to Japan. Robert Ward captured the US policy:

> Only Japan, our recently defeated and still mistrusted enemy, possessed the sort of developmental potential that we needed in a local ally. So the embarrassing decision was made upon a 180-degree shift. Within twenty-nine months of the end of the war in the Pacific, Japan, until then our most dangerous enemy, was in the process of becoming our most important ally in Asia.[57]

What was extraordinary about the Occupation reform was the Japanese acceptance of the political, economic, and social reconstruction as a consequence of a war. Importantly, no official investigation was made by the post-War Japanese judiciary itself into the validity of laws enforced during the Occupation, as the Belgian Court of Justice had examined—in the light of their own judgment—the legality of laws passed during the German Occupation after World War One.[58] Delmer Brown of the CI&E reminisced that the basis of the Occupation reform was:

> Not only American systems, but American ideals really. It was American through and through. And it is remarkable in a way that the Japanese accepted as much of it as they did. And maybe even more remarkable is that they still accept it. This phenomenon appears in various parts of the Occupation, not just in education.[59]

As shown, both American and Japanese leaders regarded the Japanese defeat in 1945 as a great opportunity to make Japan more democratic and to bring it closer to the Western countries. The education reform took place within this broader context, but with some interesting variations in the relations between the Japanese and the Americans. Given the contexts, education reforms were intensively discussed by both the Americans and the Japanese who were already alert to a range of ideas about changing the pre-1945 Japanese education system.

2. AMERICAN AND JAPANESE CO-OPERATION IN EDUCATION REFORMS

The Civil Information & Education Section (CI&E)

As shown earlier, Japan and Japanese culture were unknown to the majority of Americans at the end of World War Two. At least to solve a basic problem prior to the Occupation, the US Navy started language training for potential officers in post-War Japan in the University of California at Berkeley as early as 1941. In the middle of 1942, the Army and the Navy established a military government school at the University of Virginia, Charlottesville, where some of the CI&E officers, such as Eileen Donovan, Mark Orr, and Joseph Trainor, were trained. From 1943, these military bureaus jointly set up language schools, such as the Civil Affairs Training Schools (CATS) at Harvard and Yale and other universities. Before training, they waited for the end of the War in the Civil Affairs Staging Area (CASA) in Monterey, California. To deal with the shortage of officers, trainees were also recruited from among Americans of Japanese heritage, after they were released from detention in the Japanese-American relocation camps in Arizona and elsewhere.

At the Japanese surrender, SCAP formed its divisional section for education, the CI&E, on 22 September 1945. It started with nineteen members, including some of these trainees. The number of the CI&E staff steadily grew to 140 by April 1948.[60] This made a sharp contrast with the US unit in charge of German education reform which started with only six officers and was still a mere branch within the US Occupation authority in the same period. The first chief of the CI&E was Ken Dyke, who was later succeeded by Donald Nugent. Nugent recalled in an interview that "I was selected because of the language knowledge rather than knowledge about Japan."[61]

SCAP gave great political power to the members of the CI&E. In fact, authority was not in proportion to their modest academic and professional qualifications, if compared with American education officers in Germany.[62] Neither were the qualifications of the CI&E officers comparable to those of their counterparts in Japan, that is, the top-ranking bureaucrats of the Ministry of Education and the presidents of the universities. Disproportion between power and qualification was not unique to the CI&E. Some of the Occupation officers were able to exert greater authority than the highest-ranking officials of the Japanese government. For example, Wolf Ladejinsky, who used to work in a modest position in the Foreign Agriculture Division in Washington before the War, took the lead in the sweeping land reforms during the Occupation and became the "godfather of land reform in Japan." Theodore Cohen was also responsible for major reforms in the Japanese labor movement after he wrote a master's dissertation on the history of this issue at Columbia. Those who had such great power in occupied Japan never again had a chance to exert equivalent power after they returned to the United States. Given great authority, the officers also felt responsible for, and found themselves "extremely attentive to," the democratization of Japan.[63]

The United States Education Mission to Japan (USEMJ)

To subsidize the insufficient qualifications of the CI&E staff, the recommendations of the USEMJ benefited SCAP in moving the education reform forward. As early as January 1946, SCAP requested that the War Department dispatch a group of prominent American educators to Japan. Jointly sponsored by the War and State Departments, the mission was formed with twenty-seven members led by George Stoddard. The selection process of the members of the mission implied that one of its important purposes was to highlight the American effort for Japanese democratization. In the first discussion on the formation of the mission in October 1945, the names of prominent educators, such as John Dewey and James B. Conant, were on the list. Conant was even a candidate for chairman of the mission. However MacArthur and his aides rejected this appointment, saying that Conant was a "politically inappropriate choice of chairman."[64] MacArthur also rejected the initial idea to include some foreign educators in the mission.

The mission started its assignment in Japan in March 1946, seven months after the Japanese surrender. Prior to their arrival in Japan, the group studied Japanese education and held meetings in Hawaii and Guam. There, some major reforms were already discussed.[65] Their final recommendations for reforms were given to SCAP in the Report of the United States Education Mission to Japan. The major themes of the forty-one page report were: (1) the overall democratization of Japanese education; (2) the re-education of the Japanese people; (3) the administrative re-organization of the education system; and (4) the rehabilitation of higher education.

The valuation of the report varied on the American side. MacArthur enthusiastically endorsed on the report:

> It is a document of ideals high in the democratic tradition. In origin, these ideals are universal. Likewise universal are the ends envisaged by the mission.[66]

The Occupation authorities distributed the report along with MacArthur's statement to educational institutions throughout the country. Notably, however, the CI&E did not highly rate the report. Some of the members retrospectively stated that they had neither found the mission's study particularly profound nor felt obliged to follow the recommendations.[67]

Yet, MacArthur's acclamation had a great impact on his Japanese audience. Mark Orr, chief of the education division of CI&E, recalled that because of the MacArthur's message, some of the leading Japanese educators seemed to presume that "it was something on the order of a directive itself."[68] In the face of such reactions, Orr even worried that the "report was taken too seriously" by those Japanese. The report was read by educators in Japan—to the amazement of the CI&E and the USEMJ itself—as a Bible. Japanese educators who translated the report into English praised it to the skies in the preface:

> We regard this historical Report as one of the most distinguished pieces of educational literature in the world. This is the fruit of the idea of democratic education which human beings have achieved by the first half of the twentieth century. The Report expresses the best, the soundest tradition of American democracy. We cannot feel anything but happiness that this precious Report was offered for Japanese education and the good future of Japan. . . . Japanese parents, teachers, educational administrators and every single Japanese should read the Report three times so that they can find the future direction of current Japanese education.[69]

Indeed, some Japanese expressed critical views. The philosopher Shimizu Ikutaro, for instance, noted that the views of the report of the USEMJ were too idealistic and based on "infantile naiveté."[70] Yet these views were only a few and expressed tardily.

On 27 August 1950, the five members of the Second United States Education Mission to Japan (USEMJ2) came to observe and evaluate the result of reforms. The Japanese reception of the USEMJ2 was similar to that of the USEMJ. Nambara Shigeru, chairman of the *Kyoiku Sasshin Iinkai* [Japanese Education Reform Committee (JERC)], welcomed the mission by stating that:

> It was a matter of great admiration for us at that time that General MacArthur, before everything else, demanded that your Education Mission be sent over here—a step which bears ample witness to his superior penetration and wisdom.[71]

In the light of democratic principles, therefore, the report was very useful for SCAP, because reforms based on recommendations by educational experts were more appropriate than those based on military orders.

The Ministry of Education in Japan

The reception of the American proposals by the Ministry of Education was also cordial, if not as rapturous. In contrast to the educational authorities of the German *Länder*, ministers of education and the top-ranking bureaucrats of the ministry remained attentive to discussions with the US officers. In doing so, they were confronted with a dilemma as loyal civil servants between the policies of their government and SCAP. Although they were not as authoritarian as ministers and bureaucrats in the pre-1945 period, they worked for reforms together with the CI&E, but with frictions.

The change of characteristics of the ministers during the Occupation clearly shows the government's intention to prepare a democratic atmosphere in the ministry for co-operation with the Americans. As usual, most of the ministers and the leading bureaucrats of the ministry had followed the elite route of the "*Koto Gakko*"—the Imperial University line and entry into a ministry. Unusually, however, the Japanese government appointed mainly university academics or people from the so-called liberal professions as the ministers of education. Maeda Tamon (August 1945-January 1946) used to work as a journalist as well as a bureaucrat at the Ministry of Home Affairs. Abe Yoshishige (January-May 1946) was a Kantian philosopher of Kyoto Imperial University. Tanaka Kotaro (May 1946-January 1947) was a professor of law at Tokyo. Takahashi Seiichiro (January-May 1947) was a professor of economics of Keio University. Katayama Tetsu (May-June 1947) was a socialist and a founder of the Social Democratic Party in 1926. Morito Tatsuo (June 1947-October 1948) was an assistant professor of economic at Tokyo. In the pre-War period, Morito was imprisoned because of the publication of his work on Peter Kropotkin.

Although the pre-War professors of the Imperial Universities had been invited into policy-making circles, as shown earlier, such consecutive appointments of academics to the top position of any ministry were unprecedented. Moreover, half of the ministers of education during the Occupation were Christians, namely Maeda, Tanaka, and Katayama. Joseph Trainor, deputy chief of the CI&E, stated later that the US officers often found it interesting that so many Japanese Christians became new leaders in occupied Japan where there were so few Christians.[72] In fact, since the Meiji period, a number of Japanese leaders came under Christian influence, and some of them were actually baptized. Like Mori, without officially becoming Christian, some leaders were inspired by Christian doctrines during their study abroad. These new characteristics of the ministers created a condition for breaking the past pattern of its authoritarian and bureaucratic administration.

They, however, remained politically conservative mainly on the issues of the *Tenno* state. They maintained an ambivalent attitude toward admiration of Western ideas and faith in the political ideology of the *Tenno* state. As will be shown in the following sections, their opposition to the abolition of the *Kyoiku Chokugo* contrasted with their acceptance of the abolition of *Shushin*, moral education based on Confucian ethics. Other opposition raised by the ministry was mainly because of the administrative difficulties in implementing some costly reforms, like the speedy introduction of the 6-3-3 school system.

In general, the Ministry of Education acted as a useful channel between the Occupation authorities and Japanese towns and villages throughout the nation. With or without full agreement, the Japanese Ministry of Education followed the decisions of the CI&E and the JERC. The bureaucrats of the ministry carried out a number of extensive reforms under the chaotic situations of the defeated country immediately after the war.

Japanese Educators on the Japan Education Reform Committee (JERC)

The reform group of Japanese educators selected by the Japanese government was even more useful to SCAP and the CI&E in pursuing their reforms. As planned during the war, the Americans tried to gain support from Japanese leaders. After the first phase of the so-called "negative reform measures," such as purges and bans until the end of 1945, the Occupation authorities launched constructive measures for changing Japanese education. For successful changes, SCAP regarded influencing Japanese leading educators as vital and was quick to gather them within a centrally organized body.

Prior to the arrival of the USEMJ, SCAP ordered the Japanese government to form a co-ordinating committee of highly qualified educators to work with the mission. The Ministry of Education selected twenty-nine people and formed the *Nihongawa Kyoiku-ka Iinkai* [Japanese Educators Committee (JEC)] on 9 February 1946. The CI&E was satisfied with the selection of the members who were "of extremely high caliber," including presidents of Imperial and other universities, professors of education, prominent Christian educators, and leaders in women's education.[73] About half of the members were academics from higher education institutions. In response to the recommendations of the USEMJ, the JEC submitted proposals, which almost duplicated the American recommendations, except for the issues of the *Kyoiku Chokugo* and the reform of Japanese language. The Occupation authorities already realized the dual characteristics of Japanese leaders: a development of liberalism shown in substantial agreement with the mission on the one hand, and the somewhat conservative nature marked by their adherence to the issues related to the *Tenno* on the other.[74]

At the request of the CI&E, the Japanese government formed in August 1946 a new body, JERC, which was more independent of the Ministry of Education than the JEC. But its basic policy was followed by the JERC. This new committee comprised a chairman, a vice chairman, fifty permanent members, and some temporary members. The members were appointed on the recommendation of the prime minister from among the learned and experienced persons of the political, educational, religious, cultural, economic, and industrial circles. Nambara, president of Tokyo Imperial University and a liberal Christian, took over the Chairman's position from November 1947.

The innovative aspects of the JERC were that: (1) the committee was established under the jurisdiction of the prime minister, rather than under his supervision; (2) the committee enjoyed its autonomous position from the prime minister by reporting to him the results of its investigation of its own accord; and (3) the chairman and the vice chairman were elected through voting by the committee members. In principle, the Occupation authorities guaranteed JERC's autonomy from themselves.[75]

According to a suggestion by the CI&E, a steering committee was founded as a liaison agency which consisted of the members of the CI&E, the JERC, and the Ministry of Education. In reality, the committee was given a task to forge a close link between the former two organizations. For the CI&E, this politically independent Japanese body with many liberals was important in undertaking radical educational reforms in Japan. This connection of the CI&E and the JERC worked particularly well in arguing against some conservative policies of the Ministry of Education.

In contrast, the CI&E remained distrustful about the Ministry of Education practically until the end of the Occupation. The CI&E maintained that the ministry's function is to serve the JERC and not vice versa. Occasionally the JERC asked the CI&E for help to restrain the ministry's political interference in JERC's decisions. Nambara wrote to the CI&E that:

> the Ministry of Education has not respected the autonomy of the JERC, and as a result the Ministry of Education has not "sold itself" to the JERC at all. On the other hand, it was stated that the JERC has the greatest appreciation of the fact that the Education Division [of the CI&E] has respected its autonomy and has not attempted to inject itself or its ideas into the deliberations of the Council.[76]

Prime Minister Yoshida Shigeru called Nambara, who worked so closely with the CI&E, "a sycophant" and "an opportunist."[77] On some occasions, the JERC proposed even more radical reforms than the CI&E and took an actual lead in changing the pre-1945 education system. In his memoirs, Trainor concluded his account of the JERC with the comment:

> Thus did the Japan Education Reform Council, which more than any other agency, including the Occupation itself, had brought about the achievements in Japanese education, move itself out of existence.[78]

The American strategy in using Japanese liberals was a success, as anticipated. To deal with the Ministry of Education, the CI&E attempted to gain support from not only leading educators, but also many other school teachers. In this context, teachers' unions became powerful with the support of the Occupation authorities. The Situation Report—Japan by the Office of Research and Intelligence in the State Department noted that until the rise of the Cold War in East Asia, the CI&E strongly supported teachers' unions.[79] Ironically, after the Occupation teachers unions became solid political factions of either the Socialist or Communist parties.[80]

Concluding Remarks on US-Japanese Cooperation

The timing of the rise of the Cold War had a significant impact on the reform of Japanese education. Before around 1948, SCAP accorded a relatively high political priority to the reforms. The American emphasis on the education reform can be noted early, for example, the initiation of the USEMJ by SCAP itself a few months after the Japanese surrender. Recommendations made by the mission in the early stage of the Occupation showed specific reform directions to the CI&E and Japanese educators. The mission was also effective in showing the American alertness to the education reform to the Japanese. Throughout the Occupation, most Japanese educators enthusiastically accepted the recommendations set out in the report of the USEMJ. Except for bans and purges, most of the democratic reforms were recommended and not ordered by the Americans.

It is notable that the CI&E members served the Occupation in Japan with little knowledge and relatively low qualifications, if compared with the US officers in Germany as will be mentioned later. Despite this fact, however, the CI&E's responsibility and political power was great. This made it easy for Japanese leaders to follow American policy. In addition, the Americans were more confident about their traditions of democratic education vis-à-vis Japanese education, in contrast to the modest approach of their colleagues in Germany toward its educational traditions.

The centrally organized Ministry of Education and its capable administrators also assisted the implementation of difficult reforms. The Ministry of Education did not always agree with the proposed reforms. However, the CI&E had only one central educational authority to negotiate with. In Japan, the Americans were exempt from the obligation to discuss educational ideas with different bodies of culturally diverse and geographically distanced regions as in the US zone of Germany.

Furthermore, with the occasional disagreements between the CI&E and the Ministry of Education, the JERC often interceded on behalf of the CI&E. Its strategy of gaining the support of Japanese "liberals" worked well. This American strategy and the ready compliance of Japanese leaders laid down the conditions for the successful education reforms during the US Occupation in Japan.

3. PRIMARY AND SECONDARY SCHOOL REFORMS

The American Views of Pre-1945 Japanese Education and Reform Policy

The overall American views of the pre-1945 Japanese education system were relatively simple. They were essentially critical. From the middle of World War Two, the Americans found the Japanese education system fundamentally "out of harmony with democratic conceptions and ideals."[81] Problems were found not only in militarist, ultra-nationalist educational practices which had been offered after the 1930s, but also within the whole system of the modern Japanese education system since the Meiji period. The USEMJ stated its basic assumption that "The Japanese system of education in its organization and curricular provisions would have been due for reform in accordance with modern theories of education even if there had not been injected into it ultra-nationalism and militarism."[82] Primarily, criticisms centered on the underdevelopment of individualism and too much emphasis on the subordination of the individual to the state. During the war, the Country Area Committee (CAC) noted that:

> The system as it now operates and as it is now controlled supports an authoritarian social and political regime. It does not undertake to develop individual initiative and character but aims to create a general high level of educational attainment so that the supply of well-trained instruments will be available for national service. While equal educational opportunities are given to the rich and poor the effect of the system is in the main to produce obedient members of the state.[83]

The impairment of a sound sense of individualism was, in American eyes, a definite product of the Japanese education system and practices from the *Meiji Ishin*. Thus, the Americans envisaged the reform of the pre-1945 Japanese education system en bloc.

Initially, the United States condemned the ideological and administrative control in education by the central state bureaucracy. From the middle of the War, the CAC suggested the abolition of the Ministry of Education by pointing out that "The Japanese educational system is one of the most centralized, closely knit systems in the world."[84] This criticism, however, was not fully reflected in the actual US reform policy. From the outset of the Occupation, it was clear to SCAP that Japanese education reform could be far reaching during a few years of a military occupation without the effective use of the Japanese. In May 1944, the Committee on Post-War Programs stated that the Ministry of Education could be useful for the development of democratic education in Japan once this machinery departed from the rule of a "pernicious oligarchy."[85] More importantly, the Positive Policy noted that by maintaining the ministry, SCAP would take advantage of the Japanese "habit of obedience to authority" and "uncritical acceptance of the teachings of their leaders." In terms of the principles of democracy as well, the use of the Japanese ministry would sanction the implementation of reform schemes proposed by the Occupation authorities.

In sum, the US policy for the reform of the state education system of Japan was not only the deconstruction of state political machinery. The main objective was to eliminate the educational patterns which had created the ideological basis of the *Tenno* state. The consequence of that American solution was the wide-ranging overhaul of the existing education system. Overall, the Japanese education system was largely shifted toward the American model, although there were some points of dispute with the Japanese.

Policy Implementation

The Purge of Educational Personnel

As an imperative measure for the demilitarization of Japanese education, militarists were expelled from positions in educational administration and the schools. This was executed as a part of four major educational directives ordered by SCAP within the year of Japan's surrender: (1) administration of the educational system of Japan (22 October); (2) screening and certification of teachers and educational officials (30 October); (3) the so-called *Shinto* directive (15 December); and (4) suspension of courses in morals (*Shushin*), Japanese history, and geography (31 December).

The process and results of the purge, however, showed the lack of enthusiasm for it by SCAP, compared with de-Nazification in Germany. SCAP ordered the purge of militaristic educational personnel on 30 October. But most of the official educational purge started from May 1946, nine months after the surrender, a start far later than de-Nazification in Germany.[86] In the meantime, approximately 115,000 teachers and educational administrators escaped screening and dismissal by resigning.[87] Another difference from de-Nazification was that the Japanese took the initiative in purging militarist educators and examining pre-1945 textbooks before SCAP took any action. Maeda Tamon and Tanaka Kotaro wanted to show Japanese initiative to the Americans. This measure was based on *An Educational Direction for Building New Japan*, pronounced on 15 September 1945.

However, a remarkable difference from the denazification program in Germany was that SCAP started the purge by searching for Japanese militarists among Christians. First of all, the Americans ordered a purge of those who had co-operated with, or had not resisted, the Japanese military regime in Christian schools and universities in Japan. The order was issued quickly on 24 October 1945:

> The attention of this headquarters has been directed to certain acts on the part of officials of educational institutions, founded and supported by Christians of foreign nations, which represent [sic] inexcusable and unjustifiable subversion of such institutions to militaristic and ultra-nationalistic ends. . . . The Imperial Japanese Government is directed immediately to dismiss from their present positions, the following officials.[88]

SCAP delivered this directive to about one hundred Christian educational institutions throughout the nation. Over eighty institutions were screened within a few days after the enactment of the order.[89] This Christian purge was ordered earlier than the purge of the militarists on 30 October, and the abolition of *Kokka Shinto* on 15 December. The fact that the US government had already had a complete list of "militarist Japanese Christians" during the War explains this speedy attack on them. In fact, the Christian missionary schools had been co-operative and obedient to the Japanese government for their survival, since government control and supervision of the foreign schools were stricter than the Japanese schools.[90]

Overall, the purge and dismissal of Japanese militarists was imperative but not central to the reform scheme in Japanese education. The Occupation authorities were about to attempt to make a more fundamental change in the religious stance of the Japanese people.

The Elimination of Religious Aspects of Education

This American idea culminated in the enforcement of the principle of the separation of state and religion. The official view of *Shinto* by the Occupation authorities was that it consisted of mythology and "primitive chronicles" was inferior to Christianity.[91] From the outset of the Occupation, educational practices related to *Shinto* were the prime target of the reform of pre-1945 Japanese education. In addition to this American zeal for attacking *Shinto*, the complete elimination of religious education in the public sector was largely brought about by the acceptance of this principle by Japanese leaders.

Measures for the reform were taken in swift succession. On 26 September 1945, SCAP issued the Plan for Educational Control in Japan under Military Government. As mentioned earlier, SCAP ordered the *Shinto* directive on 15 December 1945. The title of the order referred to the political ideology of state *Shinto*, but the content of the order entirely banned *Shinto* as an indigenous religion in public life in Japan. No visits to *Shinto* shrines were permitted within any school activities. School excursions to *Shinto* shrines were entirely banned. Robert King Hall, a CI&E officer in the religious education section, later stated that the American measure for Japanese religion was more than an attempt to separate church and state. "It was," said Hall, "a direct attack on the very essence of the official national philosophy."[92]

The ideas of the separation of the state and religion, and the elimination of religious education in the public school system in Japan bore no relation to traditional American or French ideas about seeking an equilibrium between the ecclesiastical power of the church and the secular rights of civil society. In fact, in Japanese history including the War-time period, the *Shinto* authorities had barely intervened in secular politics except for the ancient period. Rather, confrontation between secular power and the Buddhist authorities had been more frequent and occasionally violent in Japan.

Consequently, the complete elimination of religion from public life was sanctioned in article 20 of the constitution of Japan, which reads that "The state and its organs shall refrain from religious education or any other religious activity." Article 9 of the Fundamental Law of Education of 1947, the canonical law of post-War Japanese education, echoes this idea. Although in theory the law forbids education "for a specified religion," religious education in general has actually been quarantined from instruction in the publicly funded schools, not to mention from the official school curricula, in post-War Japan.[93]

The Elimination of Moral Education, Shushin

As in the elimination of religion from public schools, instruction in older moral traditions of Japan disappeared from the school curricula. *Shushin*, the pre-1945 Japanese moral education largely based on Confucian ethics, had drawn the close attention of the US government. During the War, the scrupulous examination of *Shushin* textbooks had begun by experts on Japan in the State Department, the CATS, and the CASA. All three bodies judged that the contents of the textbooks, particularly before the 1932 edition, were not militaristic.[94] A number of staff members of the Occupation authorities also observed that the textbooks contained Confucian ethical values of honesty and responsibility, and the failure of *Shushin* was the imperialistic and militaristic use of these values by the Japanese military regime.[95] As a consequence, the State Department suggested the reprocessing of the textbooks during the period of so-called Taisho Democracy in the 1920s.[96]

The textbook examination group of the CI&E had investigated the learning and teaching materials of all school subjects from the early Occupation until

September 1950. The Ministry of Education was requested to continue submitting the English versions of those materials to the general headquarters.[97] The pre-1945 school textbooks were examined by a special commission, composed of American Army clergymen. Particular attention was paid to the descriptions which were antagonistic to Christianity, in particular the view of Christianity as a myth. But this textbook examination similarly concluded that the contents of *Shushin* were as not particularly militaristic or ultra-nationalistic.[98] Hall, the head of the CI&E examination group, retrospectively noted that:

> Allied public opinion, plus the fact that the Supreme Commander had already committed himself to the policy, demanded an immediate cessation of all *Shushin* instruction; a page-by-page textual analysis, however, indicated that the textbooks in question were relatively innocuous and that a wholesale ban might not be justified and, if undertaken, might lead to serious censure of the Command on the grounds of "thought control" and "book burning."[99]

Nevertheless, instruction in *Shushin* was suspended on 31 December 1945 together with that in Japanese history and geography. The latter subjects were resumed in June and October 1946 respectively.[100] The ban on the educational practices of the Japanese classical martial arts, that is, *Kendo* [Japanese fencing] and *Judo*, was also lifted in September 1950.[101] Yet, *Shushin* was never restored in Japanese school curricula.

The elimination of *Shushin* was, in a sense, a political measure rather than a pedagogical one for the Americans. Herbert Wunderlich, Hall's successor in the textbook examination, explained to Kaigo Tokiomi, one of the Japanese textbook examiners, that this measure was meant to be a "political gesture" with a "news value" which would publicize the American achievement in democratizing Japanese education.[102]

The Ministry of Education had been working for a substantial revision of *Shushin* instruction or the introduction of a new moral education from the early Occupation toward the end of it. Amano Teiyu, minister of education (May 1950-August 1952), stated that some kind of moral instruction would be necessary, and a revised version of *Shushin* would be an option. Amano's plan was strongly criticized by a wide range of Japanese educational leaders and teachers unions and was thus withdrawn. Instead, CI&E's suggestion for the replacement of *Shushin* by what the Americans called "social studies" was accepted by the Japanese. The themes of social studies consisted of politics, economics, and ethics, as well as geography and history and even civics. After the Occupation in 1958 the Ministry of Education introduced *Dotoku* [post-War moral education] which has received persistent criticisms by the teachers' unions since then.

The Elimination of the Educational Principle, Kyoiku Chokugo

In contrast to the quick decision on religious education and *Shushin*, discussions on the ultimate treatment of the *Kyoiku Chokugo* dragged on until the middle of 1948. As it expressed *Tenno*'s will, the treatment was considered as politically sensitive both by the Americans and the Japanese.

The Americans tried to handle this issue "very carefully and very skilfully."[103] Most of the American criticisms avoided direct attack on the *Kyoiku Chokugo* as such, but concentrated on the enforced rituals related to it, that is, reciting its script and making an obeisance to the imperial portraits. Without a legal measure for the abolition of the *Kyoiku Chokugo*, SCAP ordered on 8 October 1946 that the "Imperial Rescript should not be used as a basis of instruction, study, or ceremonies in schools."[104] Afterward, the final decision on the *Kyoiku Chokugo* was put aside for over two years.

Another reason for this American hesitation over its ultimate abolition was SCAP's planning to revise the script and to use the ideological influence of *Tenno*'s will on the Japanese. The GS [Government Section] of SCAP recommended to Ken Dyke on 9 December 1945 that:

> SCAP may be missing a best bet if the idea of a new rescript is rejected.... My thought is that if SCAP wishes to use the immense existing tradition of obedience and respect which pervades the schools, a suggestion could be made to Hirohito that he produce a new rescript, . . .[105]

Japanese educators also brought up the idea of drafting a new rescript, in order to retain an educational principle sanctioned by the *Tenno*. The JERC found some inappropriate words, for example, *Nanji-Shimmin* (Thou Subjects), but also the favor of morality in the *Kyoiku Chokugo*.[106] The Situation Report—Japan of April 1946 noted "The extent of the controversy is significant . . . because, unlike many similar discussions, the issue appears to have been one raised by the Japanese themselves."

SCAP set up a working group for the creation of a new *Kyoiku Chokugo*. The group was formed in Doshisha University, a Kyoto-based Christian university and one of the major targets of SCAP's early Christian purge. The group was led by Ariga Tetsutaro, a prominent professor of Protestant theology. The group was also supported by the Jesuit church.[107] The CI&E and Japanese educators worked for the revision of the *Kyoiku Chokugo* under the leadership of this Doshisha group. Therefore, in the adherence to the *Kyoiku Chokugo* by Japanese educators, the Americans perceived the lasting power of the state political ideology rather than the Japanese faith in indigenous cultural traditions.[108]

In the end, the plan for a new rescript was not realized, and the idea faded out. This was mainly because SCAP and the CI&E began to find this work time consuming and shifted their devotion to an increasing number of other reforms. After all the discussions, the final decision on the *Kyoiku Chokugo* was made on 19 June 1948. The Lower House in the Diet declared the loss of its validity by passing a Resolution Eliminating the Imperial Rescript on Education and Related Rescripts in accordance with the legal basis of the constitution of 1946 and the Fundamental Law of Education of 1947.[109] Thus apart from discussions about whether or not the *Kyoiku Chokugo* would fit with democratic ideas, the ultimate decision about the *Kyoiku Chokugo* hinged on the political negotiations of the Occupation authorities with Japanese leaders. The core question of the discussions was related, both by the Americans and the Japanese, to the politically delicate status of the *Tenno* in post-War Japan.

The Decentralization of Educational Administration

From the wartime period, the Americans had maintained that a substantial decentralization of Japanese education was contingent to its democratization. On the other hand, the retention and use of the ministry was regarded as essential for the efficient reform of Japanese education. While using effectively the power of the ministry, the CI&E was disturbed by the ministry's somewhat arbitrary intervention in reforms and the conservative political ideas of the bureaucrats. As indicated earlier, the JERC shared the view of the CI&E. Both bodies shared the idea of keeping the ministry away from discussions on reforms.[110] In fact, the JERC even considered the abolition of the ministry, and the establishment of a new organ, the *Gakugeisho* [Ministry of Arts and Sciences], with substantial reduction of ministerial power.[111] The JERC suggested transforming the ministry into a "service agency" which would provide mainly practical information and statistics.

However, the plan for a service agency jeopardized the interests of the CI&E. The Americans needed the ministry to remain powerful for the effective implementation of reform schemes. Moreover, the Ministry of Home Affairs, with which the Ministry of Education had administered educational affairs, was abolished in December 1947. In the pre-1945 period, the Ministry of Home Affairs had actually been more powerful than the Ministry of Education, and was subject to SCAP's severe criticism as "the very essence of imperial authority" with extralegal powers.[112] The CI&E was aware that the Ministry of Education would be a far better alternative than the Ministry of Home Affairs if the Americans had to establish ways to co-operate. There were, among Japanese liberals, criticisms and disappointment about the CI&E's pragmatic choice. Against these criticisms, Orr retrospectively defended the American choice by saying that:

we were dealing with a very large education system with hundreds of thousands of teachers and millions of students. And we were a very small group of people in the Education Division. . . . Given that circumstance, how could one proceed to even establish contact with the Japanese education community other than through the instrumentality of the existing Ministry of Education?[113]

The plan of the CI&E was to transfer the administration of primary and secondary education to prefectural and municipal school boards, while maintaining the ministry. This was also the idea of the USEMJ. In April 1948, the JERC concluded its plan for the establishment of the local school boards system, and proposed the idea to the prime minister. In July 1948, the Diet passed the School Board Act. Consequently, "a lay educational agency" was established at the prefectural and municipal sub-divisional levels.

However, neither the American nor the Japanese put their faith in the sound exercise of democracy by the people in Japan. In this regard, SCAP and the CI&E maintained "a distrust in the ability of the Japanese people."[114] The persistently subservient attitude of local governments to the central authority frustrated the American ideal. The CI&E also realized that teachers' unions were actually interested in exerting their own control over the contents of education, such as the curricula, textbooks, and teaching methods, rather than simply having a lay-representative group of citizens administering the schools.[115] The Americans also feared possible communist influence on the Japanese and a potential for the victory of communists at the election. Before the first election in Tokyo in September 1948, SCAP showed its concern about a danger inherent in democracy. On the teachers' side as well, there was a concern about the influence of the anti-communist ideas held by the Japanese public on the election.[116] These fears were, in fact, realized with the shattering defeat of Communist candidates in the election. The Ministry of Education was not positive about the system of public election either. Minister Abe pointed out that school teachers were not yet able to understand the meaning of real democracy. In Abe's eye, Japanese teachers were still maintaining their autocratic behavior in front of children, despite their own demand for democratic rights.[117]

On the other hand, both the US authorities and Japanese leaders effectively took up the voice of the Japanese people for the reforms which had US-Japanese agreement. The following reform illustrates that the people's voice helped both groups reorganize the school system.

The 6-3-3 School System

The introduction of the 6-3-3 school system explicitly demonstrated the powerful effect of American democratization of Japan. This does not mean that this reform was imposed by the Americans, but that the new system was mainly supported by Japanese who had already started to believe in democratic education after World War Two. With or without knowledge of "American democracy," the Japanese people believed many changes would be possible under the Occupation after witnessing radical changes guided by SCAP.

First of all, the idea of the 6-3-3 single-track school system was not new in Japan in 1945. The system was first introduced to Japan in 1926 as a democratic education system with the slogan of "secondary school for all." From the 1920s, the Ministry of Education had been drawing up plans for a simpler school system of primary and secondary education, and a gradual extension of compulsory education. The immediate concern of the Ministry of Education was how the new 6-3-3 school system could be implemented in the post-War chaos.[118]

The ministry had no intention to abolish completely the *Koto Gakko* either. It had equipped the students with superior education and sent them off to the Imperial University. The ministry wanted to retain this solid institutional basis for the creation of national leaders.[119] However, one of the main American purposes of the reform was to destroy such elite routes as the *Koto Gakko*—Imperial University line. In American eyes, the arrogance shown by *Koto Gakko* students mirrored the unsound development of elites in Japanese society.[120]

Despite the ministry's concerns, the reform was moved forward by the CI&E and the JERC. The JERC decided to implement the 6-3-3 school system with enthusiasm. Nambara and George Stoddard, chairman of the USEMJ, had a secret meeting in the absence of the Ministry of Education and agreed about the adoption of the 6-3-3 school system instead of the 6-5 system which the USEMJ had actually planned prior to its arrival in Japan.[121] The Japanese people also desired to have a simpler and more egalitarian school system. The US Occupation authorities received a large number of letters petitioning for the implementation of the 6-3-3 school system.[122] The drastic changes in people's day-to-day life made the democratization of Japan evident to the people.

As long as the Ministry of Education was concerned, its bureaucrats as well as Prime Minister Yoshida Shigeru planned an actual implementation of the system after "sensible conditions" were fulfilled, but not as early as the fiscal year of 1947. The implementation of the 6-3-3 school system would involve not only the integration of previously diversified schools, but also the extension of compulsory education from six to nine years. After the War, the national treasury was almost empty. Most of the budget of 800 million yen for the new school system went for the renovation of school facilities for girls after the introduction of coeducation.[123] Thus, extending compulsory education without any positive prospect for finance seemed to the bureaucrats to be "irrational and insensitive."[124]

Under such difficult circumstances, local governments had to take on more of the financial burden for the introduction of this new system than was initially planned. Local governments now had to bear 70% of the cost instead of the initial figure of 30%.[125] But the finances of local governments were in no better condition than those of the central government. A number of the heads of local and municipal government resigned or committed suicide because of their guilt at failing in the quick implementation of the system.[126]

The political power of SCAP, the enthusiasm of the Japanese liberals, and the voice of the population were too strong for the ministry to postpone the reform. The Ministry of Education started the 6-3-3 school system in April 1947, disregarding the suggestions of the Ministry of Finance.[127] After the introduction of the Dodge Plan, an American program for Japan's economic recovery applied to the fiscal year of 1949 onward, the national budget for education became even tighter.

As described, changes in primary and secondary education were radical. This was largely due to the support for reforms from the JERC. In higher education, however, many of the proposed reforms were unimplemented. The next section describes how the reactions of Japanese educational leaders influenced the reform processes.

4. HIGHER EDUCATION REFORMS

The American Views of the pre-1945 Japanese University and Reform Policy

The Americans were equally critical of both the school and the university systems in Japan. The criticisms of the university centered on the following three points. First, there was the close and exclusive relationship between the university and the state, exhibited in the preferential treatment given to the Imperial Universities. Second, the structure of the Japanese university was hierarchical based on the idea of extreme elitism. Third, as implied by the former two points, the university and its graduates remained aloof from community life and millions of the Japanese people.[128]

The prestigious Imperial Universities had been notorious from the pre-War period in the United States. The Occupation authorities were aware that the pre-1945 Japanese university was politically resilient in coping with state intervention.[129] After 1945, too, Japanese universities survived the purge by the Occupation authorities well, compared with not only German academics but also with Japanese in other fields. The purge of Japanese communists in education, the so-called Red Purge, or "Eells Whirlwind," was started in July 1949 by the agitating speech of Walter Eells, a Stanford academic and CI&E adviser. Yet it did not bring about many losses in the university, either.[130]

The Americans recognized that this exclusive elitism had little connection with class stratification.[131] Their criticisms centered on the point that those who performed well in the school would eventually monopolize political power. The favoritism within own university cliques, the monopoly of privileged professions particularly in the central government sector, and the "arrogant" character of the Imperial University and its graduates were, in the eyes of the Americans, antithetical to the idea of democracy. This monopoly of political power, by the graduates of the Imperial University in the state bureaucracy, was also identified as being the basis for Japanese military aggression. Alfred Crofts of the Higher Education Section claimed that:

> The hierarchy of universities is like that of the old feudal society. . . . Highest come the seven Imperial universities, with Tokyo Imperial, the great *Teikoku Digakukko*, at the apex. All the civilian war crimes defendants are *Teidai [Teikoku Digakukko]* graduates. [Italics in original text][132]

The Americans captured the character of the "feudal society" of the Japanese university in the comment that:

> Each student belongs to a professor, and within an apprenticeship he remains half-independent from his professor in terms of undertaking his own research. Within the context of this "family model" of a relationship between professor and student, the work of student was, in many cases, unfairly influenced by professor's view and practice as scientist.[133]

The feudal aspect of the Imperial Universities demonstrated in the *Koza* system came under criticism not only from the Americans but also from the Japanese private universities. The Americans believed that university autonomy based on such divisions of science into academic enclaves would retard intellectual advance and bring academic stagnation into the Japanese university.[134] Following this criticism, the USEMJ also attributed a part of such an undemocratic academic culture in Japan to its borrowing from the European, if not exclusively German, patterns of university education. For Americans, the notion of elitism, linked with class society in Europe, created the basis for the autocratic relationship of professor to students and the pyramidal model of academic authority in the university. In fact, the academics of the JERC underscored the historical preference for the German model by the Japanese university in justification of their refusal of the American models, as demonstrated in the failed reforms of the board of trustees system and the transfer of university administration to local governments.[135]

Overall, the central point of the American criticism of the Japanese university was the close relationship of mutual benefit between the Imperial University and the state. In the light of the ideal pronounced by the USEMJ, Japanese universities had to be separated from the state and opened up to the public. To achieve the goals proposed by the USEMJ, universities, particularly the former Imperial University, had to depart from the bureaucratic control of the Ministry of Education and relinquish the privileges bestowed by the State.

Policy Implementation

The Transfer of University Administration to Local Governments

The CI&E suggested the transfer of the administration of national universities to local government to reduce state control over university administration. Officially, the plan was proposed by the University Accreditation Association on 15 December 1947, given strong suggestions by the CI&E.[136] Its intention was to set free the university from the control of the state bureaucracy and to associate the university with communities. Although the reform excluded the seven former Imperial Universities and three new national universities, the CI&E considered that this reform would release the majority of the national universities from the control of the Ministry of Education. The ministry agreed with the idea of the CI&E.

However, the academics of the non-imperial universities claimed that such a political boundary among universities would destroy the traditions which had been fostered in the university under the guidance of the state since the Meiji period.[137] This reform meant for the non-imperial universities that they would cease to be entitled to privileges and financial support from the state, as well as the social prestige as a state university. These universities did not accept being distinguished from the ten prestigious ones and mixed up with the vast majority of private universities whose academic standards had never reached those of the national universities in the pre-1945 period. When a plan for the local transfer of university administration began to include the former Imperial University, strong opposition was raised by its academics. In fact, the Ministry of Education agreed to the inclusion of the Imperial Universities in this reform.[138] Nambara was one of the most powerful opponents.[139] On 24 December 1947, the JERC officially denounced the overall transfer and noted the following deficiencies in this reform: (1) a possibly harmful influence of local political interest on university administration; (2) the lack of a global view for the cultivation of national leader in local governments; and (3) their financial incapability of bearing the burden of university administration.[140]

Although Eells found these grounds "not very convincing or compelling," the CI&E after all made a concession to the JERC by giving up this decentralisation plan.[141] The ultimate decision of the CI&E was that "All new publicly controlled four-year universities should be controlled by the national government under laws passed by the Diet."[142] It is notable that the mutual agreement of the CI&E and the Ministry of Education was not strong enough to pursue this plan in the face of the opposition of the JERC. Consequently, the administration of the national university remained in the hands of the state.

The Uniform Four-Year System

In contrast to the blocking of the reform inside university administration, a radical transformation took place in the outer surface of Japanese higher education, that is, a fourfold expansion of the number of universities. This resulted from the integration of most pre-1945 higher education institutions into uniform four-year universities.

Since the enactment of the School Education Law in March 1947, Japanese education has been operated in principle within the 6-3-3-4 system: a four-year university following the 6-3-3 school system. As described, the 6-3-3 school system had been introduced on the strong recommendations of the CI&E and the USEMJ as well as the broad support of the JERC and the Japanese public. However, the USEMJ had only recommended the introduction of the 6-3-3 school system, and had not mentioned the four-year system for the university. The mission only recommended that, as a general principle, there should be wider equal educational opportunity in Japanese higher education.[143] The reform plan actually developed through discussions within the JERC. It introduced the radical idea of abolishing the *Koto Gakko*, and integrating it with the *Semmon Gakko* and the *Shihan Gakko* [normal school] into the university.

This "violent reorganization" surprised the CI&E. The American evaluation of this simple measure of university integration was rather low. The CI&E certainly supported the upgrading of higher education institutions run by Christian missionaries or institutions for women.[144] Yet, the CI&E did not believe that the institutions with a single faculty and those with multiple faculties should be uniformly classified as "universities."[145] Problems with this integration were also noted by the Japanese. Considering the amount of administrative work involved in this major reorganisation of higher education, the Ministry of Education calculated that the possible implementation of this reform would begin, at the earliest, from the fiscal year of 1949, instead of a proposed start from 1947. An additional problem of the principle of "one uni-

Table 4.2. The Number of Higher-Education Institutions in Japan, 1940-1951

	1940	1945	1950	1951
All Schools	474	566	419	425
National	120	282	72	75
Public	176	63	66	60
Private	178	221	281	290
University	47	48	223	221
National	19	19	71	71
Public	2	2	34	33
Private	26	27	118	117
Junior College	—	—	149	180
National	—	—	—	4
Public	—	—	17	24
Private	—	—	132	152
University Preparatory School	32	34	21	3
National	4	5	1	—
Public	2	2	8	—
Private	26	27	12	3
Senmon Gakko	194	309	24	21
National	60	90	—	—
Public	12	56	5	3
Private	122	163	19	18
Koto Gakko	32	33	2	—
National	25	26	—	—
Public	3	3	2	—
Private	4	4	—	—
Shihan Gakko	169	142	—	—
National	12	142	—	—
Public	157	—	—	—
Private	—	—	—	—

Source: "CI&E, Post-war Developments in Japanese Education: Structural Reorganization," April 1952 [ERJ]1 2-B-10/13].

versity per prefecture" in this reform was competition between the local governments over upgrading post-secondary schools to boost the local economy and local pride. Competition also took place among the Imperial Universities which wished to absorb the *Koto Gakkos* of high academic standards even if it meant violating the rule of geographical restrictions on merger.[146] The academic standards of the new universities, the products of "hasty patch work," were indeed far lower than those of the former Imperial Universities as well as other old national universities. "How many of them are really worthy of the name [of] university?" was the question of Japanese educators.[147]

Yet the Imperial University had a countermeasure to the problem of downgrading its academic standards. The JERC proposed the establishment of postgraduate schools. Nambara was particularly enthusiastic about this plan.[148] In principle, the plan allowed every university to establish post-graduate schools. In reality, however, only the former Imperial Universities were financially and intellectually capable of doing so. The decision was made in April 1949 that the post-graduate school should consist of a two-year master's course and a five-year doctoral course. Although the Imperial Universities did not want to be mixed up with the "new universities," the complex structure of differentiated higher education institutions could not possibly fit in with the 6-3-3 school system. Given this reality, the introduction of the graduate school system was, along with the retention of the *Koza* system in the former Imperial Universities, an operational solution to the retention of the privilege and prestige of the Imperial University.

This structural reform of Japanese higher education, therefore, did not result in a radical transformation in terms of the elimination of extreme elitism and the privileged status of the Imperial Universities.[149] The "negative heritages" left by this reform was still seen in 1970s by the OECD in the "distinctively hierarchical" structure of the Japanese university.[150] The increase of the number of universities within the academic hierarchy created a basis for the high level of competition in university entrance examinations.

The Board of Trustees System

All through the discussions on the introduction of the board of trustees system, the JERC had stood out against the idea of the CI&E. It suggested that the Japanese university should have a system following the model of the American state university, which, for the Americans, exhibited one of the "most treasured concepts" of higher education.[151] In their view, it was antithetical to democratic principles that the professors of the national university govern the university by excluding the people from communities who actually support the university through their taxes. When the USEMJ2 visited Japan in September 1950, the mission also questioned the monopoly of university administration by academics. It recommended that "every higher educational institution should have a policy-making board of men and women, . . . most if not all of whom would be unconnected with the institution in any other official capacity."[152] The Ministry of Education also agreed to adopt the American model of the board of trustees system in the Japanese university.

However, the opposition of the JERC, particularly the academics of the national universities, was emphatic. As a reason for its opposition, the JERC noted that:

> In Japan, too [as in the United States], we formerly had such trusteeship in private universities, and it is still optional if they have reasons to justify it. But in

the case of government universities, it is different. If they had had such an administrative organ during the war, the meager but treasured academic freedom would early have fallen victim to the influence of the time. This danger always threatens. In such a country as Japan, where the democratization is not easily achieved and the social state changes continually, we should protect universities not only against bureaucratic control but also against other, unjustifiable social influences.[153]

The JERC argued that such a system of layman control would lead to a severe impairment of the traditional academic culture of the Japanese university. Nambara asserted that "the whole range of university administration ought to be based on the decisions of the board of professors."[154] Despite criticisms from the representatives of private universities, Nambara insisted that the administration of the university, including personnel and finance, should be released from bureaucratic control and depend on the decisions of the faculty council alone. As well as the academics, the students of the Imperial Universities opposed inviting non-academics into the academe in its management.[155]

In the face of the opposition, American enthusiasm for the introduction of the system decreased. As Trainor has recalled, the crucial reason for the failure of this reform was that the CI&E did not predict this "most emphatically negative" reaction of Japanese liberals. Trainor noted later that:

The influence of the [CI&E] Division upon reforms in higher education was much less than it was in other fields. This is not to indicate that there was not significant contribution made by the Division staff members. There was, but much of the advice given to Japanese educators in this field was not followed by the Japanese.[156]

As a result, the administration of the university was placed in the hands of faculty councils by the University Control Law of 17 April 1949. The Japanese version of university autonomy was safeguarded. Two decades later, the OECD saw the situation unchanged and argued that the Japanese university yet again failed to develop as integrated intellectual communities.[157]

General Education

Another American attempt to make the Japanese university open to the public had some success. This proposal was readily accepted by the JERC. The report of the USEMJ claimed that the narrowly focused contents of university instruction, and the monolithic nature of academic ideals of Japanese universities hindered the cultivation of students' creativity. The mission suggested that "for the most part there is too little opportunity for general education, too early and too narrow a specialization, and too great a vocational or professional emphasis."[158]

The Americans held that the exclusive, narrowly focused contents of university instruction were also derived from the old model of the German university in the nineteenth century. Thus universities in Japan should change curricula by adopting the American model of general education in order to remove elitism from them. The recommendation of the mission went on that "The general education should, we feel, be integrated into the regular curriculum planned for each student, so that he can get full credit for it and not regard it as something extra and separate."[159]

The background of the emphasis on general education by the CI&E was also a pedagogic trend of the mid-twentieth century. The idea of general education in the Conant report influenced university circles in the West. The Report published as *General Education in a Free Society* asserted the significance of general education to train the Christian citizen. The Conant report continued that:

> We are part of an organic process, which is the American and, more broadly, the Western evolution. Our standards of judgment, ways of life, and form of government all bear the marks of this evolution, which would accordingly influence us, though confusedly, even if it were not understood. . . . Thus stated, the goal of education is not in conflict with but largely includes the goals of religious education, education in the Western tradition, and education in modern democracy.[160]

Both the CI&E and Japanese reformers believed that the introduction of general education in the university would suit a new democratic society as it would foster the idea of human development for a wider range of the population rather than the idea of specialized education for elites. This Harvard model of general education became the prototype for Japanese post-War university education.[161] However, the introduction of general education in Japanese universities resulted in a simple broadening of academic scope, for example, making gymnastic exercise compulsory and reducing academic standards. From the last half of the 1950s, requests were made strongly by Japanese industrialists for a stronger emphasis on specialized education, as in the pre-War period.[162]

5. CONCLUSION

The US Occupation authorities skilfully used their political power in discussions on the educational as well as political, economic, and social reforms of Japan. They designed the policies for the Occupation based on the interests of the Americans and their views of Japan. The relatively low level of political tension in East Asia enabled the Americans to build and change their policies without major opposition from the other Allies and countries in Asia where the political situation was less hazardous than in Europe. In addition, lessons learned in Italy and Germany resulted in detailed preparations for, and the speedy execution of, the Occupation reform as a whole in Japan.

Most of the so-called "negative measures" for prohibition were quickly imposed within 1945. The *Tenno* issue—the most difficult problem—was decided by the end of 1945, and Japan started afresh from 1 January 1946 after the *Tenno*'s demystification. This declaration marked the decisive moment of the Occupation. By the declaration, the political principle of the "positive measures" for reconstruction was defined. Making clear to all the Japanese that Japan would and had to change, SCAP created a political and social basis for making sweeping transformation in Japanese society.

In education, too, the Americans made a quick start. In March 1946, the Education Mission stated what had been wrong in pre-1945 Japanese education and how they should be changed. The tardy rise of the Cold War in East Asia permitted the Occupation authorities to maintain their commitment to education reforms, to which the Americans attached a minor importance in Germany. What made the American reforms easier in Japan were the constructive discussions on reforms with the JERC and its enthusiasm for changing Japanese education by absorbing foreign educational patterns. The active cooperation offered by the JERC for radical reform was politically as well as educationally beneficial for the CI&E, since it could claim that reforms were based on Japanese desire. With reservations about some of the reforms, the Japanese Ministry of Education too followed the CI&E policies.

The fundamental faith in Western ideas maintained by Japanese leaders created favorable conditions for constructive discussions for reform, in addition to the strong political guidance of the Occupation authorities. The inconsistency in regard to educational ideas among the Japanese, demonstrated by conflicts between Japanese educators and the ministry's bureaucrats, helped the Americans avoid monolithic counter-argument by the Japanese, as had occurred in the US zone of Germany. Both the JERC and the ministry were led by graduates of the Imperial Universities. From the Meiji period, a distinct inclination toward Western ideas had been maintained. Neither the JERC nor the bureaucrats of the ministry showed keen adherence to the retention of traditional socio-cultural values in Japanese education. The JERC also helped the CI&E carry on difficult negotiations with the Ministry of Education. The Japanese leaders were split from within.

As a whole, the effective use of the strong faith in Western ideas and ideological ambiguity of the Japanese leaders permitted the US Occupation authorities to change many aspects of Japanese education during the Occupation. The great difficulty of SCAP and the CI&E was the reforms related to the *Tenno* issue. However, once the Americans realised the political sensitivity of this issue and avoided a frontal attack on the *Tenno* system, the implementation of reforms on the American model was not difficult. The pre-1945 Japanese education system was in any case established following foreign models by deliberate absorption of foreign ideas by national leaders. Since the Japanese pattern of elite formation in the university had not changed from the Meiji period until, at least, 1945, another massive implantation of new systems and ideas in Japanese soil was not too difficult for both Japanese leaders and the US Occupation authorities.

NOTES

1. "MacArthur Gensui Atsugi Tochaku," *Asahi Shimbun*, 31 August 1945. MacArthur attributed Japan's consent to SCAP'S policy to the "slavish mentality of adulating a winner" of the Japanese. Paul Bailey, *Postwar Japan: 1945 to the Present* (Cambridge: Blackwell, 1996), 29.

2. "Positive Policy for Reorientation of the Japanese," 19 July 1945, State-War-Navy Coordinating Committee (Secret) [ERJ1 1-B-5]; "Italian Education under Allied Military Government—Based on Reports from the War Department," 30 May 1944, Post-War Programs Committee [Notter File 1411 PWC 177].

3. Douglas MacArthur, *MacArthur kaisoki* (Tokyo: Asahi Shinbunsha, 1964), 291.

4. In contrast to such British and Russian insistence on their rights to occupy Japan, Chiang Kai-shek "wisely" declined the frequent invitations of Roosevelt to the Occupation. John Bennett and Anthony Nicholls, *The Semblance of Peace: The Political Settlement and the Second World War* (London: Macmillan, 1972), 136-37. Cf. Bates claimed that there was a significant contribution of the British Commonwealth Occupation Force (BCOF) to the democratization of Japan. Of the entire occupied area of Japan (147,000 mi^2), the US force ruled 86.4% (127,000 mi^2), and the BCOF controlled 13.6% (20,000 mi^2). Peter Bates, *Japan and the British Commonwealth Occupation Force, 1946-52* (London: Brassey's, 1993), 172, 264.

5. "Message to General of the Army Douglas MacArthur Concerning the Authorities of Supreme Commander for the Allied Powers," 6 September 1945. Division of Special Records, Foreign Office, Japanese Government (DSR FO JPN), *Documents Concerning the Allied Occupation and Control of Japan, Volume 1: Basic Documents* (Tokyo: Foreign Office of Japanese Government, 1949), 109. Officially, Clay's title had been the United States deputy military governor until March 1947. The military governor's position was handed over from Dwight Eisenhower to Joseph McNarney in November 1945 and ultimately to Clay in March 1947.

6. Howard Schonberger, *Aftermath of War: Americans and the Remaking of Japan, 1945-1952* (Kent: The Kent State University Press, 1989), 40. Mayo also suggests that MacArthur's "highly assertive and colorful manner" made later studies of the Occupation overestimate his power in Japan. Marlene Mayo, "American Wartime Planning for Occupied Japan: The role of the experts," in *Americans as Proconsuls: United States Military Government in Germany and Japan, 1944-1952*, ed. Robert Wolfe (Carbondale: Southern Illinois University Press, 1984), 3-51.

7. Quoted from: Toshio Nishi, *MacArthur no 'hanzai': Hiroku Nihon senryo, vol. 1* (Tokyo: Nihon Kogyo Shimbunsha, 1983), 26. See also: Dorris James, *The Years of MacArthur, Volume III: Triumph and Disaster 1945-1964* (Boston: Houghton Mifflin Company, 1985). Assuming supreme authority in Japan, MacArthur stayed aloof from the Japanese during his service in Japan. Cohen recalled that "For more than five years, with the rarest of exceptions, the only thing MacArthur saw of Japan physically was on the automobile route between the Daiichi Building [where the headquarters was located] and his quarters at the American Embassy, a distance of about a mile." Theodore Cohen, *Remaking Japan: The American Occupation as New Deal* (New York: The Free Press, 1987), 66. It is also said that MacArthur spoke to only a total of sixteen Japanese persons during this operation in Japan. Not only for Japanese leaders, but also for many US officers, MacArthur was an unapproachable figure. John Dower, *Embracing Defeat: Japan in the Wake of World War II* (New York: WW Norton & Company, 1999), 204-205; Harry Wildes, *Typhoon in Tokyo: The Occupation and Its Aftermath* (New York: The Macmillan Company, 1954), 19.

8. Charles Spinks, "Indoctrination and Re-Education of Japan's Youth," *Pacific Affairs* 17, no. 1 (1944), 66-67.

9. Robert Ballou, *Shinto: The Unconquered Enemy: Japan's Doctrine of Racial Superiority and world conquest* (New York: The Viking Press, 1945), 4. See also: Carlton Hayes, *Christianity and Western Civilization* (Westport: Greenwood Press, 1954).

10. Taylor wrote that "Nothing is normal in German history except violent oscillations." Alan Taylor, *The Course of German History: A Survey of the Development of Germany since 1815* (London: Hamish Hamilton, 1945), 13. See also Robert Vansittart, *Black Record: German Past and Present* (London: Hamish Hamilton, 1945); Robert Gilbert Vansittart, *Lessons of My Life* (London: Fight for Freedom, 1942).

11. MacArthur, *MacArthur*, 283-84.

12. "Positive Policy for Reorientation of the Japanese."

13. Dower, *Embracing Defeat*, 218.

14. "Proposed Program for Japan," 2 July 1945, Memorandum for the president from Henry Stimson. Henry Stimson and McGeorge Bundy, *On Active Service in Peace and War* (New York: Harper & Brothers, 1948), 620-21.

15. Dower captures the role of Japanese liberals after the War: "With few exceptions (but many internecine differences), the intelligentsia assumed the mantle of being 'progressive men of letters' (*shinpoteki bunkajin*) and rallied behind the causes of democracy and liberation. . . . This was a virtuoso turnabout for the intelligentsia, precious few of whom had opposed the war." Dower, *Embracing Defeat*, 233.

16. Shiro Takahashi, "Shinto-shirei to Tenno-sei," in *Sengo kyoiku kaikaku tsushi*, ed. Meisei University Sengo Kyoiku-shi Kenkyu Centre (Tokyo: Meisei University Press, 1993), 74-90. According to Suzuki, Henderson had developed close friendship with some Japanese liberals during the Occupation. Suzuki, *Nihon senryo to kyoiku kaikaku*, 50-51.

17. Edwin Reischauer served the American Science Mission to Japan during the Occupation. His analysis about Japan, written after his service as the US ambassador to Japan (1961-1966) can be read in, e.g., his *The Japanese* (Cambridge: Harvard University Press, 1977).

18. Grew's address in Chicago on 29 December 1943, which included his appraisal of the *Tenno*, drew strong objections from the State Department. Schonberger, *Aftermath of War*, 21-36. See also: Joseph Grew, *Ten Years in Japan: A Contemporary Record Drawn from the Diaries and private and official papers of Joseph C. Grew* (New York: Simon and Schuster, 1944). Nakamura suggests that most of the pre-1945 studies on East Asia conducted by the Americans had pro-China stance, e.g., Thomas Bisson's *Japan's War Economy* and Owen Lattimore's *The*

Situation in Asia. Masanori Nakamura, *Gendai-shi wo manabu: Sengo kaikaku to gendai Nihon* (Tokyo: Yoshikawa Kobunkan, 1997), 10-11. For the conflict between the "Japan crowd" and the "China crowd," see: Dower, *Embracing Defeat*, 221-24. Orr of CI&E also recalled that he chose studies on Japan rather than those of more popular China in the pre-War period because of a desire to "know the enemy." "Mark T. Orr" (Interview Part 1 by Harry Wray on 10 January 1980, translated by Masako Shibata). *Sengo Kyoiku-shi Kenkyu Kiyo* 17 (2003): 89-110.

19. Mears's original version of 1948 was published for the first time in 1995 in Japanese: Helen Mears, *America-jin no kagami: Nihon* (Tokyo: Ainekkusu, 1995).

20. Rosenzweig, for example, claims that *"Eine japanische Morgenthau-Debatte fand nicht statt"* and suggests the absence of an American plan for imposing harsh punishment on Japan. Rosenzweig, *Erziehung zur Demokratie?*, 96.

21. Borton, *Japan's Modern Century*, 71-76. Iokibe further splits the "Japanophilistic" group in two sub-groups: progressive individuals who were keen on reforming Japan like Borton, and more conservative individuals, like Blakeslee, who suggested a more cautious approach to Japan. Makoto Iokibe, "America no tai-nichi senryo kanri koso," in *Senryo to kaikaku*, ed. Masanori Nakamura, et al. (Tokyo: Iwanami Shoten, 1995), 93-123. The members of the Japanophilistic group called themselves the Gladstone Liberals. For the role of its leading member, Joseph Ballantine, see: Edward Beauchamp, "Educational and Social Reform in Japan: The First US Education Mission to Japan, 1946," in *The Occupation of Japan: Educational and Social Reform*, ed. Thomas Burkman (Norfolk: The MacArthur Memorial Foundation, 1980), 175-92.

22. "Statement of Cordell Hull, Secretary of State," 1 January 1940, *The Department of State Bulletin*, II, 11. Division of Publication, Department of State, US Government (DP DS USA), *Postwar Foreign Policy Preparation 1939-1945* (Washington: US Government Printing Office, 1949), 5. See also: Marlene Mayo, "Psychological Disarmament: American Wartime Planning for the Education and Re-Education of Defeated Japan, 1943-1945," in *The Occupation of Japan: Educational and Social Reform*, ed. Thomas Burkman (Norfolk: The MacArthur Memorial Foundation, 1980), 21-128.

23. Lassa Oppenheim, *International Law: A Treatise*, vol. 2 (London: Longmans, Green and Co., 1944), 342. Cohen recalls that the United States "committed flagrant violations of normal democratic procedure." Cohen, *Remaking Japan,* 7. Similar accounts: Bernard Eccleston, *State and Society in Post-War Japan* (Cambridge: Polity, 1989), 17; Makoto Iokibe, *Beikoku no Nihon senryo seisaku 1* (Tokyo: Chuokoronsha, 1985), 113-14; Ray Moore, "Reflections in the Occupation of Japan," *Journal of Asian Studies* 38, no. 4 (1979): 727.

24. Churchill had maintained that "Point Three of the Atlantic Charter (the right of self-determination) applied only to the occupied countries of Europe." Cordell Hull, *The Memoirs of Cordell Hull*, vol. II (New York: The Macmillan Company, 1948), 1,478. Abe, the minister of education, stated that Japan was fortunate to have been occupied by the Americans and not by the Russians or even the British. Yoshishige Abe, *Sengo no jijoden* (Tokyo: Shinchosha, 1959), 59.

25. Quoted from: Dower, *Embracing Defeat*, 218.

26. *The Department of State Bulletin*, vol. XII, No. 318, July 29, 1945. DSR FO JPN, *Documents Concerning the Allied Occupation,* 7.

27. "The United States Initial Post-Surrender Policy for Japan," 22 September 1945. DSR FO JPN, *Documents Concerning the Allied Occupation,* 93.

28. "Tenno-sei ni kansuru sekai no koe," *Asahi Shimbun,* 5 November 1945.

29. "Treatment of the Institution of the Emperor," 11 December 1945, the State-War-Navy Coordinating Subcommittee for the Far East, Division of Political Studies (Policy Summaries) [Notter File 1520 H-128].

30. The statement of Vandenbosch, a leading member of the FEC and an expert on Southeast Asia, on 22 October 1943, quoted from: Iokibe, *Beikoku no Nihon senryo*, 259.
31. Jay Krane, "Polls, Press and Occupation Policy," *Columbia Journal of International Affairs* 2, no. 1 (1948), 72-73.
32. "Chronological Minutes of the Territorial Subcommittee (T Minutes) #53," 30 July 1943, quoted from: Iokibe, *Beikoku no Nihon senryo*, 259. Ronald Anderson, an English teacher in pre-War Japan and a CI&E officer, also recalled that some of his *Koto Gakko* students in the 1930s mocked the Taisho *Tenno*'s weird statement at the National Diet. The local police had arrested the students for *lèse majesté*, but kept them into custody only briefly. "Ronald S. Anderson" (Interview by Harry Wray on 9 February 1980, translated by Masako Shibata), *Sengo Kyoiku-shi Kenkyu Kiyo* 16, (2002): 101-33.
33. "Treatment of the Institution of the Emperor."
34. Hull, *The Memoirs*, 1,592.
35. "Imperial Rescript on Reconstruction," 1 January 1946. Religions and Cultural Resources Division, Civil Information & Education Section, General Headquarters of Supreme Commander for the Allied Powers (RC CI&E SCAP), *Religions in Japan: Buddhism, Shinto, Christianity* (Rutland: Charles E. Tuttle Company, 1948), 77-78.
36. "Apprehension, Trial and Punishment of War Criminals in the Far East," 3 April 1946 [FEC 1488, Box 223].
37. Ninety percent of the assets of the imperial households were confiscated by the state. The rest was entirely subject to the control of the cabinet within the national budget. On 13 November 1947, the new Japanese government decided to divest eleven former imperial families of their official titles and privileges and to impose taxes on them as on commoners, while retaining three imperial families in direct descent from the ancient imperial family. Yotsuya Hirota, "Kyu-shisan-kaikyu no botsuraku," in *Sengo Nihon: senryo to sengo kaikaku 2*, ed. Masanori Nakamura (Tokyo: Iwanami Shoten, 1995), 142-52.
38. Herbert Bix, *Hirohito and the Making of Modern Japan* (New York: Harper Collins Publishers, 2000), 1-13. According to Bix, this resulted from the *Tenno*'s effort to preserve his throne and his capability of exercising "give-and-take of politics" with the Americans.
39. "Office Memorandum on Emperor from G. H. Blakeslee to General McCoy," 28 May 1946.
40. RC CI&E SCAP, *Religions in Japan*, 166.
41. "Abolition of Governmental Sponsorship, Support, Perpetuation, Control, and Dissemination of State Shinto," 15 December 1945 [SCAPIN 448].
42. The General Headquarters of the Supreme Commander for the Allied Powers (GHQ SCAP), *Nihon senryo no Shimei to Seika*, (Tokyo: Itagaki Shoten, 1950), 312.
43. "MacArthur Asks Bibles by Thousand—He Bids Society Send Them for 'Every Hamlet,'" *New York Herald Tribune*, 9 June 1949 [FEC 1066, Box 165].
44. GHQ SCAP, *Nihon senryo*, 312-13. See also: "Japanese Shinto Hirohito Should Adopt Christianity to Please West," *Christian Science Monitor*, 15 April 1948 [FEC (B) 1235, Box 165]; "Christianity Spreads in Japan," *Baltimore Sun*, 7 October 1948 [FEC (B) 1238, Box 166].
45. "MacArthur's Press Release Statement on the Election of Tetsu Katayama as Prime Minister," 24 May 1947, in: GHQ SCAP, *Nihon senryo*, 770.
46. "Statement by General MacArthur on Four Hundredth Anniversary of St. Francis Xavier," 25 May 1949, SCAP Press Release [FEC 1500].
47. "Japanese Are Returning to Shinto Shrine," *New York Times*, 8 January 1949 [FEC (B) 1235, Box. 165]; "Slow Progress Made in Japan by Christianity - Small Gains Are Reported Despite Intensification of Mission Work since War," *New York Herald Tribune*, 20 November 1949 [FEC (B) 1237 Box 166]. According to SCAP's report, the Catholic Church in Japan had a

membership of 119,224 in 1940 and 130,388 in June 1949. The member of Protestants increased from approximately 200,000 to 201,321 during the same period. "The Christian Movement in Japan," *GHQ, Far East Command Public Information Bulletin* No. 30, 10 January 1950 [FEC 1066, Box 165].

48. William Woodard, *The Allied Occupation of Japan 1945-1952 and Japanese Religions* (Leiden: E. J. Brill, 1972), xi. See also for the Christian policy of SCAP: Ray Moore, "Kami no heishi: Nihon wo kirisuto-kyo-koku tosuru MacArthur no kokoromi," in *Tenno ga Bible wo yonda hi*, ed. Ray Moore (Tokyo: Kodansha, 1982).

49. John Montgomery, *Forced To Be Free: The Artificial Revolution in Germany and Japan* (Chicago: The University of Chicago Press, 1957), 26-27. Montgomery served SCAP in Japan as a political science officer and conducted a survey of the Japanese public opinion on the prosecution of militarists.

50. Hiroshi Masuda, "Kyoshoku-tsuiho no shogeki," in *Senryo to Kaikaku. vol. 2, Sengo Nihon senryo to sengo kaikaku*, ed. Masanori Nakamura et al. (Tokyo: Iwanami Shoten, 1995), 110.

51. Fusae Ichikawa, "Fujin sansei-ken," in *Showa no sengo-shi*, ed. Saburo Ienaga (Tokyo: Yubunsha, 1976), 83-96.

52. "Rural land Reform," 9 December 1945, Memorandum for the Imperial Japanese Government from the Central Liaison Office of SCAP [SCAPIN 411].

53. Bailey, *Postwar Japan*, 46-47; Masanori Nakamura, "Meiji-Ishin to sengo kaikaku," in *Sengo minshu shugi*, ed. Masanori Nakamura et al. (Tokyo: Iwanami Shoten, 1995), 277.

54. John Herz, ed. *From Dictatorship to Democracy: Coping with the Legacies of Authoritarianism and Totalitarianism* (Westport: Greenwood Press, 1982), 195-96; Yutaka Kosai, "The Postwar Japanese Economy, 1945-1973," in *The Cambridge History of Japan. vol. 6: The Twentieth Century*, ed. Peter Duus (Cambridge: Cambridge University Press, 1988), 496.

55. Nakamura, *Gendai-shi wo manabu*, 196.

56. Cohen, *Remaking Japan*, 2.

57. Robert Ward, "The Legacy of the Occupation," in *The United States and Japan*, ed. Herbert Passin (Englewood Cliffs: Prentice-Hall, Inc., 1966), 31.

58. Oppenheim, *International Law*, 342-43.

59. Interview with Delmer Brown (CI&E) on 19 January 1986, in: *Harry Wray Oral History Collection*.

60. Hideo Sato, ed., *Rengokoku-sasikoshireikan-soshireibu Minkan-joho-kyoiku-kyoku no jinji to kiko* (Tokyo: Kokuritu Kyoiku Kenkyusho, 1984), 56-58.

61. Interview with Nugent by Harry Wray on 6 February 1980. Before the war, Nugent taught English in a secondary school of commerce in Wakayama, Japan.

62. Only after the Occupation, some of the CI&E officers were awarded a Ph.D. degree by the thesis based on their experience in occupied Japan, like John Chapman, Fred Kerlinger, Mark Orr, and Herbert Wunderlich.

63. Herbert Passin, *Encounter with Japan: The American army language school* (New York: Harper & Row, Publishers, Inc., 1982), 189.

64. According to Tsuchimochi, the most probable reason for this rejection was that Conant was one of the advisers to the US president on the atomic bomb project and the chairman of the National Defence Research Committee. Moreover, MacArthur believed that Conant would also become a Republican candidate in the presidential election, like MacArthur himself. Gary Tsuchimochi, *Education Reform in Postwar Japan: The 1946 U.S. Education Mission* (Tokyo: University of Tokyo Press, 1993), 23-28.

65. A document in the Wanamaker collection shows that in the preliminary meetings in Guam, the group of Wanamaker designed a plan for a single-track structure of the 5-6 school

system, instead of the 6-3-3 system. Based on this document, Tsuchimochi argues that the 6-3-3 system was not imposed by the Americans but was based on the wish of the Japanese themselves. Gary Tsuchimochi, "Beikoku tai-nichi kyoiku shisetudan hokokusho no seiritu jijo ni kansuru sogoteki kenkyu," *Bulletin of the Faculty of Education, Nagoya University* 31 (1984): 256-63; Tsuchimochi, *6-3 sei kyoiku no tanjo*.

66. "General MacArthur's statement to the Report of the United States Education Mission to Japan," 30 March 1946 [ERJ1 2-A-6].

67. This view was commonly held by the former CI&E officers and was overtly expressed by Edwin Wigglesworth (CI&E), in an interview on 29 July 1985, in: *Harry Wray Oral History Collection*.

68. "Mark T. Orr."

69. Hiroshi Sugo, Seiichi Miyahara, and Seiya Munakata, eds., *America kyoiku shisetudan hokokusho yokai* (Tokyo: Kokumin Tosho Kankokai, 1950), 1-2. Translation is mine.

70. Ikutaro Shimizu, "Konnichi no kyoiku tetsugaku," *Shiso* 322 (1951), 2-4.

71. "Address of Welcome on the Occasion of the Second Visit from the American Education Mission by Shigeru Nambara," undated [ERJ1 1-L-46].

72. Interview with Joseph Trainor by Harry Wray on 9 June 1980.

73. "Comments on the Situation Report—Japan of the Office of Research and Intelligence, Division of Far East Intelligence," 7 June 1946 [ERJ1 1-B-15]. Cf. Suzuki sees the conservative aspects of these members. Eiichi Suzuki, "Haisen chokugo no Kyoiku Chokugo hihan," *Kyoiku* 396 (1981): 70-81.

74. "Comments on the Situation Report."

75. "Organization of the Educational Reform Committee," 9 August 1946, Imperial Ordinance 373. Nihon Kindai Kyoiku Shiryo Kenkyukai (NKK), ed., *Kyoiku Sasshin Iinkai, Kyoiku Sasshin Shingikai Kaigi-roku: Sokai 1*, vol. 1 (Tokyo: Iwanami Shoten, 1995), v. Cf. Argument about the restricted autonomy of the JERC: Kanji Katsuoka, "Trainor no shiso to sengo kyoiku kaikaku," in *Sengo kyoiku no sogo hyoka*, ed. Hoichi Tsuchimochi (Tokyo: Kokusho Kankokai, 1999), 314-19.

76. "Memorandum: Special Conference," 23 November 1946, from J. C. Trainor to Lt. Col. D. R. Nugent. Nihon Kindai Kyoiku Shiryo Kenkyukai (NKK), ed., *Kyoiku Sasshin Iinkai, Kyoiku Sasshin Shingikai Kaigi-roku: Shiryo*, vol. 13 (Tokyo: Iwanami Shoten, 1998), 27.

77. Debates between Yoshida and Nambara in: "President Nambara Blasts Premier Yoshida in Counterblast", translation of *Asahi Shimbun* on 7 May 1950 [ERJ2 1-K-6].

78. Trainor, *Educational Reform*, 119.

79. "Situation Report—Japan," 26 April 1946, Department of State, Office of Research and Intelligence, Division of Far East Intelligence [ERJ1 1-B-14].

80. Benjamin Duke, *Japan's Militant Teachers* (Honolulu: University Press of Hawaii, 1973).

81. "Japan: The Education System under Military Government," 15 July 1944, Country Area Committee [Notter File 1090 CAC 238].

82. "Report of the United States Education Mission to Japan", 30 March 1946, 4 [ERJ1 2-A-6].

83. "Japan: The Education System under Military Government."

84. "Japan: The Education System under Military Government."

85. "Japan: Suspension of Powers of Government", 9 May 1944 [SCAP File 1411 / PWC 112).

86. "Investigation, Screening, and Certification of Teachers and Educational Officials," 30 October 1945, Memorandum for Imperial Japanese Government by the Central Liaison Office [SCAPIN 212]; The Imperial Rescript No. 263 of 7 May 1946.

87. "Violation of Religious Freedom," 24 October 1945, Memorandum of the Office of Supreme Commander of the Allied Powers for Imperial Japanese Government. Rikkyo Gakuin Hayku-niju-go-nen-shi Henshu Iinkai (Rikkyo), ed., *Rikkyo Gakuin hyaku-niju-go-nen-shi*, vol. 1 (Tokyo: Dainippon Insatsu, 1996), 478-79; Reiko Yamamoto, "Educational Purge (Part I): Purges by SCAP Memorandum (Memo Case)," *Research Bulletin of Educational History of the Postwar Japan* 4 (1987): 133-54.

88. "Violation of Religious Freedom."

89. "Rikkyo Gaikuin socho ika juichi shi no taishoku yokyu," *Asahi Shimbun*, 29 October 1946; Rikkyo, *Rikkyo Gakuin*, 489.

90. Masao Terasaki, "Nihon no kindai kyoiku to kirisuto-kyo-shugi gakko," *Kyoshoku Kenkyu* 8 (1997), 11; Shunsuke Tsurumi, *Senjiki Nihon no Seishin-shi* (Tokyo: Iwanami Shoten, 1982), 87-95.

91. "Civil Affairs Handbook Japan, Section 15: Education," 23 June 1944, the Headquarters, Army Service Forces [ERJ1 1-B-9]; "In Support of Appropriations for Occupation Purposes," 2 September 1947, MacArthur's statement; Supreme Commander for the Allied Powers Government Section (GS SCAP), *Political Reorientation of Japan: September 1945 to September 1948*, vol. 2 (Washington: US Government Printing Office, 1948), 763.

92. Robert Hall, ed., *Kokutai No Hongi: Cardinal Principles of the National Entity of Japan* (Cambridge: Harvard University Press, 1949), v.

93. Masako Shibata, "Religious Education Reform under the US Military Occupation: The Interpretation of State Shinto in Japan and Nazism in Germany," *Compare* 34, no. 4 (2004): 423-41; Masako Shibata, "Education, National Identity and Religion in Japan in an Age of Globalisation," in *World Yearbook of Education 2005: Globalisation and Nationalism in Education*, ed. David Coulby, Crispin Jones, and Evie Zambeta (London: Kogan Page, 2005).

94. Shigeki Kaizuka, "Senryo-ki no 'Sankyoka Teishi Shirei' no seiritsu katei ni kansuru ichi-kosatsu," *Bulletin of Institute of Education, University of Tsukuba* 18, no. 1 (1993), 2-3.

95. Spinks, "Indoctrination and Re-Education", 68.

96. "Japan: The Education System under Military Government."

97. "Application of SCAP Directive AG 350 (22 Oct 45) CIE on Administration of the Educational System of Japan," 18 September 1950, Memorandum of K. B. Bush, CI&E, for Japanese Government [SCAPIN 612/1].

98. "Textbooks on Religion," 1 September 1948, Far Eastern Section Japan [FEC 1238, Box 166].

99. Robert Hall, *Shushin: The Ethics of a Defeated Nation* (New York: Bureau of Publications, Teachers College, Columbia University, 1949), 15.

100. "Suspension of Courses in Morals (Shushin), Japanese History, and Geography," 31 December 1945 [SCAPIN 519]; "Reopening of School Courses in Japanese Geography," 29 June 1946 [SCAPIN 1046]; "Reopening of School Courses in Japanese History," 12 October 1946 [SCAPIN 1266].

101. "Education Policy for Japan," 2 July 1946, Far Eastern Commission [SCAP File AG 350]; "Memorandum for Japanese Government from K. B. Bush, CI&E, for lifting the ban of classical sports such as *Kendo* and *Judo*," 13 September 1950 [SCAPIN 7265-A].

102. Quoted from: Kaizuka, "Senryo-ki," 6.

103. "Memorandum of Education Steering Committee to Nugent," 17 August 1946. NKK, *Kyoiku Sassin*, vol. 13, 11.

104. "Policy for the Revision of the Japanese Education System," 21 November 1946, Far Eastern Commission, Committee No. 4 [SCAP File C4-005/6].

105. "Letter of J. J. Schieffelin, Military Government Section (Kyoto, Honshu) to C.I. and E. Section, Ken R. Dyke," 9 December 1945 [Trainor, Roll 27 Box 30].

106. Japanese Education Reform Council, *Education Reform in Japan: The Present Status and the Problems Involved* (Tokyo: Japanese Education Reform Council, 1950), 5. Nambara also agreed with the idea about its revision. Takashi Kato, *Nambara Shigeru: Kindai-Nihon to chishiki-jin* (Tokyo: Iwanami Shoten, 1997), 159-69.

107. Yoshizo Kubo, *Tainichi senryo seisaku to sengo kyoiku kaikaku* (Tokyo: Sanseido, 1984), 281-307; Suzuki, "Haisen chokugo," 75-76; Suzuki, *Nihon senryo to kyoiku kaikaku*, 108-25.

108. "Situation Report—Japan."

109. GS SCAP, *Political Reorientation*, 585. Problems left out by this measure of abolition: Teruhisa Horio, *Nihon no Kyoiku* (Tokyo: University of Tokyo Press, 1994), 150-67.

110. "Letter from Nambara to Orr," 15 July 1948 [Trainor, Roll 26 Box 29]; "Memorandum: Monbusho, J. E. C., and Education Division," 26 August 1946, from Trainor to Orr, in NKK, *Kyoiku Sassin*, vol. 13, 15-16.

111. The discussion on this idea, held on 23 January 1948, was recorded in a strictly confidential file, Nihon Kindai Kyoiku Shiryo Kenkyukai (NKK), ed., *Kyoiku Sasshin Iinkai, Kyoiku Sasshin Shingikai Kaigi-roku: Tokubetsu Iinkai 5*, vol. 10 (Tokyo: Iwanami Shoten, 1998), 170-79.

112. GS SCAP, *Political Reorientation*, 135-36.

113. "Mark T. Orr."

114. "Conference with GS on Election of Local School Boards," 4 September 1948, Memorandum of Mark Orr [Trainor Box No. 17, HM-A2].

115. "Mark T. Orr."

116. It was reported that 75% of the electorates detested communists. "Kyoiku Iinkai Senkyo eno Kanshin," *Tokyo Shimbun*, 11 September 1948 [Trainor Box 17 HM-A2].

117. Abe, *Sengo no jijoden*, 94.

118. Because of the war, Japan lost 1,396 primary school buildings. The buildings of 581 lower secondary schools were burned down, and 753 were severely damaged. As of 1947, 1.59 million students out of the 3.19 million in the lower secondary school had no adequate classroom. Toshihiro Kennoki, *Zoku ushi no ayumi* (Tokyo: Shogakkan, 1977), 41.

119. Interview with Abe Yoshishige by *Asahi Shimbun* on 31 January 1946. Hoichi Tsuchimochi, "Gakko seido kaikaku," in *Sengo kyoiku kaikaku tsushi*, ed. Meisei University Sengo Kyoiku-shi Kenkyu Centre (Tokyo: Meisei University Press, 1993), 130.

120. Trainor, *Educational Reform*, 226.

121. "Special Report by Shigeru Nambara, President, Tokyo Imperial University and Chairman of Japanese Committee to G. D. Stoddard, March 21, 46," Wanamaker Papers Box No. 36. Tsuchimochi, "Beikoku tai-nichi kyoiku shisetsudan," 258.

122. Tsuchimochi, "Gakko seido kaikaku," 144. According to Horio, the public survey of *Mainichi Shimbun* in September 1948 showed that 60% of parents and 70-80% of the principals of the lower secondary school welcomed the new 6-3-3 system. Teruhisa Horio, *Kyoiku wo sasaeru shiso* (Tokyo: Iwanami Shoten, 1993), 537-38.

123. The Ministry of Education noted that in April 1947, 60% of lower secondary schools in the public sector adopted coeducation. The figure increased to 99.5 in September 1949. Ministry of Education, Japan, "Nihon ni okeru Kyoiku Kaikaku no Shinten," *Monbu Jiho* 880 (1951), 19-20.

124. Jiro Arimitsu, *Arimitsu Jiro nikki* (Tokyo: Daiichi Hoki, 1989), 969-70, 989; Toshihiro Kennoki, "Sengo bunkyo fu'un-roku," *Bunkyo* 66 (Spring 1994), 37-38.

125. Toshio Nakauchi et al., *Nihon kyoiku no sengoshi* (Tokyo: Senseido, 1987), 97.

126. Nakauchi et al, *Nihon kyoiku*, 97; Kennoki, "Sengo bunkyo," *Bunkyo* 66, 53.

127. Arimitsu, *Arimitsu Jiro*, 949, 989.

128. "Report of the United States Education Mission to Japan," 35.

129. Hugh Keenleyside and A. Thomas, *History of Japanese Education and Present Educational System* (Tokyo: Hokuseido Press, 1937); "The Historical and Psychological Background of Japanese Higher Education," Analysis for the United States Education Mission to Japan 1946 [ERJ2 1-K-196]; Interview with Morito Tatsuo, Minister of Education (June 1947-October 1948), by the NIER on 12 January 1963, in: *Meisei University Oral History Collection*.

130. Ienaga, *Daigaku no jicchi*, 112-16; Reiko Yamamoto, "Senryo-ka ni okeru kyoshoku tsuiho kensho: CIE staff no shisaku to sono haikei," in *Sengo kyoiku no sogo hyoka*, ed. Hoichi Tsuchimochi (Tokyo: Kokusho Kankokai, 1999), 206.

131. "Universities of Japan," a radio program broadcast on 29 April 1947. Tsuchimochi, *Education Reform*, 149.

132. "Universities of Japan."

133. Kindai Nihon Kyoiku-seido Shiryo Hensan-kai, ed., *Kindai Nihon Kyoiku-seido Shiryo*, vol. 19 (Tokyo: Dainihon Yubenkai Kodansha, 1957), 176. English translation is mine.

134. Daigaku Kijun Kyokai Junen-shi Henshu Iinkai (DJH), ed., *Daigaku Kijun Kyokai junen-shi* (Tokyo: Daigaku Kijun Kyokai, 1957), 109; "Post-War Developments in Japanese Education, vol. 1: Education in Japan," April 1952, CI&E Report [ERJ1 2-B-10].

135. NKK, *Kyoiku Sassin*, vol. 10, 105-6.

136. Eells was one of the most ardent advocates of this reform. DJH, *Daigaku-kijun-kyokai*, 35.

137. Kaigo and Terasaki, *Sengo Nihon no kyoiku kaikaku 9*, 93.

138. Takashi Hata, *Sengo daigaku kaikaku* (Tokyo: Tamagawa University Press, 1999), 43, 74.

139. "Nambara's Statement at the 5th General Assembly of the JERC on 26 December 1947." Nihon Kindai Kyoiku Shiryo Kenkyukai (NKK), ed., *Kyoiku Sasshin Iinkai, Kyoiku Sasshin Shingikai Kaigi-roku: Sokai 3*, vol. 3 (Tokyo: Iwanami Shoten, 1996), 230.

140. "The Minutes of the 10th Special Committee on 24 December 1947." NKK, *Kyoiku Sassin*, vol. 3, 230-31; NKK, *Kyoiku Sassin*, vol. 10, 95-96.

141. "Reorganization of Higher Education," 12 January 1948, Memorandum from W. C. Eells, Adviser on Higher Education, to Mark T. Orr, Chief, Education Division [Trainor, Roll 26 Box 29].

142. "Suggested Plan for Publicly Controlled Universities in Japan," undated [Trainor, Roll 26 Box 29].

143. "Report of the United States Education Mission to Japan," 18, 35-36.

144. Prior to the official start of the new system in April 1949, the CI&E permitted twelve public and private institutions, including five women's and six Christian schools, to be upgraded to the university in 1948 without an agreement with the Ministry of Education.

145. Trainor, *Educational Reform*, 228; "Report of the Second United States Education Mission to Japan," 22 September 1950, 9-10 [ERJ1 2-A-9].

146. Toshihiro Kennoki, "Sengo bunkyo fu'un-roku," *Bunkyo* 67 (Summer 1994), 46.

147. Takashi Hashimoto, "The Idea of University and the General Education," *Education Research Magazine* 18, no. 4 (1950) [ERJ1 2-A-42].

148. Masao Maruyama and Kanichi Fukuda, eds., *Nambara Shigeru Kaikoroku* (Tokyo: University of Tokyo Press, 1989), 372.

149. Amano, *Koto-kyoiku*, 57-58; DJH, *Daigaku-kijun-kyokai*, 109.

150. Organisation for Economic Co-Operation and Development (OECD), *Reviews of National Policies for Education: Japan* (Paris: OECD, 1971), 69-70.

151. Trainor, *Educational Reform*, 239.

152. "Report of the Second United States Education Mission to Japan," 10.

153. Japanese Education Reform Council, *Education Reform*, 65; "Japanese Universities and University Students," Publications Analysis No. 237 of the Military Intelligence Section, Cultural Staff of SCAP, undated [ERJ2 1-K-63].

154. "Aim and Function of the Japanese University," address of Nambara Shigeru delivered at the General Meeting of the Professional Association, in May 1947 [ERJ1 1-I-52];Terasaki, *Daigaku no Jiko-henkaku,* 210-11.

155. Cummings, "The Conservative Reform" 423; DJH, *Daigaku-kijun-kyokai,* 139.

156. Trainor, *Educational Reform,* 223.

157. Organisation for Economic Co-Operation and Development (OECD). *Nihon no Kyoiku Seisaku* (Tokyo: Asahi Shimbunsha, 1971).

158. "Report of the United States Education Mission to Japan," 39.

159. "Report of the United States Education Mission to Japan," 39.

160. Harvard University Committee, *General Education in a Free Society: Report of the Harvard Committee* (Cambridge: Harvard University Press, 1946), 44-46.

161. Masako Seki, *Nihon no daigaku kyoiku kaikaku: rekishi, genjo, tembo* (Tokyo: Tamagawa University Press, 1988), 78.

162. Kaigo and Terasaki, *Sengo Nihon,* 385-86.

Chapter Five

The Occupation Reform in the US Zone of Germany, 1945-1949

1. THE CHARACTERISTICS OF THE OCCUPATION IN GERMANY

Dissension and Power Struggle among the Allies

The Occupation in Germany was more complex than that in Japan in terms of the power structure among the Allies. The quadripartite structure of the Occupation caused dissension about policies for Germany. In addition, the German tradition of the autonomy of the individual *Länder* hampered the construction of an effective communication channel between the Office of Military Government for Germany of the US (OMGUS) and the German authorities.

During World War Two, the discussions of the Allied powers about surrender terms started in Casablanca in January 1943. Roosevelt abruptly introduced the expression, "unconditional surrender." The term denoted "the total elimination of German and Japanese war power."[1] After the United States, the Soviet Union and the United Kingdom had confirmed the "atrocities of the Hitlerites" in Moscow in October 1943, the idea of stern and punitive measures for Germany developed among the Allied powers toward the end of the war. The formation of the so-called Morgenthau Plan in the United States and the ideas of the British diplomat Robert Vansittart were the explicit articulation of such ideas. Henry Morgenthau, the secretary of treasury (1934-1945), suggested that Germany should be reconstructed as an agricultural country without a potential for industrial development. His idea was initially supported by President Roosevelt and had its highest influence on American Occupation policy around September 1944.[2] However, this plan for the "pastoralization" of Germany created controversies inside and outside the US. Borton later recalled that "As soon as he won the ear of President Roosevelt on his pastoralization policy for Germany, most of the people that were working on German policy in the State Department resigned because they realized that all of their work was for naught."[3] Stimson condemned this revanchist idea as "a crime against civilization itself."[4] In Europe, criticisms were even stronger. The British foreign minister, Anthony Eden, asserted that "A starving and a bankrupt Germany in the midst of Europe would poison all of us who are her neighbors."[5] General Clay also admitted that the Allies could not afford to waste the industrial potential in Germany, which was larger than any industrial potential in Europe.[6]

Economically, the Europeans were in real trouble. In the early Occupation period, Britain had already insisted on the withdrawal of its troops from Germany unless Britain could receive so-called "occupation payments" from the US.[7] Retaining the power of veto in certain issues, the British actually handed over educational issues to the Germans in December 1946, after their eighteen-month operation in Germany. The economic conditions of France were worse. The French Occupation authorities were almost incapable of accepting refugees returning to Germany, let alone conducting the adequate operation of a military occupation.[8] For France and in particular Britain, the objective of the Occupation in Germany was in principle to restore the German economy; not to paralyze it.

Increasing ideological confrontation between the US and the Soviet Union also broke down the joint effort of the Allies. As early as July 1945, Clay showed his concern to Washington that the Soviet Union had begun to appoint communists to key positions in the German administration.[9] In addition, thorough land reform in the Russian zone between August and September 1945 had created strong American skepticism about any agreement with the Soviet Union on Germany as "an economic unit."[10] The resumption of mass production in German military industries by the Russians brought a furious American accusation against the Russian violation of the Potsdam Agreement.[11] Not only in Germany were the Americans concerned about the expansion of communism in Europe as a whole. The Russian approach to the British Labour Party and the growth of socialist movements in France magnified the concern.[12] Communists were, said Clay, "almost everywhere in Europe."[13]

The concern directly influenced the US Occupation policy. The government gave a higher priority to the quick recovery of the political independence of Germany. It was also necessary to lighten the American economic burden brought by the Occupation at least in Germany. On 6 September 1946, James Byrnes, secretary of state (1945-1947), spelled out in Stuttgart the US policy for a speedy settlement of Germany. This Stuttgart Speech, however, received harsh criticism from German neighbors. The Polish government claimed that such a reckless suggestion from the Americans, who had not been terribly harmed by Germans, was not acceptable.[14] The French ambassador to Poland sustained the Polish criticisms by saying that Byrnes's idea was "inadvisably premature."[15] The ambassador asserted that the reconstruction of countries which fell victims to Germany should be first and not second to that of Germany.

Around late 1947, no country could foresee the possibility of the restoration of a unified Germany. *Times* reported that:

> Mr. Marshall said at Moscow that the partition of Germany would reopen the door to militant German nationalism; and Mr. Molotov pronounced a similar and no less emphatic warning. Yet it would be rash to suppose that any one of these statesmen now expects the London conference to produce the kind of agreement upon which a unified Germany might be restored.[16]

In January 1948, the US government reached the conclusion that "Soviet policies and motives are not in accord with the best interests of free nations."[17] The US, the UK, and France agreed in London in March 1948 that "close cooperation should be established among themselves."[18] The allied confrontations became evident even to the Germans.[19]

Initially, the ideas of a Long-Range Policy Statement for German Re-Education had quadripartite endorsement for the rehabilitation of Germany as "an integral part of a comprehensive program."[20] However, the allied countries each had a view of the so-called German problem. The continuous negotiation with Stalin's communist totalitarianism as well as Europeans' stubborn suspicion of, and antipathy to, Germany made the US Occupation difficult. Hans Speier noted later that the idealistic, missionary American zeal for the re-education of Germany was shattered by the disunity which the Allies showed "with startling rapidity and unmistakable clarity."[21] American naiveté in understanding the problem in the European context invited further troubles. Even at the crucial moment of the rise of the Cold War, the Americans were unable to make a timely policy shift in Germany, as they could do in Japan without major conflict with other Allies and Japan's victims.

In addition, the policies of the various departments of the US government often differed from Clay's ideas. The political power of Clay as well as the OMGUS was limited. The duty of military governor was conducted by the open, impartial personality and faith in democratic principles of General Clay: "benevolent despotism," in the term of John McCloy, assistant secretary of war (1941-1945). There was no MacArthur in occupied Germany. Neither Clay nor the OMGUS enjoyed the use of a centrally organized administration to spread their voices to every hamlet throughout Germany as efficiently as MacArthur and SCAP in Japan were able to do.

The American Views of Germany

Like the German problem, the policy for the re-education of Germany had differing interpretations by each allied power. The Soviet Union had a somewhat different view about the basic cause of the German problem. It was relatively straightforward—the socio-economic contradictions of capitalist society as a whole.

Among the three Western Allies, the European Allies shared critical views of Germany. They were mainly historically based. John McCloy, assistant secretary of war, said that:

> Twice in his [F. Roosevelt's] lifetime and mine, due to this antagonism between France and Germany, we had to move across the Atlantic with our blood and treasure, and it was getting a little bit tiresome every generation having to go over and fight another war because of Franco-German antagonism.[22]

In France, the government as well as the public maintained strong skepticism about, and fear of, the political and economic recovery of Germany.[23] General de Gaulle said that France had constantly been irritated by "the illusions of the Anglo-Saxons" who stick to appeasement solutions for the German problem.[24] French insistence on continuous, strict control over Germany, on the one hand, and a reluctance to bear the burden, on the other, prevented the Allies from making feasible plans for the reconstruction of Germany.

In Britain, Germany was often considered as a country without a history of a civil revolution, unlike France and Britain itself, and as an "inherently authoritarian" society. An extremist idea of such views could be seen in so-called Vansittartism:

> We [the British] live at opposite poles. We have not a main idea in common, because . . . words have entirely different meanings in our respective tongues. Our terms and concepts, our aims and admirations, are in complete contrast, even if the labels are the same. We have no real mental relations with Germans.[25]

"The German nation needs the most drastic cure in history," said Robert Vansittart, or "the world will die of the German disease."[26] But this Vansittartian idea brought no actual change in the major policy of the British government for the Occupation. In fact, because of their colonizing experience, the British actually took a pragmatic policy, demonstrated in the early withdrawal of the British troops from Germany in the actual Occupation.[27] Some critical voices were also raised by, among others, Victor Gollancz, a major opponent of Vansittart, about his one-sided idea of the German problem and the "exaggeration of the Holocaust."[28]

The American views of Germany were particularly complex due to various reasons, such as political stances and ethnic origins of the US citizens, which included a large number of émigrés and exiles from Nazi Germany. In fact, toward the end of the war, Jewish exiles had already established a number of lobbying groups which could make collective appeals to the US government.

However, all four Allies shared a view of Nazi aggressions as a part of the German "national tradition."[29] During the war, the psychological remolding of the German people gained ground in allied discussions. Curative measures were called for the "collective neurosis" of the German people. The Committee on Post-war Programs noted that:

> The basic assumption underlying this approach [of re-education] is that Germany is ill rather than guilty. The cure will involve measures of social and mental therapy calculated to reduce paranoid tendencies.[30]

The Occupation authorities set up their administrative organ, the Psychological Warfare Division. The US State and War Departments ran this body with the cooperation of the British Foreign Office. The Zonal Advisory Council of the Control Commission for Germany (British Element), or CCG (BE), noted that "The authoritarian state of the Prussian *Junker* class with its cunningly thought-out system of complete subordination of the individual, which debases a man to the state of a petty fly-wheel in the military state machine, is their highest ideal."[31] Thinkers from Prussia, such as Kant, Fichte, and Treitschke, were rebuked as the vanguard of German reactionarism.[32] The failure of the Weimar Republic and the consequent rise of the Nazis were attributed to the legacy of the incomplete social modernization in the *Kaiserreich* under Prussian hegemony. The state of Prussia, "a bearer of militarism and reaction in Germany," was eliminated in February 1947.

At the same time, at least the Western Allies generally shared a sense of esteem for German traditions as a precious inheritance of Western civilization. The United States, in its relatively short history, shared strong cultural interactions with Germany. The Long-Range Policy valued a sense of German self-respect, that is "the justifiable pride of Germans in their former great literary, artistic, scholarly, scientific, and religious contributions to civilization."[33] The underlying idea of the re-education of Germany rested on the fact that Germany was an important component of the association of the European states. For all the Allied powers, Germany belonged to Europe and would continue to do so, politically, economically, and culturally. As Henry Kellermann of the Area Division for Occupied Areas (ADO) has noted, this was the strong reality of Europe and the US Occupation in Germany.[34]

The Basic Principles of the Occupation in the US Zone of Germany

As described, the dissension among the Allies and the political and economic devastation in Europe were the pragmatic exigencies of the Occupation in Germany. Immediately after the German surrender, there was no central government or authority in Germany capable of maintaining political order in the country. The end of the total war and the consequent unconditional surrender brought a political void as well as psychological vacuum to Germany.[35]

The eventual restoration of political independence and the quick recovery of the economy in Germany were important objectives especially of the British and the Americans. Clay believed that "full bellies" were a "first requisite to receptive minds."[36] The arguments of John Keynes and others about the rise of the Nazis in Germany as a direct consequence of the Versailles Treaty were not forgotten. A potential for social upheavals in Europe followed by economic crisis was also a serious concern of Europeans.[37] The prime principle of the Occupation in Germany was to eradicate the conditions of Nazi aggression without wasting the German capability for economic recovery. Surpassing the other Allies in its economic power, the United States was confident that the recovery of the German economy was its key task and duty. Clay was directed from Washington to "not let hunger occur where you have the American flag flying."[38]

The basic principle of the social reform of Germany also rested on the bringing of Germany back to the community of Western civilization. In reconstructing the social order in Germany, the US Occupation authorities carefully avoided interfering in sensitive matters, such as religious issues. As will be shown later, this non-interference policy for German religion was frequently discussed in preliminary discussions on post-War Germany and became one of the major principles of the United States as well as the other Western Allies for their operation in Germany.

In the eyes of the Western Allies the reaffirmation of Christianity was vital for moral recovery among the German people and the consolidation of their society. Thus, despite the principle and despite Russian and French objections, the OMGUS supported German churches with finance and materials, including the reconstruction of 383 church buildings in the US zone.[39] Clay legitimized the contradictions in the principles and practices of the Occupation policy:

> Military Government has never interfered in the internal affairs of the Church. Religious institutions have been recognized, however, as a significant element in the social structure of Germany and have been given commensurate consideration in the program of re-education and reorientation conducted for the building of a peaceful and democratic Germany.[40]

The OMGUS did not look for the extensive overhaul of the political and the central value systems in German society. In the Occupation in Germany, the demise of every Nazi element and the revitalization of the economy were both the maximum and the minimum reform agendas of the OMGUS.

The Major Reform: Denazification

Putting aside most of the other reforms, the OMGUS maintained the policy of denazification as central to the Occupation in Germany. Clay declared in front of the representatives of the German *Länder* that:

> Regardless of its effect on German economy, regardless of the additional time which it may take, if this will [for denazification] does not develop, Military Government will necessarily have to take measures to see that denazification is carried out in that zone of Germany for which we are responsible. Let us have no misunderstanding. Denazification is a 'must.'[41]

The OMGUS was also anxious about potential hostilities by the remaining Nazis.[42] Importantly, furthermore, the completion of denazification was an eloquent proof of the American democratization of Germany. The State Department stated that:

> efforts should be directed toward: first, insuring that peoples of the world are convinced that US policies and motives, together with the fact that the US has the capability of carrying them out, are in their own best interests: secondly, making certain that the seriousness, reliability and consistency of the US and its policies are impressed on the peoples of the world.[43]

This purpose of denazification explains the tone of Clay's *Monthly Reports*. While often expressing his irritation about the sluggish progress in denazification, Clay had continued to report to Washington of "considerable progress" in this program.[44]

In December 1945, the Allies reached quadripartite agreement on uniform criteria for the denazification program and issued the Directive No. 24 of the Control Council (CC) on 12 January 1946.[45] Subsequently, CC Directive No. 38 of 12 October 1946 established a clear policy for the classification and punishment of war criminals, Nazis, and militarists.[46] Yet, the actual co-ordination of the Allies for denazification was delayed. At the end of 1946, Clay noted, in contrast to his report to Washington, the inefficiency and the consequent enormous bureaucratic difficulties of the denazification program.[47]

The program was chiefly operated by the Special Branch of the OMGUS Internal Affairs and Communications Division (IA&C), consisting of 2,900 officials including 2,400 German civilians. More than 13,400,000 Germans over eighteen years old were subject to a register for screening. As of 15 January 1946, 1,194,000 *Fragebogen* forms were distributed to the German adults in the US zone.[48] By then, about 987,000 Germans had been processed, and 184,000 people were classified as (1) non-employment mandatory. This classification indicated the highest rank of involvement in Nazi activities followed by the other ranks: (2) discretionary-adverse recommendation; (3) discretionary-no adverse recommendation; (4) no evidence of Nazi activity; and (5) evidence of anti-Nazi activity. Those who were classified in the highest rank, non-employment mandatory, were relatively numerous overall in Bavaria and among high-ranking public officials throughout the US zone.

By November 1945, the *Land* governments already possessed full legislative, executive, and judicial powers which were subject only to the military governments. In the denazification program as well, partial responsibility for the program had rested with the Germans of the local review boards from November 1945.[49] Initially, the OMGUS received "a general favorable reaction among the German populace" to this measure.[50]

However, as the program progressed, the criteria for denazification were loosened, and the number of chargeable persons gradually dropped. This derived from the decrease of Washington's political interest in it. The growing tension of the Cold War had major impact on decisions in Washington. In August 1946, the Pentagon and the State Department actually planned to end the denazification program. Clay tried to prevent the laxity of the program which, in his view, would become an "open sesame" to the return of ex-Nazis.[51] Because of his enthusiasm and in spite of it, the OMGUS continued the program by reducing its size and severity.

Along with the increasing inconsistency of the criteria, the American de-Nazification program ended in the punishment of too many "little Nazis" and too few "big Nazis," as Clay has admitted. The OMGUS gradually noted dissatisfaction among the German public because of this inconsistency in denazification. The criteria for denazification were different from *Land* to *Land* and even within a *Land*. The Senate of the Central Committee in Hamburg claimed that "*Wir stehen daher dem Verfahren der amerikanischen Zone mit grösster Skepsis gegenüber.*"[52] Apart from what Karl Jaspers has called the "silent disappearance of the Nazi leaders," either by suicide or exile, other lower-ranking Nazis were often found in the public sector in the Federal Republic of Germany.[53] William Griffith, chief of denazification in Bavaria, noted later that "denazification had failed to come even near achieving any objective set forth for it."[54] The ambitious attempt at thorough denazification brought about great complexity and confusion in its actual conduct and consequently left former Nazis at large.

Table 5.1. The Trend of Denazification: Percentage Distribution of Special-Branch Findings by Regions in the US Zone, November 1945-February 1946 (%)

Area	Bavaria				Württ.-Baden				Greater Hesse*				TOTAL			
Phase**	I	II	III	IV	I	II	III	IV	I	II	III	IV	I	II	III	IV
(1) Non-employment	24	23	22	20	20	18	17	16	21	19	16	14	22	21	20	18
(2) Discr.-adv. recom.	7	7	7	7	10	10	10	9	8	7	7	6	8	8	8	7
(3) Discr.-no adv. recom.	21	22	23	23	22	22	22	24	18	20	23	25	21	21	22	24
(4) No evidence Nazi act.	47	47	47	49	48	50	52	50	52	53	53	54	48	49	49	50
(5) Anti-Nazi act.	1	1	1	1	—	—	—	1	1	1	1	1	1	1	1	1
TOTAL	100	100	100	100	100	100	100	100	100	100	100	100	100	100	100	100

*Including the Bremen Enclave
** Phase I: November 1945; II December 1945; III: January 1946; and IV February 1946
Source: *Denazification Report*, 20 November 1945 (No. 4), 2; 20 December 1945 (No. 5), 2; 20 January 1946 (No. 6), 4; 20 February 1946 (No. 7), 4.

Regarding other reforms, the American attempt at land reform resulted in near failure, in contrast to radical changes in the Soviet zone and Japan. On average, more than one half of the land submitted to the OMGUS was actually seized by the *Land*, and the rest was exempted from confiscation.⁵⁵ The reform lacked, first of all, a feasible statute endorsed by the OMGUS for the reform. There was also a strong voice from the Bavarian landed aristocracy, who protested its innocence and claimed that only the Prussian *Junker* was to be punished for supporting the Nazis.

The *Grundgesetz* was written at the near end of the Occupation. In the writing process, the OMGUS employed older and experienced Germans as its staff. In August 1948, the delegates of the Western *Länder* assembled in Herrenchiemsee for the final agreement about the constitution of West Germany. In September 1948, the Parliamentary Council met in Bonn to draft a new constitution. A number of American political scientists of German heritage contributed to this work.⁵⁶ In this process, Clay—in contrast to MacArthur's aloofness from Japanese leaders—constantly paid visits to the meetings with the representatives of the German *Länder*.

As a whole, the re-education program for Germany started with, and ended in, denazification. In contrast to massive changes in Japanese society, many traditional aspects of German society survived the re-education program. The shaping of the American reform of German education was similar to the political and social reforms. However, in education, there were specific causes for the "failed reforms" more than such elements as the complex power structure of the Occupation authorities.

2. AMERICAN AND GERMAN COOPERATION IN EDUCATION REFORMS

The Education and Religious Affairs Branch (E&RA)

For the Americans, education reform was not the central concern of the Occupation in Germany. As Clay has confessed, education reform had never been the major priority of US policy for Germany from Roosevelt's presidency.⁵⁷ This policy continued in Truman's administration. This low level of enthusiasm for education reforms was clearly shown in the delayed formation of specific reform schemes. After its establishment, the E&RA, a branch of the OMGUS in charge of education, merely existed without a specific policy.⁵⁸ In fact, the E&RA started, as mentioned earlier, with only six staff members in Berlin in July 1945 as a part of the Public Health and Welfare Division (PH&W). The E&RA remained a branch within the OMGUS until March 1948, when the E&RA, the IA&C, and the ICD (Information Control

Division) were merged into the Education and Cultural Relations Division (E&CR). Such low political priority given to education reform provoked the distrust of German leaders of the US Occupation authorities. Crucially, by the time the Americans started education reform with specific reform schemes, the influence of the Occupation authorities on German leaders had already waned.

In these circumstances, the OMGUS took little advantage of the high quality of E&RA officers. Due to the relatively strong interaction between the US and Germany, the OMGUS did not have great difficulties in finding qualified educational officers, unlike the uneasy staffing of the CI&E. The chiefs of the E&RA, John Taylor and his successor Thomas Alexander, were experts on German education. Alexander, in particular, had already been recognized as a distinguished scholar through his studies on pre-Nazi German education, which were often referred to by the Occupation authorities.[59] Edward Hartshorne, the head of the E&RA's Higher Education Section, had also shown a profound understanding of German higher education in his publication, *The German Universities and National Socialism*. It was written in Berlin where he studied as one of the young American students drawn to renowned German scholarship and Friedrich Meinecke. Edwin Costell recalls that "I was the only non-Ph.D. ever to serve on the professional staff on the Higher Education Section."[60] Paradoxically, in Germany, the more knowledgeable officers were not necessarily valued highly or welcomed. Rather the confidence with which each side held their views of German education often invited confrontation between them. The frequent clashes between Alexander and German educators were an illuminating example. The OMGUS attempted to support the chronically understaffed E&RA by establishing close co-ordination with the administration of all the *Länder* of the US zone.[61] However, this was not possible because of rejection by the Germans and opposition by the countries of Nazi victims and, above all, because the attempt was in contradiction with American democratic principles of the decentralized administration system.

All of these circumstances created difficulties with the education reform on the American side. However, changes in German education were necessary for the OMGUS to make American efforts for the creation of a democratic Germany visible to the world. Clay also needed to prove his strong leadership in the Occupation in Germany.

The United States Education Mission to Germany (USEMG)

The effective influence of the USEMJ on the reforms of Japanese education caused Clay's sense of rivalry with SCAP in Japan.[62] Criticisms of sluggish progress in education reform in Germany were raised both within the US government and by the American public.[63] From the onset, the idea of sending the Education Mission to Germany was largely political.

This idea was put forward in lobbying from the National Education Association. Based on the suggestion of the association, Clay requested Taylor in July 1946 to form an education mission similar to the USEMJ. In the first instance, Taylor did not favor Clay's idea. Taylor stated that proposals by such a mission would not move education reform forward in Germany as easily as in Japan. However, the political pressure on the OMGUS for noticeable progress in the re-education of Germany was strong enough to shift the ideas of the OMGUS and Taylor. William Benton, assistant secretary of state (1945-1947), stressed the American tasks in his letter to James Byrnes:

> to break up the caste system which pervades the German school system and to educate the German people away from authoritarianism and aggression and toward democracy and peace. . . . Democracy, by its nature, cannot be imposed. The methods employed by Goebbels, even if we were willing to use them would defeat our purpose. Nevertheless, so long as the United States has the ultimate authority it has the ultimate responsibility to see that the German people work out their own educational salvation.[64]

The mission was dispatched in August 1946, over one year after the German surrender. It consisted of eleven delegates, headed by the chairman, George Zook, the president of the American Council on Education. The selection of the mission's members was largely based on their reputations as prominent educators rather than on their knowledge of German education. Some members of the mission regarded the appointment of Zook as inappropriate. Robert Patterson, secretary of war (1945-1947), admitted that the mission was "a political mission and not an educational mission."[65]

In Germany, both educators and administrators received the American recommendations far less favorably than had the Japanese. The press also showed strong skepticism about the relevance of the recommendations included in the mission report. The German press was not shy about labeling it as a step toward the *"Entartungen der deutschen Kultur"* [the degeneracy of German culture].[66] Even some American scholars did not speak highly of the report. They often found the recommendations strange and attributed this deficiency to mission's lack of understanding about the role of education in German society.[67]

Furthermore, the report of the USEMG itself lacked powerful assertion that German education would need radical reforms. The USEMG was conscious of its own dilemma:

> The difficulty of the task is due in no small part to the special character of German culture, with its peculiar defects and virtues. The virulent disease of Nazism developed in a culture of very profound dimensions. No country—unless it be ancient Greece or Rome—has contributed more generously to the common treasures of our civilization. No approach to the German educational problem dare be blind to this achievement or lacking [sic] in gratitude for it.[68]

Strategically as well, the Americans were very cautious about offending the dignity of the Germans by denouncing many aspects of pre-war German education, as Clay has admitted.[69]

The E&RA, rather than the German side, was probably most influenced by the mission report. Given specific reform targets, the OMGUS and the E&RA came to devote more energy to education reform. Based on the recommendation of the USEMG, Clay issued a directive called the MGR8s (Military Government Regulations Title 8): Control and Supervision of Education of January 1947. The major effect of the USEMG was thus on the American side, and not the German. The report of the USEMG was by no means read as a Bible by German educators, though it was not ignored.

The Ministries of Education in the German *Länder*

The approach of German educational administrators toward the US authorities and education reform as a whole also greatly differed from that of Japanese bureaucrats. From the outset, communications between the Americans and the Germans were difficult. First of all, the German administrative machinery was almost destroyed in the sudden collapse of the Nazi regime and consequent denazification. In addition, the German tradition of decentralized administration blocked channels for communication between the OMGUS and the diverse German representatives in different *Länder*.

Although in theory the Americans valued the tradition of *Kulturhoheit*, they found that the absence of a central co-ordinating organ was a crucial obstacle to discussions on, and implementation of, reforms. Thus the *Länderrat* was established in Stuttgart on 17 October 1945. The OMGUS also considered establishing a sub-organ, the *Kulturausschuss* [Education Committee], to discuss specifically educational matters with German representatives. After a long argument, the Germans agreed on 28 September 1946. Upon its establishment, the Bavarian minister insisted that the indigenous educational patterns of each *Land* should be protected. Although the ministers of Hesse and Württemberg-Baden suggested the simultaneous foundation of branch committees, the Bavarian minister opposed this suggestion, still fearing a danger of centralization in education. In this context, the *Kulturausschuss* did not take on the key function in actual reforms. Taylor's vindication of it as a mere "technical apparatus" had no effect.⁷⁰ Consequently, the E&RA had to cope with the different educational policy and even the educational ideas of each *Land*.

Among the German representatives, those from the politically liberal *Länder*, such as Greater Hesse and Bremen, were more willing to discuss reform with the Americans. Greater Hesse was artificially created for the Occupation with the former *Land* Hesse and the former Prussian province of Hesse-Nassau. Erwin Stein, the Hessian minister of education, cooperated with the OMGUS by calling for support from the administrators of his office and educational specialists. In the Bremen Enclave, Christian Paulmann played a central role in the relatively radical reform as the senator for school and education. He made progress in education reforms which were relatively close to the American model. But he was also a leading member of the SPD, *Sozialdemokratische Partei Deutschlands*. To protect the voice of Bremers, his constituents, and to defend the traditional educational patterns were his professional duty. In this sense, Paulmann was tactical in safeguarding his position both as a politician in Bremen and as a German representative in front of the Occupation authorities.

Württemberg-Baden reacted to the American suggestions slowly but with some compliance. This *Land* was also created for the Occupation by the Americans and the French by merging two traditionally rival *Länder*, Baden and Württemberg, and dividing the merged area in half, that is, North Württemberg and north Baden for the US zone and former Württemberg-Hohenzollern and south Baden for the French zone. The slow and inefficient administration of Württemberg-Baden partly derived from this abrupt and unnatural creation of the *Land*. Theodor Heuss, a prominent liberal historian and journalist, and his successor Theodor Bäuerle led the reform in their own way as the ministers of education.

In contrast, Bavaria, a *Land* with the original boundaries of the former Second and Third Reichs, continuously opposed American reform policy and was often indifferent to discussions on reforms. At first, the OMGUS contacted the Bavarian Catholic church to find a "politically suitable" person to fill the position of the minister of education in Bavaria. The church's favorite was Otto Hipp, the *Bürgermeister* of Munich.⁷¹ But his sluggish execution of denazification frustrated the OMGUS. Hipp's position was replaced initially by Franz Fendt (1945-1946) and ultimately by Alois Hundhammer (1946-1950). The conflict between the Americans and the Bavarians was aggravated over the period of these changes. Hundhammer's political power as an influential member of the Bavarian *Landtag* helped him maneuver Bavarian policy against the American reforms. He gained this power after his detention in the Dachau concentration camp. Hundhammer was a clear example of those anti-Nazi Germans who were, in the American eye, not necessarily politically liberal. Hundhammer said that American reform proposals would lead to "a complete overturning of and a radical break with a cultural pattern developed during the growth of centuries" in his country.[72] His strong affirmation of indigenous educational patterns received support from a wide range of German intellectuals and most ardently from the Catholic church in Bavaria.[73]

Overall educational administration in Germany pursued the strategy, what the British called "go-slow" tactics, in dealing with the Occupation authorities and waited until they ran short of time. The French were also annoyed with the customary response of "next year" by the Germans.[74] Despite some disagreement among the *Land* ministries, German bureaucrats demanded—strongly like Bavarians or tactically like Bremers—self-administration in educational matters and the retention of the traditional educational patterns.

German Educators

A lack of enthusiasm for, or aversion to, education reforms on the lines of the American model was also persistent among leading educators. In Germany, there was no centrally organized co-ordinating committee which consisted of selected educators who were always ready for discussions with the Americans, like the JERC.

In principle, German educators were not against the idea that radical changes were needed for post-war German education. For instance, Bäuerle formed the School Planning Commission, consisting of the representatives of the *Schulräte* [school superintendents], teacher-training institutions, elementary and secondary schools, and universities. The situation on university reform was similar. The University Planning Committee (UPC) was established first in Marburg University. Later, the UPC was found in other universities and discussed reforms within each institution.

However, the major idea of education reform held by the Germans was not the absorption of foreign models. Their watchword was "*von Weimar vorwärts*" [forward from Weimar]. The nostalgia of conservatives for the pre-Nazi period hindered the Occupation-sponsored reforms. The British noted that "The persistent attempts to find a solution under the WEIMAR regime had done no more than poison the whole political atmosphere."[75] Many educational leaders in Western Germany maintained the idea of "*innere Schulreform*" [internal school reform], an axiom that did not work in the Soviet zone.[76] In the Western zones, the Germans wanted neither conceptual nor structural reforms in their education under a foreign military occupation. They asserted their pedagogic principle of "*sich bilden*," to cultivate the qualities of one's own self. This renowned idea, so cherished by the Americans, ironically thwarted the American democratization of German education.

Thus essentially education reform during the Occupation was, for the Germans, full of contradictions. In the first place, some Germans found the idea of *Umerziehung* [re-education] "intellectually offensive."[77] Meinecke viewed the Allies' re-education of the German people as a severe ordeal and "a test of endurance."[78] Julius Ebbinghaus, rector of Marburg University, suggested to his colleagues and students:

> It seems to you an intolerable, an impossible thought that we should receive our instructions from foreigners, that we should be reprimanded and told how to behave, that we should be thwarted in our right to form a state of our own; it is a thought you feel it your duty to rebel against.[79]

Along with the other prominent academics, Karl Jaspers also played a key role in calling for the moral and spiritual recovery of the German people from within. Jaspers addressed to his audience at Heidelberg University:

> It is a miracle that we have survived. But it is also our own decision. This decision implies our readiness to accept the consequences of life under such conditions. Our sole dignity in this time without dignity is truth, and the infinite patience of work in spite of all obstacles, of all failures, as long as it is granted to us. The life we have saved we also want to merit. Faithful to our elders and to our country; faithful to our homeland which we recognize in Kant, in Goethe, Lessing, and the other lofty figures, in all that has nobility among us, in our language, in our woods, and mountains, and rivers, and lakes; obedient to the eternal moral commands, we want our true heritage to form us.[80]

Geoffrey Giles characterized Jaspers' role that "Jaspers saw the central need to build a German identity for the future, based on the positive legacy of the past, rather than rejecting all national identity when throwing out the perverted nationalism of the Nazis."[81]

Eduard Spranger—another academic who pursued the "German ideal" in the post-war period—emphasised *Volksbewußtsein* [folk consciousness]. For Spranger, like many other German scholars, learning education from foreigners was something which would make him blush.[82] He argued that it was not a matter of teaching people Germanness, but a matter of educating people in the consciousness of being a German.

For most of the German educators, the American reform programs were poor in quality. The strong resistance of German educational and political leaders to American proposals was often encouraged by German journalists. Hundhammer's victory over the American recommendations for a new educational model was extolled by the German press. In it, he was a *"wahrer Tri-*

umphator" [real victor].⁸³ *Die Berlin* also gave a critique that "the school reforms were decided not by educators but by politicians."⁸⁴ Despite their high qualifications, the Americans recognized a barrier between German intellectuals and themselves:

> The quality of our staff in charge of cultural and educational affairs has failed to impress German academic circles and has elicited the comments that our cultural efforts are aimed to the level of the "little man" rather than at the achievement of top level performances. Consequently, there exists in Germany an evermore noticeable trend on the part of intellectual circles to draw away from any form of association or identification with Military Governments and to establish the independence of the German intellectual in his struggle for rehabilitation.⁸⁵

German intellectuals maintained their belief in the fundamental values and quality of German *Kultur* and urged a deliberate return to pre-1933 Germany. There were few opportunities for the Americans to transform the education system in Germany after their own model.

Concluding Remarks on US-German Cooperation

As sketched above, the difficulty of the US Occupation authorities in Germany was to establish a system and atmosphere for cooperative and constructive discussions with German leaders. Structurally, educational administration in Germany was far more complex than that in Japan. In Germany, there was no central Ministry of Education through which the OMGUS could deliver its military orders to every single city and village throughout the nation. Moreover, based on the tradition of *Kulturhoheit*, the educational authorities in each *Land* had formed different administrations and had developed a range of educational ideas. Not only with administrators, but also with German educators, the US authorities failed to establish reciprocal understanding about education reform policy. German insistence on *Kulturhoheit* slowed down the establishment of a centrally organized co-ordinating organization which would promote efficient communication between the OMGUS and the German educators who were spread over various areas and organizations within the Zone.

Political circumstances in Europe were not favorable for American education reform in Germany either. Confrontation with the Soviet Union reduced the political significance of education reform for the Americans. The minimal enthusiasm of the United States, shown in the late start and weak organization of the education section of the OMGUS, triggered the German feeling of distrust in the American reform.

Ironically, the historically developed cultural interaction between the United States and Germany did not help or perhaps even hindered the progress of the American-led education reform in Germany. Despite the wealth of qualified leading personnel, the OMGUS failed to establish a cooperative relationship with the Germans. Because of the strong assertion of *Kulturbewußtsein* by German intellectuals, the Americans were unable to establish constructive communication with the Germans about changing their educational patterns. By lacking incisive criticisms of German education, the report of the USEMG had less impact on German leaders than on Japanese leaders.

3. PRIMARY- AND SECONDARY-SCHOOL REFORMS

The American Views of pre-1945 German Education and Reform Policy

Indeed, the Americans did not draw a close parallel between the German and the Japanese education systems in their valuation. Their views of German education were more complex. While criticizing authoritarian and class-affected aspects of the education system in pre-1945 Germany, the Americans also recognized that they were indebted to the traditions of the German education system for the development of American schools and universities.

The situation was made even more complex by American awareness of the rather low valuation of "American democracy" by most European intellectuals. The American ideas and practices of educational equal opportunity were particularly in contrast with those of the Germans. The report of the USEMG illustrated the system of pre-1945 German education:

> This system has cultivated attitudes of superiority in one small group and of inferiority in the majority of the members of German society, making possible the submission and lack of self determination upon which authoritarian leadership has thrived.[86]

Compared with American egalitarian education, German education was framed by various social divisions in class, gender, region, and religion. Specifically, the class-affected multi-track school system and the charging of tuition fees were in opposition to the American idea of egalitarian education.

The German notion of academic freedom was also viewed only as a privilege reserved exclusively for teachers in the *Gymnasium* and the university. For the Americans, this monopoly of privilege shaped the authoritarian atmosphere of educational institutions and cultivated the submissive attitude of students toward teachers.[87] The paternal authority prevalent in German society and schools was condemned for poisoning democratic principles and cultivating the *Führerprinzip* [leadership principle]. Dewey as well as his contemporaries traced the origin of these "undemocratic" patterns of German education back to discipline training in Kantian pedagogy. Dewey by no means identified educational patterns during the Wilhelmine empire with those of the Nazi regime. But Kantian pedagogy was labeled widely by Deweyans as one of the bases of German totalitarianism. In the eyes of many American educators, the dominant power of authority—both that of teachers and the state in Germany—seemed to be a spiritual basis of "a narrowly conceived nationalism and the almost total lack of understanding of the meaning of democracy."[88]

The educational differentiation by religious creed was also identified as the source of social divisions. But what was more problematic, for the Americans, was the state's political involvement in religious matters. In their view, the church-state-school relationship split the German people along confessional lines and resulted in a weak development of democratic education in the German school. However, on religion, the Americans reduced their critical tone, as shown earlier. The policy of non-interference with internal ecclesiastical affairs had been maintained from the war-time period. In November 1944, the US government directed SCAP in Germany that:

> You will not intervene in questions of denominational control of German schools or religious instruction in German schools except insofar as may be necessary to ensure that religious instruction and the administration of such schools conform to such regulations as are or may be established for all subjects and all schools.[89]

This was an echo of the allied decision at the Versailles Education Conference in January 1945 that "the question of denominational control in Germany is one in which the Supreme Commander does not intend to intervene."[90] This political principle was strictly kept in the Western zones, regardless of the religious policy of the individual Allies at home.

Despite those criticisms, the nineteenth-century German school system as a whole had established its prestige among American educators. Horace Mann had praised Prussian education as that which "among the nations of Europe has long enjoyed the most distinguished reputation for the excellence of its schools."[91] At the same time, the intellectually and physically well-equipped *Gymnasium* was for American educators the ideal academic institution: *mens sana in corpore sano*.[92] A Stanford study reported to the E&CR that "no educational system in the world has ever set and maintained" such high standards of education as in Germany.[93] The Institute on Re-Education of the Axis Countries also noted that "The problem of re-educating Germany is not that of teaching an ignorant or an untutored people."[94] Culturally, Japan and Germany were incomparable for most Americans. Taylor stated that:

> Japan is an oriental country, the culture of which never reached a level comparable to that of Germany, the Nazi interregnum notwithstanding. . . . The so-called negative aspects of present Military Government policy with respect to the German educational control by their application [sic], tend to re-establish an already highly developed and well articulated system of education. Hence the situation in Germany is not analogous to that in Japan.[95]

Overall, the cultural confidence of the Americans was more modestly expressed in Germany than in Japan. In fact, most European intellectuals viewed North America as a cultural infant in the immediate post-war period. Alonzo Grace, director of the E&CR, said that "the thinking American is somewhat embarrassed and chagrined at the average European concept of American culture."[96] Gerard Willem van Loon of ICD also sensed that:

> These people [the German people] have been brought up to believe that *Kultur* was a distinctly Teutonic invention and that Americans were all illiterate millionaires whose sole ambition was to live in a skyscraper on a diet of gin and jazz.[97]

The relatively quiet cultural confidence of the Americans toward Germany created their uncertainty about the thorough-going education reform in Germany.

Policy Implementation

Denazification in Education

Immediately after the German surrender, what the OMGUS did at first in German education was denazification. Its clearest policy was the elimination of Nazi influence from all aspects of German education. A heavy emphasis on denazification was a common policy of all the allied powers from the wartime period.

Upon the unconditional surrender of Germany, the OMGUS closed down all academic institutions and began to scrutinize former Nazis among educational personnel and Nazi themes in learning materials before reopening. The official definition of denazification was given in CC Directive No. 32, which declared in June 1946 that any member of the administrative or teaching staff and any student of any educational institution, from kindergarten to university, "who in any way whatsoever spreads or assists in spreading or connives at spreading militaristic, Nazi, or anti-democratic doctrines, will be dismissed from such institution . . . without prejudice to any other disciplinary measure or criminal sanction."[98] Denazification was also extended to the students of the former Nazi schools, such as the *Adolf Hitler Schule* and five *Napolas* (*Nationalpolitischen Erziehungsanstalten*). It was vital to democratize Germany and, more crucially, to eliminate the potential for hostility of former Nazis to the Occupation authorities. The Germans who failed to conform with the military government's instructions and directives were regarded as Nazi sympathizers.[99]

As the program progressed, the stern measures for denazification proved to be unfeasible. The schools were therefore re-opened hastily. All the *Volksschulen* and the secondary schools in the US zone were re-opened in October 1945 and September 1946 respectively. The OMGUS continued to re-open schools without a substantial improvement in physical and personnel problems, while dealing with increasing population influx. As of December 1945, the average teacher-pupil ratio in the primary school was 1:73.[100] The ratio was still 1:75 in October 1946.[101] To cope with the shortage of teachers, the criteria of the purge were loosened. While in the Russian zone only 8,000 out of 28,000 school teachers survived denazification screening, the denazification programs in the Western zones ended somewhat incoherently.[102] The US Occupation authorities had to recognize that complete political purity comes only by miracle, as the USEMG had predicted.

The textbooks of the Nazi period were also scrutinized. After eliminating Nazi influence, there were practically no usable ones left in the schools. As early as October 1944, the Americans and the British actually began to screen the textbooks of the Weimar period before the end of the war. The textbooks, stored in microfilm form, were obtained from the library of Teachers College in Columbia University and were transferred to London for scrutiny. In it, the Americans were less strict than the British, who judged the pre-Nazi textbooks to be also nationalistic and militaristic.[103] As the Occupation started, the OMGUS launched its own examination. The result of 1 August 1946 also showed a somewhat lenient judgment of the Americans. They censored 1,885 textbooks and approved 1,430 in total, of which 987 (52.3%) were unconditionally and 443 (23.3%) were conditionally approved.[104] Thus the Americans chose to reprint textbooks used before 1933 rather than to write ones afresh. Between late 1944 and early 1945, an edition of 40,000 sets was printed in Aachen and Bonn as emergency textbooks. Additionally 5,328,616 copies were produced in Munich and distributed throughout the US zone.[105]

In planning for the re-writing of the textbooks, the Americans and the British by and large agreed that the Allies should not impose anything on the Germans, but would let the Germans re-write textbooks by themselves. The French always remained skeptical about this Anglo-American policy.[106]

On the other hand, the descriptions of European colonial expansion were deliberately deleted as a taboo.[107] Denazification of learning materials also ended up as a political compromise.

The Principle of State-Church Relationship

The Allies recognized that in Germany religious education had been an indispensable part of education before the establishment of the modern school system. There, differences in religion and religious sect were closely related to people's official life, such as schooling and taxation. Thus, the Allies agreed not to interfere in this long-established custom of the German denominational school. To the Germans, the US Education Mission said that:

> Ideally, it is nobody's business in a democracy what anybody else believes or does not believe about matters over which reasonable men have always differed. ... Counsels of prudence no less than considerations of humility stop us from trying to impose upon Germany the pattern of church-and-state which has proved so advantageous to both parties in America.[108]

For the Occupation authorities, this policy of non-intervention in German religion did not contradict their recognition of the political relationship between the Nazis and the Christian churches and between Nazi ideology and Christianity. The CC remarked that the Nazi educational authorities had safeguarded the "far-reaching privileges" of the Roman Catholic community.[109] The E&RA also knew of a close political relationship between the German Evangelical and Catholic churches, and the minister for ecclesiastical affairs of the Nazi regime.[110] In Britain as well, there had been harsh criticism from the war-time period about the political negotiation of the German church leaders with the Nazis.[111] It is often argued that the Allies were aware that the basis of the Nazi *Weltanschauung* had much to do with the Germanization of Christianity by the Nazis.[112] Post-war assertions by several Jewish groups that the Nazi *Endlösung* was undertaken nowhere else than in Christendom and that "the Holocaust was an extreme pattern of political and cultural expression" in European Christendom were never really confronted.[113] The Jewish allegation about the association of the Nazi *Weltanschauung* and Christian creed was abandoned in discussions on the re-education of Germany.

It is argued that the Jews had been abandoned during the war and the Occupation, by being treated by the Americans and the British as "a skeleton in the democracies' political closet," a matter rather not to mention.[114] In fact, the chairman of the American Jewish Conference wrote a letter of regret to the US assistant secretary of war and criticized that "the report of the US Education Mission to Germany contained no special evaluation of German anti-Semitism and that no expert of an appropriate Jewish institute was included" in the mission.[115] Notwithstanding Russian, French, and British disapproval or hesitation, the US Occupation authorities also defended the wish of the German Catholic church to maintain part of the *Reichskonkordat* of 1933, a political contract between Hitler and Pope Pius XII.[116]

At the same time, the OMGUS helped the German churches open campaigns to demonstrate their war-time resistance to the Nazis. Indeed, during the Nazi period, there was some resistance to the Nazis by Christian individuals and groups. For example, Catholic priests Rupert Mayer and Bernhard Lichtenburg were central in the Catholic resistance movement. Evangelical theologian Karl Barth was forced to leave his position at a university, because of the explicit confrontation of his position with the Nazi *Weltanschauung*.[117] The bishop of Munich exhibited Catholic Church's struggles with the Nazis in a space offered by the OMGUS in Bavaria.[118] The Evangelical Church later followed. The Occupation authorities sought to support the Germans to restore a sound religious creed in German mind. It is true that there were many observations of the feelings of hopelessness among the German people immediately after the war. *Stuttgarter Zeitung* reported that most Germans showed cynicism and political disinterest because of "their duty toward national honor to close their minds and conscience against facts they cannot deny."[119] Similarly, Barth remarked that the Germans in the immediate post-war period revealed this cynicism in order to escape responsibility for their war-time thought and actions by "descending into the abyss of the unconscious."[120]

Overall, the US Occupation authorities more than the other two Western allies adopted a policy of appeasement to the German churches. The French were particularly critical about that the state-church relationship in Germany, which had, in the French eye, undermined the organizational and pedagogic independence of the school from religious authorities. Moreover, for the French, the German churches were responsible for impeding the development of independent, free thinking among students and for cultivating their submissive, obedient mentality in the German school.[121] But the idea of a complete separation of state and church yet again fell short of implementation after the earlier failure in the Weimar period.

The aid of the OMGUS for the German churches was partly political. There was deliberate intention to reduce confrontations between the Occupation authorities and the churches, in particular those in Bavaria. The Bavarian minister of education, Hundhammer, was most explicit in appealing to the Occupation authorities about the significance of religious education in the German school. He wrote to the OMGUS for Bavaria (OMGBY) to assert that:

> The supreme objects and aims of education are reverence for God, respect for religious conviction and human dignity, self-control, a sense of responsibility, a

zest for self-reliance, a readiness to help and to appreciate the true, the good and the beautiful.[122]

When the E&RA planned to introduce social studies as a part of moral education, Hundhammer counterattacked by reinstalling the old tradition of *Prügelstrafe* [corporal punishment] in the school. Hundhammer's measure was unpopular even among the Germans.[123] Willy Vieweg, Stein's deputy, also made clear that the Hessian Ministry of Education had no intention to reinstall *Prügelstrafe* in the *Land*. In fact, in Hesse, the American model of social studies was introduced as *Staatsbürgerkunde* with some adjustment to German socio-cultural circumstances.[124] But the objection to the US principle of the separation of state and church was unanimous, though in different degrees, in all the *Länder* of the US zone. The German people found this principle irrational, which created the basis of the absence of stability and order in the American culture.[125] The state-church-school relationship thus remained legal and was enshrined in Article 7 in the *Grundgesetz* of the Federal Republic of Germany. It states that "Religious instruction shall form part of the ordinary curriculum in state and municipal schools, except in secular (*bekenntnisfrei*) schools."

The Reorganization of School Structure and Denominational Problems

The Americans and the Germans discussed the reform for the demolition of the multi-track school system in different perspectives. For the Germans, the mixing up of primary and secondary education would destroy the traditional pattern of specific education in the *Volksschule*, in particular religious instruction, and the basis of German society. The Germans expected from the American system the destruction of the heterogeneity of secondary education which had played a so-called social-conservative role vital in maintaining the traditional social order. German academics argued that "*Ob man der Grunsschule vier oder sechs Jahre zubilligt, ist keine Frage der Demokratie.*"[126]

For the Americans, the introduction of the single-track school system was an essential means of the democratization of German education as well as German society. The Americans pictured the differentiated pattern of German education as a system of caste. Within the US policy, the introduction of the single-track school system was "one of the crucial points in any reform plan of the present educational system."[127] As practical measures for the broadening of educational equal opportunity—what the Germans call *Chancengleichheit*—the Americans planned to introduce the *Einheitsschule* [comprehensive school] and the abolition of school tuition. The USEMG proposed that primary education should be provided from grades one to six, and secondary education, including the vocational strand, should uniformly consist of grades seven to twelve.[128]

With few exceptions, the proposal received severe criticisms from many sectors of German society—educators, educational authorities, local parliaments, parents, and above all the Christian churches. For the Germans, this reform was not a question about the principle of *Chancengleichheit*. In fact, the idea of the *Einheitsschule* had been discussed in Germany from the nineteenth century, and in vigorous discussions during the Weimar period, though without actual implementation.[129] The greatest obstacle to the introduction of the *Einheitsschule* had been the strong wish of the German people to maintain the traditional pattern of religious education specific to the individual *Volksschulen*. Even the powerful state bureaucracy of the *Kaiserreich* had failed to establish a uniform type of the *Volksschule* as the "state school" in the face of the appeal to the principle of *Kulturhoheit* by the individual *Länder*.[130] After the Nazis mixed up these differentiated patterns of religious education, the German people fervently desired to restore the traditional form of the *Volksschule* and to "re-confessionalize" it.

Failing to understand the significance of the religious aspect of the school system, the Americans unsuccessfully tried to change the traditional system. The prolonged education reform in Germany frustrated the OMGUS and, above all, General Clay. Clay actually ordered in January 1947 that the *Land* governments in the US zone should submit basic and long-term reform plans for each *Land*. Clay's telegram of 10 January 1947 stated that the basic plan was due in April 1947 and that the long-term plan was due on 1 July 1947. However, all the plans of the *Länder* satisfied neither Clay nor Alexander and even frustrated them because of the still-existing gap between American plans and German ones.[131] The further pressure of Alexander on the *Land* governments worsened the relationship between the E&RA and the German authorities. The OMGUS finally issued a military order, CC Directive No. 54, in June 1947 to make the Germans accede to the reform along others. The directive stated that "Schools for the compulsory periods should form a comprehensive educational system."[132] The E&RA also distributed its memorandum to the OMGUS offices in all the *Länder* to say that "in general it may be assumed that this office will not approve any educational reform which does not provide a six-year *Grundschule*."[133]

The strongest objection to the American proposal came, as with other reforms, from Bavaria. Regarding its reform plan submitted to the E&RA, Alexander wrote to Clay that "The so-called 'reform' proposal is totally unacceptable."[134] Hundhammer brushed aside the American request for the submission of a revised plan. He maintained that *"Die Volksschulen sind die Grundlagen unseres Schulwesens überhaupt."*[135] He also wrote to the OMGBY that "it was and is my conviction that in no case may a school reform, weaken, or destroy the peculiar character of our education, which is rooted in the entire culture of our country and people."[136] This was not only the idea of Hundhammer but also that of the Bavarians, including the majority of *Landtag* members and *Gymnasium* teachers. This support enabled Hundhammer to claim that his ideas represented the wish of the people. Whereas in Japan the Americans obtained much public support for this implementation, they received letters from *Gymnasium* teachers appealing to their right to maintain the multi-track school system in Germany. The Catholic church in Bavaria resolutely and persistently opposed the American proposal and claimed the moral and natural right of the German people to reject forceful education reform.[137] The church even asked the Vatican to help the Bavarian Ministry of Education decline the American proposal. In the face of such a triple pressure, the OMGUS and E&RA were unable to impose the single-track system.[138]

Greater Hesse was, according to the early observation of the OMGUS, in the forefront of reform in the US zone. The first Hessian minister of education, Franz Böhm, for instance, suggested maintaining the traditional confessional school but making it interdenominational.[139] Later under the administration of Franz Schramm, debates on religious education tended rather to break various traditional demarcations in education. A strong voice for the retention of the traditional confessional school system was raised only by the Liberal Democrats. Both the Christian Democratic Union and the Social Democratic Party believed that Hesse would need some adjustment of the existing school system on confessional lines. The heterogeneity of Greater Hesse, a *Land* artificially formed by the Allies, brought about a more balanced political party structure and the exclusion of church dominations in educational matters which created a basis for a relatively radical approach to education reform. Erwin Stein, the new minister of education, advocated in public the simplification of the multi-track school system of secondary education.[140] When compulsory education was extended in Hesse from eight to nine years, the OMGUS stated that "almost all the respondents welcomed this change."[141] But toward the end of the Occupation, the relationship between the Hessian ministry of education and the OMGUS for Hesse (OMGHE) worsened, as the Hessian ministry continuously modified the American schemes before implementation. Stein claimed that "*so wird nur eine aus deutschem Geist geschaffene Erziehungs- und Bildungsreform dauernden Bestand haben.*"[142] Stein, also protested about the imposing of a military order for educational reforms by appealing to the Hague convention.

In Württemberg-Baden, as stated earlier, education reform went in slow but relatively harmonious co-ordination with the E&RA. In April 1947, Bäuerle proposed a plan for a new school structure, similar to the American model of the single-track system. Bäuerle also formed the *Hauptausschuss*, the central committee for education reforms in the *Land*, in November 1947. Under Christian Caselmann, the Chairman of the *Hauptausschuss*, it produced proposals for education reforms—the Caselmann Plan. Although the plan was more precise and progressive than proposals from the other *Länder*, the E&RA claimed that the plan still carried the inertia of tradition. In the German context, the retention of the traditional educational pattern was the desire of almost the whole of German society, especially that of educated Germans. Alexander reported to Clay that:

> This office is disappointed in the progress made. Minister Bäuerle has shown much good will, but he stands pretty alone. The Church, the University and the secondary school forces have opposed his efforts.[143]

Similar plans were made in the Bremen Enclave. Christian Paulmann proposed the introduction of the modified model of the *Einheitsschule*, consisting of the six-year *Grundschule*, the three-year lower *Mittelschule* [lower-secondary school], and the differentiated three-year *Oberschule* [upper-secondary school]. Within this proposal, flexibility was given to permit changing the school types in upper-secondary education. The proposal also included the introduction of free education and of teacher education into higher education. But the case of the Bremen Enclave was an exception. As a politically liberal area within Germany, Bremen had a powerful SPD.[144] The plan was created under the leadership of Paulmann, as a leading member of the SPD in Bremen, with the support of the Bremers.

In sum, the major American difficulty in reforming German education derived from the view of American proposals as foreign by German leaders. German leaders maintained that the American proposals disregarded the indigenous elements of German society, which were essential for sensible reflection on past deficiencies and future plans for education. Despite the fact that the US officers in Germany were more knowledgeable about German education, compared with the case of Japan, the Americans were condemned for their cultural naiveté by the Germans. The crucial failure of the OMGUS and the E&RA had two major aspects. First the Americans attempted to change the long tradition of *Kulturhoheit* by implementing uniform educational patterns in various regions within a few years or occasionally several months. The Bavarian criticism of this attempt was the strongest opposition to the OMGUS. An American officer said that "the people [in Bavaria] are first of all Bavarians, then Catholics or Lutherans, and thirdly Germans."[145] Second, the Americans failed to understand the significance of gaining the acceptance of German leaders. As seen above, the Americans were occasionally more

134   *Chapter Five*

forceful in trying to realize their educational reforms in Germany than in Japan. In the face of strong rejections expressed by German leaders, the political pressure of the OMGUS had no effect. The Germans began to solve their long-standing educational problems by themselves after Germany became a sovereign state again.

4. HIGHER-EDUCATION REFORMS

The American Views of the Pre-1945 German University and Reform Policy

For the reform of the German university, the OMGUS was even less enthusiastic than for that of primary and secondary education. The US authorities started later and had less precise plans for higher education. The reform was not even on the agenda at the Versailles educational conference in January 1945.

Culturally, this can be explained by the favorable views of the German university held by the Americans through a long process of intellectual interaction. From the nineteenth century, the German university had long enjoyed fame. Those who were inspired by the scholarship of the German university visited universities throughout Germany. The universities in Berlin, Leipzig, Heidelberg, Halle, Göttingen, Bonn, and Munich were particularly popular, but Würzburg, Marburg, and Breslau also received a number of American scholars.[146] German professors were also enthusiastically invited by American universities. Another tribute was paid to the solid organization of the German university, including its administration. Harvard, Columbia, Cornell, Wisconsin, Philadelphia, Pennsylvania, and Northwestern Universities were influenced by the German model of university administration. Johns Hopkins University was once called the university of Göttingen-in-Baltimore. The mutual relationship between some German universities and the University of Chicago was celebrated by the personal tributes of *Kaiser* Wilhelm and President Roosevelt. Abraham Flexner, the director of the Institute for Advanced Study at Princeton University, admitted that his feeling toward the German university was "one of reverence."[147]

Those who maintained the view about the German university during the Nazi interregnum even encouraged German academics to resist US-lead reforms. Roger Adams at the University of Illinois, Urbana, wrote in November 1947 to Karl Freudenberg at Heidelberg:

> My own conviction is that as few changes as possible from the system which you have had in the past will in the long run work out the best. Unfortunately,

the educational people in the Military Government are for the most professional educators [i.e., administrators] who are only mildly interested in scholarly work.[148]

Intellectually, the academic culture and practices of the German university did not lose much of their past reputation within the Western intellectual communities.

In terms of political irresponsibility, however, accusation against the German university was acute. The fame of the university was debased not only by the distortion of science but also by the political surrender of university academics to the Nazis. Western intellectuals accused most of the German academics of turning a blind eye to Nazi atrocities suffered by their colleagues and to book burnings.[149] The decision for Brownshirts over Gown by the German university ended in the near destruction of its long tradition of neo-humanism. Post-War Western intellectuals sought answers to critical questions: Why had the university system known for autonomy and academic freedom become the victim and partly the collaborator of the Nazi regime? And why in Germany, where so many scholars had been renowned for their critical thinking, had academics surrendered to the Nazi Party? This issue was broadly discussed in educational conferences and meetings during the Occupation.[150]

The Americans pointed out a number of conditions which had permitted the political vulnerability of the university against Nazism. These conditions were viewed as inherent in the system and character of the German university. First of all, the professional hierarchy of the university was denounced. Because of this, it was argued, young German teachers and students were prevented from cultivating critical views of their professors and the authorities as a whole. The USEMG found the power of the *Ordinarien* [tenured professors] autocratic and regarded its relationship with *Nichtordinarien* [non-professor university teachers] as dictatorial. In addition, German elitism was characterized as egoistic and arrogant. The character was seen in the "peculiar aloofness" and social naiveté of a university-educated elite.[151] The Institute on Re-Education of the Axis Countries pointed out a number of beliefs with which the German elite had been indoctrinated:

> Extreme arrogance and brutality toward 'inferiors' is desirable, if expedient ... Lies and treason against friends are to be praised as virtues if they serve the ends of warfare. Individual and student life, as in the Student Corps at a university, properly follow the patterns of militarism. . . . envy and 'Schadenfreude' [gloating over another's pain] are legitimate and morally justifiable emotions, properly glorified in epics and children's books as a desirable part of education.[152]

136   Chapter Five

In American eyes, the German university had failed to cultivate adequate moral leadership and consequently built a perverted and egocentric society. Taylor stated that:

> I speak of the guild, which is very aristocratic, the social organization of the students, which neither in the time of the republic, nor under the Nazis, nor today has changed enough.[153]

Thus, student associations, such as *Burschenschaften* and *Altherrenbünde*, were also severely accused for their reactionary and para-military character and actions.[154] The Americans saw the spiritual conditions for the neglect of democracy inherent to the mind-set of the German people apart from the influence of National Socialism:

> Impartial observers of past-Hitler Germany conclude that the Nazification of German youth was less thorough-going than we generally feared in Allied countries during the war. . . ., the number of fanatical Nazis among young Germans is relatively small. On the other hand, the German youth who have cast off Nazism, or even the ardent anti-Nazis among them, are not necessarily democrats in our sense of this word.[155]

In Germany, the spiritual recovery of the youth was a great concern of all the Allies. The need for the re-education of the German youth was a shared value. In fact, in every zone of the Occupation, the Allies founded a special institution for the re-education of German prisoners of war.[156] The Occupation authorities were anxious that these desperate, confused young people might yet again be attracted by extreme political thought. The OMGUS actually found out that the students who were defined as "non-Nazi" disseminated propaganda of Nazism and anti-Occupation authority rhetoric as late as a year after the war.[157] Even in the late period of the Occupation, the Americans still insisted that the Occupation authorities had to maintain strong control over the German university, or it would "become the center of agitation against the Occupation forces."[158]

Thus much of the American effort was devoted to making the German university correct its political mistakes in an American way. Taylor criticized "the lack of civil courage of too many university teachers" in front of the German ministers of education and made clear to them that "where mistakes have taken place, the dismissals will be recalled after close examination of each individual case."[159]

Policy Implementation

Denazification in Higher Education

At the end of the war, the allied powers immediately closed down all the schools and universities in Germany. Besides the university, a large number

Erlangen Universities frustrated the Occupation authority.[166] In Munich University, denazification under the rector, Albert Rehm, did not satisfy the OMGUS, although he was appointed by the OMGUS. After the speedy resignation of Rehm's successor, Georg Hohmann yet again conducted denazification reluctantly. In the end, denazification at Munich was "completed" with the dismissal of thirty-three professors and forty-six other teaching and administrative staff members. It was reported to the OMGUS, however, that "Munich's law faculty was full of Nazis."[167] Having diverse outcomes depending on the leadership of each university, the denazification of the university in the US zone of Germany resulted in the screening of 2,477 staff and faculty members and the dismissal of 236 people in the middle of October 1947.[168] Much of the effort of the US Occupation authority was devoted to this program, although dismissed professors were reinstalled in the university within a few years.[169]

Not only professors but students were also screened and punished. As mentioned earlier, the hostility of the German youth to the Occupation authorities was their great concern of the Americans in Germany. This concern had practically never been felt by the US officers in Japan.[170] In their eye, young Germans in the immediate post-War period appeared to be vulnerable and dangerous:

> Military defeat, preceded and followed by the rapid disintegration of the nazi system that had over [and] again exhorted the population never to capitulate, left the young generation with shattered ideals and deprived of the accustomed controls by paramilitary organizations and political police. In the vacuum thereby created there was room for new ideals, but even when groping for them the majority of German youth was still a totalitarian youth in search of new leadership. . . . there were few traditions available inside Germany to guide the reorientation of the younger generation.[171]

The order Non-Admittance of Persons with Former Nazi Affiliations as Students to Institutions of Higher Learning, issued on 14 January 1946, restricted admissions for those who have taken an active part in the Nazi Party's activities.[172] In Heidelberg University, for instance, 767 students were surveyed, and 194 (25%) were accused of being related to the Nazis. *Fragebogen* conducted in Württemberg-Baden showed similar results: in *Technischhochschule* Stuttgart 270 students out of the total number of 1,108 (24%) were accused; in *Technischhochschule* Karlsruhe 25 out of 100 (25%); and in *Pädagogischinstitut Stuttgart* 16 out of 50 (32%).[173] A number of student associations were also subject to severe scrutiny, allegedly having attacked Jewish students. The Americans often identified the characteristics of the German student associations with those of Prussian militarism.[174] Besides, the membership of German fraternities was, in the American point of view, basically class conscious and improper for educational institutions.

of so-called "war-research establishments" were closed, includir
institutions in Bavaria, nine in Württemberg-Baden, and two in G
as of 1 January 1947.[160] The reopening of these academic institu
wait until they were decently equipped with teaching personnel ;
materials.[161] The actual reopening of the university moved forwar
planned. Initially for urgent healthcare reasons, the medical fac
delberg University were reinstated on 15 August 1945. By Dece
all the faculties of the University were reinstated.

In the university, the UPC of each university acted as the leadi
undertake denazification. The UPC was initially established in the
1945 by the co-ordination of Hartshorne of the E&RA and Ebl
Marburg University. The early start to university reform by the Br
pation authorities gave stimulus to this co-ordination.[162] In reo
university had to appoint five to ten "politically acceptable" perso
present and former faculty members as the official members of tl
tee. It consisted of not only professors, but also of *Dozenten* [as:
fessors]. While retaining the authority for the appointment of the c
each UPC, the E&RA remained at a good distance. The initial pur
UPC was to make policies for the overall reconstruction of the uni\
is, (1) a constitution for the university; (2) an operational plan for
istration of the university until a constitution is approved; (3) e
policies and objectives, both general and for separate faculties; (4
tions of teachers in the various faculties whom they consider ac;
and politically acceptable; (5) a list of the university personnel who
excluded for political reasons; (6) curricula; (7) selection and ad1
students; (8) supervision of student affairs, housing, and extra-cur
tivities; (9) university property; (10) examinations, degrees, and pr
licenses; (11) control and financing of the university, including p;
salaries and pensions; (12) such other matters concerning the uni
may be required by the responsible military government authority.[1]
prime objective of the UPC task was to screen former Nazis among
ics and replace them with the new ones.

The severest scrutiny of former Nazis took place within six mo
the war, but harsh measures had continuously been taken until arou
1948.[164] In Marburg University, 50% of the law faculty and 44% of
ical faculty were purged under Ebbinghaus. In Heidelberg Universi
"a Nazi showcase" by James Tent, only a few were purged unde
Rector Hoops.[165] The members of the screening committee of the H
UPC, led by Karl Jaspers, suspected Hoops's commitment to denaz
Under the leadership of Karl Jaspers, 64% in the medical faculty, 6:
faculties of political science, and 60% in the natural sciences facu
dismissed, whilst in Bavaria the "insufficient" denazification at Mu

The skepticism about the democratic foundation of German society, the fear of the resurgence of extreme radical thought among German youth in the vacuum of political and social life, and the urgency of re-education of future generations became of growing importance in the Occupation policy. The Committee for the Reform of University Constitution in the US zone discussed the significance of the spiritual recovery of young Germans and concluded that:

> Indem sie [die Verfassungen der Länder] den Hochschulen die Pflege freier Wissenschaft und die Erziehung der akademischen Jugend zu den geistigen und sittlichen Werten abendländischer Kultur zur Pflicht machen, weisen sie nicht nur der geistigen Tradition und der unabhängigen Entfaltung schöpferischer Kräfte einen eigenen Raum zu, sondern begründen zugleich eine hohe Verantwortung.[175]

Similarly, the *Hochschulgespräche* at Marburg, founded in January 1946, confirmed that emphasis on the Western spirit especially through religion was an important task of the university in order to foster sound youth.[176]

With the rise of ideological confrontation with the Soviet Union, the OMGUS placed more emphasis on US-German cultural exchange programs than denazification. As Kellermann has revealed, the US government deliberately intended to spread American culture and the American way of life in the postwar world. This cultural exchange program was largely supported by Congress, represented by the Advisory Commission on Educational Exchange, and actually undertaken by the Office of the US High Commissioner for Germany (HICOG) from the last phase of the Occupation through the 1950s.[177]

By the same token of the declaration of the University Constitution's committee, the Americans aimed at the recovery of occidental moral and cultural values among the German youth. This emphasis on moral recovery among the German youth explains the early re-opening of the theology faculty, along with that of the urgently needed medical faculty, in most of the universities in the US zone.[178] The OMGUS believed that theological seminaries and faculties would play a significant role "in determining future social trends in Germany."[179] Permission was granted for a number of theological students from Germany to attend seminaries in Switzerland and Italy. In university education as well, the Americans and the Germans saw the recovery of Christianity among the German people as a key for a new Germany.

The Board of Trustees System

Apart from denazification, the American indifference to the reform of the German university was apparent. The introduction of the American model of the board of trustees system was barely a success.

Initially, the USEMG suggested that the German university should construct democratic relationships between the university and the community through the adoption of the board of trustees system. The board had to be "advisory bodies broadly representative of social groups."[180] It was also suggested that the invitation of external influence in the university would break the servile relationship of autocratic *Ordinarien* and *Nichtordinarien*. In the *Kultusministerkonferenz* on 24 April 1947, this American model was introduced by the *Ministerrat* [Council of the Ministers] of Württemberg-Baden.[181] German academics and educational administrators discussed the system as well as the aloof and hierarchical character of the university. In December 1947, for instance, the meeting in Bad Schwalbach concluded that "*Die Hochschulen dürfen sich nicht auf Inseln fern von politischer Verantwortung zurückziehen.*"[182]

At the same time, the discussions on the reforms of university administration went hand in hand with the reaffirmation of the *Selbstverwaltung* [self-administration] of the university by German academics. They argued that the key to the democratisation of the university would rest on the recovery of what it had lost during the Nazi regime.[183] The Germans claimed that the university should maintain close contact with society but at the same time must not be enslaved by external power outside the university. In consideration of violent intervention by the Nazis into university affairs, the OMGUS yielded the point of the German argument.

In addition, the American model of the board of trustees system was too radical to German academics and administrators. The system would not only be administered by the representatives of the municipality but also be funded by it. In German contexts, this purpose applied to the elimination of the *Land* government and the involvement of smaller municipal units in university administration. The American model was different from the precedents of the *Kuratorium* [board of regents] in Frankfurt and Cologne Universities during the period of World War One. Moreover, after the sudden collapse of the Nazi regime, many new state officials were inexperienced, and their political status was inferior to that of professors. As a result, state authority in university affairs was reduced and the autonomous power of the university increased.[184] Thus, the result of the discussions on the board of trustees was that the post-war German universities adopted the old notion of the university and its autonomy from the pre-1933 period. No existing university wanted substantial structural change in university administration, except for the restoration of the administrative power of the academics after the thirteen-year infringement of university autonomy.

The only university which started with a new concept of university administration and academic freedom was the Free University of Berlin, which was founded by the US Occupation authorities in 1948. The system of the board of trustees symbolized the "Berlin Model" as a prototype of the democratic university and of the restoration of the Humboldtian idea of *"Gemeinschaft von Lehrenden und Lernenden"* [community of teachers and learners].[185] The *Kuratorium* of the University comprised the *Oberbürgermeister* [lord mayor] as the chairman, three representatives of the city, three leading citizens, the university rector, and a representative of the professors and students respectively.[186] Furthermore, the constitution of the university endorsed the direct participation of students in the university's government and the permanent membership of students representatives in the university's senate, all senate committees, faculty boards, and admission committees. Initially, the university consisted of liberal professors and students who had fled from Humboldt University in the Soviet zone. As a result, the university became the most liberal university in West Germany.

The rest of the German universities remained insulated from local communities, appealing to the principle of *Selbstverwaltung*. In 1951 in Tübingen, the academics of universities in West Germany put forward the *Tübinger Beschlüsse*, declarations of their autonomous right to make decisions on many aspects of university administration. Radical changes in the majority of universities in West Germany as a whole did not occur until after the student unrest in 1966. Before its effects became evident, the OECD criticized the German university as bluntly as it did the Japanese university:

> Schools will normally reflect the values of the society that supports them, and German universities and higher technical schools have mirrored only too well the hierarchical and authoritarian society they served.... Reforms ... were seriously delayed by the resistance of the professors who would not concede that their virtually untramelled power over assigned funds, staff, students, and curriculum was now out moded. Assistants, even Dozenten, were the professor's men, to be made or broken as he wished. Such was the reality of Lehrfreiheit.[187]

The major reason for the failure of the introduction of the American system of the board of trustees was that the idea was foreign to the German university. The claim for the retention of self-administration by German academics was their deliberate effort to safeguard the social and academic bases of the university and the school in their country. While rejecting the introduction of the board of trustees system, German academics attempted to introduce a *Studium generale* [general education] as an alternative channel between the university and society in their own ways.

General Education

The introduction of a *Studium generale*, although partial in a number of universities, was the only reform in higher education which was seriously considered by German academics. Like the tradition of the *Kuratorium* system, the German university used to practice instruction in *Studium generale*. Therefore, the conditions for the introduction of the American model of general education were different from those in the Japanese university. This reform was partly adopted by some universities in Germany, but in a largely internalized way.

As Taylor has pointed out, Americans judged that the neglect of social sciences and education for citizenship by the German university had created a crucial condition for the ideological penetration of Nazism among the elites.[188] The recommendation of the USEMG was "preparing students for the responsibilities of informed and intelligent citizenship" and "bringing instruction into immediate contact with current politics and social problems."[189] *Studium generale* in Germany was understood as a means of making university education more interdisciplinary, by breaking the particularism and isolationism of the faculties and the university as a whole. As a consequence, the introduction of general education and more emphasis on political science were proposed.

The contents of older academic subjects and newer subjects of the Nazi period were eliminated as a part of denazification in the university curricula. For example, "Nazi subjects," such as *Deutschtum* [German studies] and *Rassenkunde* [racial studies], were immediately abolished. Apart from these subjects, the academic orientation of the German university was regarded as too philosophical and too abstract and led university-educated people to be inclined to theoretical speculation which was alien to the rest of the people. The OMGUS received a study of the German university, which argued:

> The German university was not an educational institute in the American sense of the term. It was not concerned with the human person, with character, with the art of living; it was concerned exclusively with knowledge per se, knowledge for the sake of knowledge.[190]

The USEMG proposed that new faculties and new studies should be introduced to resolve this academic insularity of the German university. The other Western Allies also attempted to introduce a course of general study, the *Studium generale*, in universities in each zone. As the Cold War broke out, the US Occupation authorities emphasized the importance of political science more than before. Led by the HICOG, several conferences and lectures on political science courses were organized. Consequently, Marburg, Frankfurt, and Darmstadt Universities introduced political science courses. This academic trend was followed by universities in other zones, for example, Tübingen, Hamburg, Mainz, Göttingen, and Cologne Universities.[191]

German academics and educational administrators also agreed that the German university should aim at fostering a sound sense of good citizenship among the youth and making the university more open to the public by broadening the scope of education.[192] The Germans introduced the courses of general study in different models which would suit the situations and traditions of individual institutions. The first model required a minimum change in the organization of study and curriculum, by inserting some contents of general study in regular lectures. The second model was to set aside a specific time per week for the special lectures and seminars for the *Studium generale*, which were called "*Dies academicus*." The third model required a large-scale re-organization of university education as well as a part of the later stages in secondary education. The idea of the third model was that upon the completion of secondary education and prior to university studies, students should take special courses of general study. This model had a particularly positive effect for those who had had to interrupt their study because of the war. The intermediate course of study offered these people a chance to bridge a gap in their intellectual life before resuming or starting university study.[193] Among higher education institutions which introduced this model, the Leipniz College in Tübingen University in the French zone offered stimulating *Studium generale* courses to about sixty students on a board-in basis. Similarly, the *Colloquium Politicum* in Freiburg University provided a solid study of general education as well as political science. In the US zone, the *Collegium Heidelberg* became the center of *Studium generale*, with 165 students living in dormitories and the tutors of young Ph.D.s.[194] In those attempts to connect university studies with politics and society, the work of German scholars like Spranger, Theodor Litt, and Wilhelm Flitner, gained ground in the development of the *Geisteswissenschaften* in the German university.[195]

5. CONCLUSION

Germany experienced some changes in its political system, economic structure, and social configuration during the Occupation. The purge had an impact on political and social life in post-war Germany, if an attempt of the nation-wide implementation of the *Fragebogen* for all adult Germans is considered. Nonetheless, much room was left for the ultimate decisions to be taken by the German people, and consequently many traditions were maintained. A question then remains whether this was a consequence of the political compromise of the Western Allies to develop the German economy or the outcome of the cultural respect valuation of the Western Allies for Germany. After all the discussions of the "German Problem," the condemnation of the Germans for their inherited militarism and authoritarianism did not play a crucial part in the Allied Occupation policy. In every respect, the European Allies regarded Germany as a European state. Not only the wishes of the Germans, but also the political and economic interests of the Americans and Europeans, meant that new Germany was seen as an *abendländisch* nation.

In education, the strong assertion of *innere Schulreform* based on the indigenous pattern by German leaders made American reform plans difficult to implement. The Germans proclaimed their firm belief in traditional sociocultural values and indigenous educational patterns. Despite regional differences, this belief was cohesively maintained. The German leaders were acting as guardians of indigenous socio-cultural values and a traditional social order by retaining many aspects of German education related to these old values. In addition to political negotiation between the Americans and the Germans, Christianity—a common, basic factor of German and the Western communities—also played a significant role in the retention of the traditional pattern of German education. The issues of religious education thus remained political rather than pedagogical in German as well as European educational history. The Western Allies understood this history well. The nineteenth-century multi-track school system remained unmodified. The US military government failed to introduce the single-track school system of the comprehensive school in the face of a strong European belief in the elitist purposes of education. American egalitarian pedagogic ideas did not impress German educators. Moreover, a high respect for *Kulturhoheit* was a considerable obstacle for the military government in implementing its reform policy within the zone. For the Germans, within the fundamental principle of *Kulturhoheit* and respect for regional cultural differences, the value of German *Kultur* was supreme.

The US policy for education reform in Germany failed. Except for denazification, no major changes could be made. The impact of *Stunde Null* was doubtful. The consequence was American irritation and dissatisfaction. The next radical reform took place in West Germany in the middle of the 1960s.

NOTES

1. "The 'Unconditional Surrender' Meeting." *The Times*, 27 January 1943. Beate von Oppen, ed., *Documents on Germany under Occupation 1945-1954* (London: Oxford University Press, 1955), 1.

2. James Tent, *Mission on the Rhine: Reeducation and Denazification in American Occupied Germany* (Chicago: University of Chicago Press, 1982), 14-17.

3. Wolfe, *Americans as Proconsuls*, 2. See also: John Backer, "From Morgenthau Plan to Marshall Plan," in *Americans as Proconsuls: United States Military Government in Germany*

and Japan, 1944-1952, ed. Robert Wolfe (Carbondale: Southern Illinois University Press, 1984), 155-65; "Germany: Post-War Reeducation," 13 December 1943, the Committee on Post-War Programs (secret), Division of Political Studies (Policy Summaries) [Notter 1520-H-128].

4. Stimson and Bundy, *On Active Service*, 578.

5. Quoted from: Alec Cairncross, *The Price of War: British Policy on German Reparations 1941-1949* (Oxford: Blackwell, 1986), 11.

6. "Drafts of the Statement of Clay: General Occupation Policy Religious Affairs," undated [Z45 F 5/340-3/10].

7. *"Eine neue Schlacht um England,"* 9 August 1947, the Cultural Politics Committee of the Zones [Z2 85]; "The Fate of Germany," *The Times*, 4 October 1947.

8. By October 1946, the Occupation authorities had accepted altogether 9,476,900 refugees, of which 3,598,400 (38.0%) were in the Soviet zone; 3,055,300 (32.2%) in the US zone; 2,744,900 (29.0%) in the British zone, and only 78,300 (0.8%) were accepted in the French zone. Walter Vogel and Christoph Weisz, eds., *Akten zur Vorgeschichte der Bundesrepublik Deutschland 1945-1949. Band 1. Teil 1* (Munich: R. Oldenbourg Verlag, 1989), 25. Stolper also noted that "Unlike the Americans and the British, but like the Russians, the French have succeeded in making their zone self-supporting. . . . They lived far better than they would in France and drew a large part of their food from their starving zone." Gustav Stolper, *German Realities* (New York: Reynal & Hitchcock, 1948), 70.

9. *Denazification Report*, 20 August 1945 (No. 1), 1; *MG Monthly Report*, 20 December 1945 (No. 5), 1.

10. Ulrich Enders, *Die Bodenreform in der amerikanischen Besatzungszone 1945-1949 unter besonderer Berücksichtung Bayerns* (Ostfildern: Scripta Mercaturae Verlag, 1982), 2.

11. "Alleged Soviet Violations of the POTSDAM Protocol and CC Directives," 6 June 1946, from the Office of the Assistant Chief of Staff to Robert Murphy (Top Secret) [Z45 POLAD/33/1].

12. Jacques Bariety, "Die deutsche Frage aus französischer Sicht, 1945-1955," in *Die deutsche Frage in der Nachkriegszeit*, ed. Wilfried Loth (Berlin: Akademie Verlag, 1994), 172-94; Wilfried Loth, "Die Historiker und die Deutsche Frage: Ein Rückblick nach dem Ende des Kalten Krieges," in *Die deutsche Frage in der Nachkriegszeit*, ed. Wilfried Loth (Berlin: Akademie Verlag, 1994), 11-28; Franz Neumann, "Military Government and the Revival of Democracy in Germany," *Columbia Journal of International Affairs* 2, no. 1 (1948): 3-20.

13. Lucius Clay, "Proconsul of a People, by Another People, for Both Peoples," in *Americans as Proconsuls: United States Military Government in Germany and Japan, 1944-1952*, ed. Robert Wolfe (Carbondale: Southern Illinois University Press, 1984), 107.

14. An angry protest by the Polish public called the US government "imperialists and Guardians of Germans." "Telegram from Warsaw," 20 September 1946 [Z45 F 45-46/82/8].

15. "Telegram from Warsaw."

16. "The Fate of Germany."

17. "A Top Secret prepared Massage sent to Certain US Diplomatic Personnel," 17 January 1948, the Department of the Army [Z45 F AGTS/3/11].

18. "London Communiqué on Germany," 6 March 1948. Committee on Foreign Relations, US Senate, *Documents on Germany, 1944-1961* (Washington DC: The US Government Printing Office, 1961), 88.

19. *"Widerspruchsvoll Programm der Stellvertrete,"* 13 November 1947 (Confidential) [Z2 85 III].

20. "Long-Range Policy Statement for German Re-Education," 28/29 May 1945, the State War Navy Coordinating Committee on German Re-Education (released as SWNCC 269/5 on 21 August 1946) [Z45 F 5/310-2/22].

21. Hans Speier, *Social Order and the Risks of War: Papers in Political Sociology* (Cambridge: The MIT Press, 1952), 400.

22. John McCloy, "From Military Government to Self-Government," in *Americans as Proconsuls: United States Military Government in Germany and Japan, 1944-1952*, ed. Robert Wolfe (Carbondale: Southern Illinois University Press, 1984), 117.

23. A public survey in 1949 showed that the presence of Germany in Europe was still seen to be a "potentially big danger" for the majority of the French. Bariety, "Die deutsche Frage," 173-74; John McCloy, *The Challenge to American Foreign Policy* (Cambridge: Harvard University Press, 1953).

24. De Gaulle's declaration on 9 June 1948, quoted from: Raymond Aron, *Memoirs: Fifty Years of Political Reflection* (New York: Holmes & Meier, 1990), 183. See also: "*Frankreichs Gretchenfrage*," the minutes of the meeting of the Cultural Political Committee of the Zones, 27 September 1947 [Z2 85].

25. Quoted from: Sigrid Fretlöh-Thomas, "Education for Democracy: A New Analysis of an Example of Intercultural Influence," *Oxford Review of Education* 24, no. 3 (1998), 385. Similar views are in: "Establishment of a Training Centre in Citizenship," 24 May 1946, CCG(BE) Zonal Advisory Council [FO 1037/29]; Jérôme Vaillant, "Was tun mit Deutschland?: Die französische Kulturpolitik im besetzten Deutschland von 1945 bis 1949," in *Umerziehung und Wiederaufbau: Die Bildungspolitik der Besatzungsmächte in Deutschland und Österreich*, ed. Manfred Heinemann (Stuttgart: Klett-Cotta, 1981), 201-11.

26. Vansittart, *Lessons of My Life*, 203.

27. Hellmut Becker, "Retrospective View from the German Side," in *The British in Germany: Educational reconstruction after 1945*, ed. Arthur Hearnden (London: Hamish Hamilton, 1978), 269; Werner Burmeister, "Were the British too neutral?," *Adult Education* 51, no. 1 (1978), 98.

28. Victor Gollancz, *Shall Our Children Live or Die? A Reply to Lord Vansittart on the German Problem* (London: Victor Gollancz Ltd., 1942); Victor Gollancz, *In Darkest Germany* (London: Gollancz, 1947).

29. "What's Wrong with Germany?" in Departments of State and Public, Army USFET (DSP USA), *Occupation: A Handbook for Troops Proceeding on Service in the U.S. Occupation* (Washington: 1946), 42. For views of the German state and society as authoritarian, see in particular: Theodor Adorno et al., *The Authoritarian Personality* (New York: Harper & Brothers, 1950); Beck, *The Origin of the Authoritarian Welfare State*; Friedrich, "The Failure of a One-Party System"; Mommsen, *Imperial Germany*; Neumann, *The Democratic and the Authoritarian State*; Stern, *The Politics of Cultural Despair*. The authoritarian aspects of Germany were also intensively argued about by the scholars of the Bielefeld School, e.g.: Kocka, "Capitalism and Bureaucracy," Jürgen Kocka, *Facing Total War: German Society 1914-1918* (Leamington Spa: Berg, 1984); Kocka, "German History before Hitler"; Jürgen Kocka, "Book Review: Eley, G. (1986). From Unification to Nazism: Reinterpreting the German Past. Boston, Allen & Unwin.," *Journal of Modern History* 62, no. 1 (1990): 200-202; Wehler, *The German Empire*; Wehler, *Deutsche Gesellschaftsgeschichte*, vol. 3. Cf. Nipperdey criticizes the Bielefeld School by arguing that the control of education by the state bureaucracy was intended to be, and worked as, a guardian against the parties, capitalists, and class conflicts in the political, economic, and social contexts of the rapid modernization and industrialization of the last third of the nineteenth century. Nipperdey, "Wehlers Kaiserreich"; Nipperdey, *Deutsche Geschichte*. For similar accounts, see: Blackbourn and Eley, *The Peculiarities of German History*; Eley, *From Unification to Nazism*. In the 1980s in German intellectual circles, the so-called *Historikerstreit* involving many leading scholars in Ger-

many broke out in debates on the location of the Third Reich in German history. The fierce debates started with Jürgen Habermas's article "Eine Art Schadensabwicklung: Die apologetischen Tendenzen in der deutschen Zeitgeschichtsschreibung" in *Die Zeit* (11 July 1986) which criticized Ernst Nolte's "relocation of the Holocaust" as "only one of a whole pattern of twentieth-century genocides," shown in *Frankfurter Allgemeine Zeitung* (6 June 1986). Part of the debates are in: Reinahrd Piper, ed., *"Historikerstreit" Die Dokumentation der Kontroverse um die Einzigartigkeit der nationalsozialistischen Judenvernichtung* (Munich: Humanities Press, 1987). The English translation in: James Knowlton and Truett Cates, eds., *Forever in the Shadow of Hitler?: The Dispute about the Germans' Understanding of History, Original Documents of the Historikerstreit, the Controversy Concerning the Singularity of the Holocaust* (Atlantic Highlands: Humanities Press, 1993). See also: Ian Kershaw, *The Nazi Dictatorship: Problems and Perspectives of Interpretation* (London: Edward Arnold, 1989 [1985]).

30. "Germany: Post-War Reeducation." See also: "Declaration on Atrocities Issued after the Moscow Conference," 30 October 1943, in: von Oppen, *Documents on Germany*, 1-3; "What's Wrong with Germany?," in: DSP USA, *Occupation*, 42; Richard Brickner, *Is Germany Incurable?* (Philadelphia: J. B. Lippincott, 1943); Uta Gerhardt, "The Medical Meaning of Reeducation for Germany: Contemporary Interpretation of Cultural and Institutional Change," *Paedagogica Historica* 33, no. 1 (1997): 135-55.

31. "Establishment of a Training Centre in Citizenship." See also: "Memorandum on Postwar Education Reconstruction in Germany," by B. Q. Morgan and F. W. Strothmann, Stanford University, undated [Z45 F 5/307-3/20].

32. Office of Military Government for Germany US (OMGUS), *Textbooks in Germany* (Internal Affairs and Communications Division, Education and Religious Affairs Branch), 1946.

33. "Long-Range Policy Statement for German Re-Education."

34. Henry Kellermann, *Cultural Relations as an Instrument of U.S. Foreign Policy: The Educational Exchange Program between the United States and Germany, 1945-1954* (Washington, DC: Bureau of Educational and Cultural Affairs, US Department of State, 1978), 22. See also: *"Richtlinien für den Aufbau der deutschen Republik,"* 23 July 1947, the British zonal commission to the minister, Dr. Walter Menzel in Hamburg [Z2 73]; Paul-Ludwig Weinacht, "Steps toward Westernization in the German Educational System 1945 and 1989," *Paedagogica Historica* 33, no. 1 (1997): 351-67.

35. "Memorandum by the State, War and Navy Coordinating Committee (SWNCC) for Europe regarding Long-Range Policy Statement for German Re-Education: US Policy on German Youth Activities of January 1947" [Z45 F 5/307-3/10].

36. Clay, "Proconsul of a People," 99. Clay also stated that "You cannot teach education on an empty stomach."

37. "Re-Education of Germany and Teaching Democracy," 4 November 1947, from William Houlton to Sergeant J. Conner of the United States Army [Z45 F 5/308-1/27]. Also see: Bennett and Nicholls, *The Semblance of Peace*, 179, 266.

38. "Re-Education of Germany and Teaching Democracy."

39. "Report on the US Occupation of Germany (Religious Affairs Program)," 23 September 1947 [Z45 F 5/337-2/6]; "Working Party on Public Subsidies to the Catholic Church in Germany," undated, the Directorate of IA&C, the Allied Religious Affairs Committee [Z45 F 5/337-2/20].

40. "Statement of Lucius Clay of 13 April 1949" [Z45 F 5/340-3/10].

41. Clay's speech on 5 March 1946, in: Vogel and Weisz, *Akten zur Vorgeschichte der Bundesrepublik Deutschland 1945-1949*, 1,017.

42. "Denazification," confidential memo from Clay to Hilldring, 14 January 1946, Clay Paper 21576, in Jean Smith, ed., *The Papers of General Lucius D. Clay: Germany 1945-1949* (Bloomington: Indiana University Press, 1974), 148.

43. "Paraphrased Message Sent to Certain US Diplomatic Personnel," undated, attached to "Provisional Information Policy of the Department of State in Countering Soviet and Communist Inspired Propaganda Against the United States," 15 December 1947 (Top Secret) [Z45 F AGTS/3/11].

44. Clay maintained this tone of confidence in his *Denazification Report* until the end of 1946.

45. *Denazification Report*, 20 January 1946 (No. 6), 1; Department of State, USA (DS USA), *Occupation of Germany: Policy and progress* 1945-1946 (Washington DC: The US Government Printing Office, 1946), 18. The Control Council was defined as "the agency established by the allied governments concerned for the military government of Germany as a whole," in: "Organization for Military Government of US Zone and Areas in Which US Forces are Deployed, Section II: Definitions," 24 May 1945, US Army European Theater of Operations (Top Secret) [Z45 F AGTS/9/1].

46. DS USA, *Occupation of Germany*, 19.

47. "Denazification," Confidential paper from Clay to Echols of 15 December 1946, Clay Paper 7373, in Smith, *The Papers*, 285.

48. "Denazification Report: 15 January 1946: Summary," 5 February 1946, Headquarters USFET, OMGUS Public Safety Branch [Z45 F 5/307-2/31]; Elmer Plischke, "Denazification in Germany," in *Americans as Proconsuls: United States Military Government in Germany and Japan, 1944-1952*, ed. Robert Wolfe (Carbondale: Southern Illinois University Press, 1984), 198-225. The figure excludes *Fragebogen* already submitted under CC Law No. 8 "Prohibition of Employment of Nazi Party Members in Positions Other Than Ordinary Labor."

49. "Besprechung der Vertreter der Länder der Britischen Zone am 18. November 1946" [Z1 1338]; "Zweizoneneinrichtungen: Allgemeines" [Z1 1276].

50. *Denazification Report*, 20 September 1945 (No. 2), 4.

51. Clay's words, quoted from: John Teschke, *Hitler's Legacy: West Germany Confronts the Aftermath of the Third Reich* (New York: Peter Lang, 1999), 22. Discussions on the change of criteria: "Denazification," Confidential paper from Clay to Echols, 15 December 1946, Clay Paper 7373, in: Smith, *The Papers*, 285.

52. "We oppose with the greatest skepticism the procedure of the American zone." "*Niederschrift Über die 1. Sitzung des Denazifizierungsausschusses des Länderrats mit Vertretern der britischen Zone am 24. 10. 1946*" [Z1 1338]; *Denazification Report*, 20 January 1946 (No. 6), 6-7.

53. Herz, "Denazification and Related Policies"; Teschke, *Hitler's Legacy*; Manfred Kittel, *Die Legende von der "Zweiten Schuld": Vergangenheitsbewältigung in der Ära Adenauer* (Berlin: Ullstein, 1993). Quotation in: Karl Jaspers, "The Rededication of German Scholarship," *The American Scholar* 15, no. 2 (1946), 180. Fitz-Gibbon also argued that "Few Germans felt or feel any humiliation at having been convicted by an American-run denazification court for the crime of having been Nazis at a time when to be so was not only legal but normal and, as many thought, patriotic." Constantine Fitz-Gibbon, *Denazification* (London: Michael Joseph, 1969), 171.

54. William Griffith, *The Denazification Program in the United States Zone of Germany* (Harvard University, 1950), 553. As of 1949 in the Bavarian Ministry of Education, 6% of the total employees were former Nazis. The ratio was higher in other ministries: e.g., 81% in Judicial; 77% in Food, Agriculture, and Farming; 60% in Finance; 22% in Labor; and 18% in Transportation. Montgomery extracted these figures from *New York Times* (30 November 1949, 12).

See also: Hans Woller, *Gesellschaft und Politik in der amerikanischen Besatzungszone: Die Region Ansbach und Fürth* (Munich: R. Oldenbourg Verlag, 1986), 111-15.

55. Enders, *Die Bodenreform*, 24.

56. Among them, Carl Friedrich at Harvard was a prominent member. In the post-war period, he offered a number of extensive studies on the totalitarian aspects of the Nazi regime: e.g., Carl Friedrich, ed., *Totalitarianism* (Cambridge: Harvard University Press, 1954); Friedrich, "The Failure of a One-Party System"; Carl Friedrich, Michael Curtis, and Benjamin Barbar, *Totalitarianism in Perspective: Three views* (New York: Praeger, 1969).

57. "Education and Information Policy," 31 January 1947, Clay Paper 13662, in: Smith, *The Papers*, 309.

58. John Gimbel, *The American Occupation of Germany: Politics and the military, 1945-1949* (Stanford: Stanford University Press, 1968), 246; Robert Lawson, "Die Politik der Umstände: Eine Kritik der Analysen des Bildungswandels im Nachkriegsdeutschland," in *Umerziehung und Wiederaufbau: Die Bildungspolitik der Besatzungsmächte in Deutschland und Österreich*, ed. Manfred Heinemann (Stuttgart: Klett-Cotta, 1981), 23-39; Christoph Weisz, ed., *OMGUS-Handbuch: Die amerikanische Militärregierung in Deutschland 1945-1949* (Munich: R. Oldenbourg Verlag, 1994), 112-13.

59. For example: "Memorandum on Postwar Education Reconstruction in Germany." His work can be read in: Thomas Alexander, *The Prussian Elementary Schools* (New York: Macmillan, 1918); Thomas Alexander and Isaac Kandel, *The Reorganization of Education in Prussia* (New York: Columbia University Press: 1927); Thomas Alexander and Beryl Parker, *The New Education in the German Republic* (New York: John Day, 1929).

60. Edwin Costell, "An American University Officer in Occupied Germany: A personal account 36 years later," in *Hochschuloffiziere und Wiederaufbau der Hochschulwesens in Westdeutschland 1945-1952. Teil 2: Die US-Zone*, ed. Manfred Heinemann (Hildesheim: Verlag August Lax, 1990), 25. Though the rest of the officers in the Higher Education Section (Isidore Barnett, Nils van Steenberg, J. Glenn Gray, Cliffton Winn, and Roger Shaw) were not as highly qualified as Hartshorne, they each had doctorates.

61. As of 1946, the staff of the E&RA numbered fifty-five. Gimbel, *The American Occupation*; Kellermann, *Cultural Relations*.

62. Tent, *Mission on the Rhine*, 112; Tsuchimochi, *Education Reform*, 180.

63. Harold Zink, *The United States in Germany: 1944-1955* (Westport: Greenwood Press, Publishers, 1957), 195.

64. "Letter of William Benton to James Byrnes," 12 October 1946 [Z45 F 5/304-2/4-5].

65. Taylor's letter to Tsuchimochi on 15 November 1984 indicates that Zook was selected after the other members were decided. Some members called him a salesman. Gary Tsuchimochi, *Senryo Doitsu no kyoiku kaikaku: America taidoku kyoiku shisetsudan to America taidoku shakai-ka iinkai* (Tokyo: Meiji University Press, 1989), 59.

66. "Schwierigkeiten der Umerziehung," *Frankfurter Rundschau*, 17 October 1946 [Z1 1029]. *Frankfurter Rundschau* was the first German newspaper which was allowed to operate in the American zone.

67. Heavy criticisms about the USEMG by the Chicago Study Group are in: "Secondary Education in Germany: A memorandum on the Report of the United States Education Mission to Germany," October 1947 [Z45 F 5/304-2/6].

68. "Report of the United States Education Mission to Germany," 20 September 1946, 4 [Z45 F 5/304-2/4-5].

69. Clay, *Decision in Germany*, 305.

70. "American Education Policy: Address to German Ministries by Dr. John W. Taylor in February 1947" [Z45 F 5/344-1/5]. Discussions about the *Länderrat* are in: Ingrid Krüger-Bulcke, ed.,

James K. Pollock: Besatzung und Staatsaufbau nach 1945 - Occupation Diary and Private Correspondence 1945-1948 (Munich: R. Oldenbourg Verlag, 1994).

71. Sinfried Müller, *Schulpolitik in Bayern inm Spannungsfeld von Kultusbürokratie und Besatzungsmacht 1945-1949* (Munich: R. Oldenbourg Verlag, 1995), 13-14.

72. "Erziehungsplane auf weite Sicht," April 1947, the Bavarian minister of education [Z45 F 5/344-1/5]. Although Hundhammer held two doctorates, he gave up the "politically vulnerable life of an academic." He was a member of the *Landtag* in 1932-1933 and 1946-1970 and was also one of the founders of the CSU, the sister party of the CDU.

73. Edward Peterson, *The American Occupation of Germany: Retreat to Victory* (Detroit: Wayne State University Press, 1977), 252; Dennis Bark and David Gress, *A History of West Germany: From Shadow to Substance 1945-1963*, vol. 1 (Oxford: Blackwell, 1989), 167.

74. "Against go-slow tactics by Germans," 16 April 1946, Top Secret message by Office of the Deputy Military Governor, CCG(BE) Schleswig-Holstein Region [FO 1006]; "Educational Reforms in the French zone of Occupation in Germany," 24 January 1948, a report of Ernest de Mayer, American Consul [ERG 1-A-119].

75. "Brief for Visitors General Survey," October 1948, CCG (BE) [Z45 F 5/297-1/10]. In textbook screening, the British were indeed more critical about the relevance of the pre-1933 books than the Americans. Brigit Braun, *Umerziehung in der amerikanischen Besatzungszone. Die Schul- und Bildungspolitik in Württemberg-Baden von 1945 bis 1949* (Münster: LIT Verlag, 2004), 94-100. See also Ingeborg Koza, *Deutsch-britische Begegnungen in Unterricht, Wissenschaft und Kunst 1949-1944* (Köln: Böhlau Verlag GmbH & Cie, 1988); David Phillips, *Universitätsreform in der britischen Besatzungszone 1945-1948* (Cologne: Studien und Dokumentationen zur deutschen Bildungsgeschichte, 1983b).

76. The Soviet Union was well prepared for the implementation of various reforms on communist lines, e.g., a new concept of education, a new system of school structure, systematic learning plans, and the effective use of youth movements, mass media, and social rituals. One of the most important Russian strategies was the reconstruction of the new national identity of the East Germans within the education system. "Erfolgreiche Schulreform," *Berlin Tribüne*, 6 December 1947 [Z1 1029]; Lawson, "Die Politik der Umstände."

77. Phillips explains that this Germans' sentiment partly derived from the strong connotation of the prefix "*um*" in German, which implies "definite change or turning round" compared with the subtler connotation of "re" in English, which merely means "back or again." David Phillips, "British Educational Policy in Occupied Germany: Some problems and paradoxes in the control of schools and universities," in *International Currents in Educational Ideas and Practices*, ed. Peter Cunningham and Colin Brock (Leicester: History of Education Society of Great Britain, 1988), 81.

78. Quoted from: Christoph Führ, *The German Education System since 1945* (Bonn: Inter Nationes, 1997), 7.

79. "The Post-War University Situation: Excerpt from a speech to new students by the Rector Marburg University," 17 December 1945 [Z45 F 5/308-2/8].

80. Jaspers, "The Rededication of German Scholarship," 181-82. Cf. In the post-War period, Jaspers continued to ask himself about the identity of a German. His letter to Hannah Arendt on 29 December 1952, in: Lotte Kohler and Hans Saner, eds., *Hannah Arendt Karl Jaspers Correspondence 1926-1969* (New York: Harcourt Brace Jovanovich, Publishers, 1992), 204.

81. Geoffrey Giles, "Reeducation at Heidelberg University," *Paedagogica Historica* 33, no. 1 (1997), 209.

82. Quoted from: Noboru Murata, *Kokka to kyoiku: Spranger seiji kyoiku shiso no kenkyu* (Kyoto: Minerva, 1969), 3. Spranger also claimed that the cultivation of *Volksbewußtsein* through education could draw interest in Germany more than in many other European coun-

tries: Eduard Spranger, *Volk, Staat, Erziehung. Gesammelte Reden und Aufsätze* (Leipzig: 1932), 57-58.

83. "Dr. Dr. Alois Hundhammer zum 50. Geburtstag," *Süddeutsche Zeitung*, 25/26 February 1950.

84. "Vier Zonen - vier Schulreformen?," *Die Berlin*, 30 November 1947.

85. "Memorandum from Tom Goldstein to Henry J. Kellermann," 10 December 1947 [ERG 1 A 97].

86. "Report of the United States Education Mission for Germany."

87. "Schools for Children and Adolescents," the Office of the Military Governor to the Director, undated [ERG 3-B-445].

88. "Report of the United States Social Studies Committee to Germany," 19 November 1949, submitted to Warren M. Robbins [ERG 3-A-468]; Otto Schlander, "Der Einfluß von John Dewey und Hans Morgenthau auf die Formulierung der Re-educationspolitik," in *Umziehung und Wiederaufbau: Die Bildungspolitik der Besatzungsmächte in Deutschland und Österreich*, ed. Manfred Heinemann (Stuttgart: Klett-Cotta, 1981), 47-48.

89. This was the revised version of the "Directive for Military Government of Germany Prior to Defeat or Surrender."

90. "Minutes of Education Conference," 11 January 1945, SHAEF G-5 in Versailles [Z45 F 5/306-1/25]. The British also showed a great reluctance about handling religion: "British Brief for Official Visitors General Survey."

91. Quoted from: Schleunes, *Schooling and Society*, 3.

92. Speck von Sternburg, "American and German University Ideals; An address at the commencement of the University of the South," *Sewanee Review*, no. July (1904), 365.

93. "Memorandum on Postwar Education Reconstruction in Germany."

94. "Report on the Re-Education of Germany."

95. Address of John W. Taylor, 29 April 1946 [ERG 3-A-467].

96. "Report from Germany: Information of Dr. Grace, Director E&CR for American People," 1 February 1949, in the OMGUS Newsletter [Z45 F 5/310-2/1].

97. Quoted from: Birgit Bödeker, *Amerikanische Zeitschriften in Deutscher Sprache, 1945-1952* (Frankfurt am Main: Peter Lang, 1993), 30-32.

98. "CC Directive No. 32: Disciplinary Measures against Managing and Administrative Staff of Educational Institutions, Teaching Staff, and Students Guilty of Militaristic, Nazi, or Anti-Democratic Propaganda," 26 June 1946 [Z45 F AGTS/123/4-18]; "Memorandum of the OMGUS to the all *Länder* in the US Zone," 16 July 1946 [Z45 F AGTS/123/4-18].

99. "Proposed Definition of 'Nazi Sympathizers,'" 2 February 1945 (Top Secret) [Z45 F POLAD/32/72].

100. *MG Monthly Report*, 20 January 1946 (No. 6), 20.

101. *MG Monthly Report*, 1-31 October 1946 (No. 16), 24.

102. Führ, *The German Education System*, 13. About 28,000 individuals were trained as teachers, but over half of them had no higher education qualification.

103. Braun, Birgit. *Umziehung in der amerikanischen Besatzungszone. Die Schul- und Bildungspolitik in Württemberg-Baden von 1945 bis 1949*. LIT Verlag, 2004, 94-100.

104. OMGUS, *Textbooks in Germany*, 4.

105. OMGUS, *Textbooks in Germany*, 2.

106. General Raymond Schmittlein, Director of the *Education Publique*, asked of the OMGUS officers "Are you really going to allow the Germans to write their texts and to decide which they want to use?" "Report of the OMGUS Internal Affairs and Communications Division, Public Health and Welfare Branch, Education Section," 30 March 1946 [Z45 F 5/307-3/17].

107. Edith Davies, "British Policy and the Schools," in *The British in Germany: Educational Reconstruction after 1945*, ed. Arthur Hearnden (London: Hamish Hamilton Ltd., 1978), 100.

108. "Report of the United States Education Mission to Germany," 21.

109. "Vatican to Open Secret Archive on War Pope," *The Times*, 15 February 2003; John Cornwell, *Hitler's Pope* (New York: Viking, 1999); "Brief for Visitors General Survey."

110. "Divisional Recommendations for Assignment of Powers and Functions to German Governmental Levels: II Brief Description of Assignment of Jurisdiction over this (church's) Function and of its Administration," 25 June 1946, the E&RA [Z45 F 5/304-1/33].

111. "The Protestant Churches Welcomed Hitler," in: Franklin Littell, "The Protestant Churches and Totalitarianism (Germany 1933-1945)," in *Totalitarianism*, ed. Carl Friedrich (Cambridge: Harvard University Press, 1954), 110.

112. Karl Demeter, *The German Officer-Corps in Society and State, 1650-1945* (London: Weidenfeld & Nicolson, 1965), 221; Littell, "The Protestant Churches," 110-11.

113. Rubenstein notes that "In May 1944, Jewish leaders in Budapest requested that the US Air Force bomb the rail link between that city and Poland to hamper the deportation of Hungarian Jews to Auschwitz. . . . There is no other way to explain the refusal of the American and British governments to take even the slightest action directly to hinder the Final Solution in the face of the very precise knowledge they had of the program." Richard Rubenstein, "Holocaust and Holy War," *The Annals of the American Academy of Political and Social Science*, 548 (1996), 41.

114. David Wyman, *The Abandonment of the Jews: America and the Holocaust, 1941-1945* (New York: Pantheon Books, 1984), 337. Wyman also notes that in public announcement, American and British officials did not use the word "Jew"; instead they used: unfortunate people, persecuted peoples, oppressed minorities, etc.

115. "Report of US Education Mission to Germany," 18 November 1946, record of Civil Affairs Division [ERG 2-A-181].

116. "Internal Affairs and Communications Division, Public Heath and Welfare Branch Religious Affairs Branch," 22 April 1946 [Z45 F 5/340-3/21]; "Validity of the 1993 Concordat," 31 January 1948, Memorandum from Allied Control Authority, Directorate of Internal Affairs and Communications to Allied Secretariat [Z45 F 5/340-3/19].

117. "*Widerstehen aus christlichem Glauben*," No. 5.1-5.3, pamphlets published by Gedenkstätte Deutscher Widerstand Berlin.

118. "Report of the US Occupation of Germany, Religious Affairs Program," 23 September 1947.

119. Quoted from: William Moore, "Some German Attitudes Toward U. S. Occupation," *Columbia Journal of International Affairs* 2, no. 1 (1948), 77.

120. Quoted from: Clara Menck, "The Problem of Reorientation," in *The Struggle for Democracy in Germany*, ed. Gabriel Almond (Chapel Hill: The University of North Carolina Press, 1949), 283.

121. In the French zone, the German Catholic church protested against this French view strongly. René Cheval, "Die Bildungspolitik in der Französischen Besatzungszone," in *Umerziehung und Wiederaufbau: Die Bildungspolitik der Besatzungsmächte in Deutschland und Österreich*, ed. Manfred Heinemann (Stuttgart: Klett-Cotta, 1981), 197-98.

122. "The Article 131 II of the Bavarian Constitution," 30 September 1947, to the OMGBY from the Bavarian Ministry of Education [Z45 F 5/344-1/5]. See also: Bernhard Lehmann, *Katholische Kirche und Besatzungsmacht in Bayern 1945-1949 im Spiegel der OMGUS-Akten* (München: Kommissionverlag UNI-Druck, 1994).

123. Hundhammer noted that "*Ich hatte es für richtiger, einem Jungen rechtzeitig eine Tracht Prügel zu verabreichen, als ihm spätter dem Kopf auf das Schafott legen zu lassen.*" [I thought it would be more right to give a youth a beating at the right time rather than to let his

head later be placed on the scaffold.] Quoted from: Paul Hussarek, *Hundhammer: Weg des Menschen und Staatsmannes* (Munich: Treuga-Verlag, 1950), 154. In regard to *Prügelstrafe*, an OMGUS survey showed that only a minority of the Germans regarded *Prügelstrafe* as a basic right of teachers. "Bavarian Minister of Education Complains about Press Attacks," 21 October 1947, Report of S. E. Woods, American Consul General, to Secretary of State [ERG 1-A-93]. Even the German press harshly criticized Hundhammer. "Bavarian Minister of Education Complains about Press Attacks," 21 October 1947, Report of S. E. Woods, American consul general, to secretary of state [ERG 1-A-93]; Anna Merritt and Richard Merritt, *Public Opinion in Occupied Germany* (Urbana: University of Illinois Press, 1970), 204.

124. "Schulfragen in Hessen," *Frankfurter Rundschau*, 27 March 1947 [Z1 1029]; "E&RA Summary Report," 13 October 1947 [Z45 F 5/304-2/7]; *MG Monthly Report*, 1-30 November 1946 (No. 17), 18.

125. Val Rust, "The German Image of American Education through the Weimar period," *Paedagogica Historica* 33, no. 1 (1997), 28-29; Robert Birley, "British Policy in Retrospect," in *The British in Germany: Educational Reconstruction after 1945*, ed. Arthur Hearnden (London: Hamish Hamilton Ltd., 1978), 48-49.

126. "Whether one accepts the primary school of four or six years is not a question that involves democracy." *"Denkschrift der Universität Heidelberg zur Frage Schulreform,"* undated [Z1 1029].

127. "Analysis and Criticism of the Bavarian School Reform Plan of 1 October 1947," 6 October 1947 [Z45 F 5/344-1/5].

128. "Report of the United States Education Mission to Germany," 35.

129. The idea of the *Einheitsschule* was discussed by school teachers as early as 1848 in Germany. Richard Samuel and Hinton Thomas, *Education and Society in Modern Germany* (London: Routledge & Kegan Paul Limited, 1949), 27.

130. Between 1886 and 1906 about 90% of Catholics and 95% of Protestant Germans maintained their own denominational provision in schooling. Berg, *Handbuch*, 185. As of September 1946, 53% of the population in the US zone was Catholic and 43% was Evangelical: "Report of the United States Education Mission to Germany."

131. "Comments on the Reform Proposal of Württemberg-Baden"; "Comments on the Reform Proposals of Hesse"; "Comments on the Reform Proposals of Bavaria," 2 November 1947, from Alexander to Clay [Z45 F 5/344-1/5].

132. "CC Directive No. 54: Basic Principles for Democratisation of Education in Germany," 25 June 1947 (Restricted) [Z45 F AGTS/124/12]. The directive also indicated the introduction of free tuition and free learning materials (Article 2) and of compulsory education between the ages of six and fifteen (Article 3).

133. "Memorandum from the E&RA to the Director of the OMGUS in the Länder," 1 December 1947 [Z45 F AGTS/124/12]: "Interpretation of CC directive No. 54 with Reference to Certain Aspects," 1 December 1947, delivered to the Office of the Military Government in Bavaria, Württemberg Baden, Hesse, Bremen and Berlin [Z45 F 5/344-1/5].

134. "Letter from Alexander to Clay," 2 November 1947 [Z45 F 5/344-1/5].

135. "The *Volksschulen* are in essence the basis of our school system." Quoted from: Hussarek, *Hundhammer*, 15.

136. "School Reform," 23 December 1947 [Z45 F 5/344-1/5].

137. Frequent correspondence occurred between Cardinal Faulfaber, Archbishop of Munich, and Murry van Wagoner, Director of the OMGBY from late 1947 toward the summer of 1948 [Z45 F 5/344-1/5].

138. The three authorities were represented by Hundhammer, Cardinal Faulfaber, and Bishop Aloysius Muerch. The detailed negotiations are in: Tent, *Mission on the Rhine*, chapter 4.

139. Robert Lawson, *Reform of the West German School System, 1945-1962* (Ann Arbor: The University of Michigan, School of Education, 1965).

140. Stein delivered a speech at the educational reform meeting on 22 July 1947. His ideas were also introduced in *Frankfurter Hefte* (October 1947) and *Pädagogische Provinz* (Nov/Dec. 1947) [Z45 F 5/344-1/5].

141. "Laws and Regulations Concerning Elementary School," 1 May 1948 [Z45 F 5/344-1/5].

142. "Only education reform based on the German spirit will last." Quoted from: Rosenzweig, *Erziehung zur Demokratie?*, 178-79.

143. "Comments on the Reform Proposal of Württemberg-Baden."

144. The local government in Bremen consisted of seven SPD members, including the head of the *Land*, out of a total of sixteen members. Klaus Mehnert and Heinrich Schulte, eds., *Deutschland Jahrbuch 1949* (Essen: Im West-Verlag, 1949), 467-70.

145. "Report of the Education and Religious Affairs in Bavaria," 30 June 1945 [Z45 F 5/307-3/21].

146. Charles Thwing, *The American and the German University: One Hundred Years of History* (New York: Macmillan Company, 1928), 42-45. Toward the end of the nineteenth century, American students who matriculated universities in Germany exceeded 2,000.

147. Quoted from: Thomas Bonner, "Abraham Flexner and the German University: The progressive as traditionalist," *Paedagogica Historica* 33, no. 1 (1997), 103. See also: Abraham Flexner, *Universities: American, English, German* (New York: Oxford University Press, 1930).

148. Roger Adams to Karl Freudenberg, 13 November 1947, quoted from: Giles, "Reeducation at Heidelberg University," 206. Adams was the chair of the chemistry department of the University of Illinois-Urbana. Freudenberg was the rector of the University.

149. Spranger, as a leading member of *Mittwochgesellschaft*, and other German intellectuals, such as Friedrich Meinecke and Karl Jaspers, urged the German people to self-criticism about Nazi Germany after the war. Cf. Recent literature shows the somewhat reactionary aspects of Spranger's political stance before 1945. Uwe Henning and Achim Leschinsky, eds., *Enttäuschung und Widerspruch. Die konservative Position Eduard Sprangers in Naitonalsozialismus - Analysen, Texte, Dokumente* (Weinheim: Deutscher Studien Verlag, 1991).

150. *Richtlinien für die Reform der Hochschulverfassungen in den Ländern des amerikanischen Besatzungsgebietes. Vorschläge eines Sachverständigenausschusses 1947*, in: Rolf Neuhaus, ed., *Dokumente zur Hochschulreform 1945-1959* (Wiesbaden: Franz Steiner Verlag GmbH, 1961), 284-85.

151. "Memorandum from James L. Sundquist to Donald C. Stone," 10 June 1947 [ERG 2-A-408]; "Memorandum from Tom Goldstein to Henry J. Kellermann," 10 December 1947 [ERG 1-A-97].

152. "Report on the Re-Education of Germany."

153 "American Education Policy: Address to German Ministries by Dr. John W. Taylor."

154. "Reopening of Universities and other Institutions of Higher Learning: Supplementary Directive to Section VII, Part 1, Administration of Military Government in the US Zone in Germany," 7 July 1945 [Z45 F 5/309-1/28].

155. "School for Self-Government and Civil Leadership in Germany," 16 May 1946, the Civil Affairs Division of the War Department [Z45 F 5/300-1/33].

156. Rosalind Pritchard, *The End of Elitism?: The Democratisation of the West German University System* (New York: St. Martin's Press, 1990), 68; "The Education Control Instruction No. 10, Plan for the Resumption of German Youth Activities," CCG(BE) Sub-Commission [FO 1033/29]; "Recruitment for German Universities," 27 May 1946, addressed to the Education Branch of the Main Headquarters of the British Military Government by Dr. Grimme, CCG(BE) Zonal Advisory Council [FO 1037/28].

157. "Political Sanctions to be Applied against Students and Professors of Higher Education Institutions Who Carry on Fascist or Anti-Democratic Propaganda," 14 May 1946, the OMGUS IA&C [Z45 F 5/307-2/31].

158. Statement of C. C. Winn, the US delegate and the chairman, in "The Minutes of the Tri-Zonal University Officers Meeting in Bad Nauheim," 21-22 July 1949 [Z45 F 5/298/1/15].

159. "American Education Policy: Address to German Ministries by Dr. John W. Taylor."

160. "CC Directive No. 47: Liquidation of German War Research Establishments," 17 April 1947 [Z45 F AGTS/124/6].

161. The ratio of the reconstruction of university buildings in the US zone, 1945-1949: Erlangen 100-100 (%); Heidelberg 100-100; Marburg 85-90; Frankfurt/M 50-65; Munich 40-55; Würzburg 10-25, in: Ulrich Schneider, "The Reconstruction of the Universities in American Occupied Germany," in *Hochschuloffiziere und Wiederaufbau der Hochschulwesens in Westdeutschland 1945-1952. Teil 2: Die US-Zone*, ed. Manfred Heinemann (Hildesheim: Verlag August lax, 1990), 1.

162. In the British zone, all the six universities were also reopened by mid-December 1945. For the British reform of the German university, see: David Phillips, "Lindsay and the German Universities: An Oxford Contribution to the Post-War Reform Debate," *Oxford Review of Education* 6, no. 1 (1980): 91-106; David Phillips, ed., *German Universities after the Surrender: British Occupation Policy and the Control of Higher Education* (Oxford: University of Oxford Department of Educational Studies, 1983a); Phillips, *Universitätsreform*; Phillips, "British Educational Policy in Occupied Germany."

163. "Supplementary Directive for the Re-opening of Universities and other Institutions of Higher Learning," 7 July 1945, submitted to the Headquarters of USFET [Z45 F 5/309-1/28].

164. Vogel and Weisz, *Akten zur Vorgeschichte, Teil 2*, 1015-18.

165. Because of Nazi penetration, invitations to the 550th anniversary of Heidelberg were declined by the universities in England, led by Oxford and Birmingham Universities, and consequently Heidelberg withdrew the invitations. It was noted 47 dismissals out of 189 entire faculty members (25%) by the Nazis in 1936. Charles Burlingham et al., eds., *Heidelberg and the Universities of America* (New York: The Viking Press, 1936), 61.

166. Tent, *Mission on the Rhine*, 65. See also: Steven Remy, *The Heidelberg Myth* (Cambridge: Harvard University Press, 2002).

167. Karl Lowenstein's report to Alfred Pundt, Legal Division, of 23 April 1946. The figures presented by Tent show the situation in November 1946.

168. "E&RA Summary Report," 13 October 1947 [Z45 F 5/304-2/7]; "Denazification Report - 15 January 1946: Summary." Cf. In the Russian zone, only 17.5% of total university teachers (28% of *Ordinarien*, 9.4% of *Dozenten*) survived denazification in the universities Rostock, Greifswald, Berlin, Leipzig, Halle and Jena as of 1947. Ralph Jessen, "Diktatorischen Elitenwecksel und universitäre Milieus. Hochschullehrer in der SBZ/DDR (1945-1967)," in *Universität und Eliten im Osten nach 1945*, ed. Jürgen Kocka (Göttingen: Vandenhoeck & Ruprecht, 1998), 31.

169. Reinhard Heydenreuter, "Office of Military Government for Bavaria," in *OMGUS-Handbuch: Die amerikanische Militärregierung in Deutschland 1945-1949*, ed. Christoph Weisz (München: R. Oldenbourg Verlag, 1994), 230. In the post-War period, the US government held some former-Nazi scientists to use them for the scientific development at home rather than prosecuting them in Germany. This political scheme, called by the code name "Operation Paperclip," was largely supported by American officials, including Clay: Smith, *The Papers*, 432-33.

170. "Mark T. Orr" (Interview Part 2 by Harry Wray on 1 January 1980, translated by Masako Shibata). *Sengo Kyoiku-shi Kenkyu Kiyo* 17, (2003): 89-110.

171. "Long-Range Policy Statement for German Re-Education."

156 Chapter Five

172. "Non-Admittance of Persons with Former Nazi Affiliations as Students to Institutions of Higher Learning," 14 January 1946, the Directorate of IA&C, CC Co-ordinating Committee [Z45 F 5/301-3/29].

173. "Report on Political Attitudes and Activities in German Institutions of Higher Learning (American Zone)," July 1946 [Z45 F 5/298-2/25].

174. "Report on the Re-Education of Germany"; "Memorandum on Postwar Education Reconstruction in Germany." Giles suggests that there were many cases of attacks on the Jewish students, including members of the NSDStB during the Nazi period. Geoffrey Giles, *University Government in Nazi Germany: The Example of Hamburg* (New Haven: Institution for Social and Policy Studies, Yale University, 1976), 5-7; Geoffrey Giles, *Students and National Socialism in Germany* (Princeton: Princeton University Press, 1985).

175. "The *Land* constitutions made it an obligation for the university to cultivate free science and the education of academic youth to foster their sense of the spiritual and moral values of occidental culture. The obligation is not only to construct spiritual tradition and the independent development of creative powers in spiritual space, but at the same time to establish a great sense of responsibility." "Minutes of the University Committee Meeting in Bad Schwalbach, 13-18 November and 30 November-9 December 1947" [Z1 1019].

176. *Marburger Hochschulegespräche 1948*, in: Neuhaus, *Dokumente zur Hochschulreform*, 261-62.

177. This large-scale cultural exchange program received criticism from some American intellectual circles, since it exhibited American "quasi-authoritarian power" and an "American posture of paternalism." The criticism was also raised about a huge expenditure for "a people whose government had twice caused a world war and the second time around adopted and mercilessly carried out the unparalleled atrocities of the Nazi regime." Kellermann, *Cultural Relations*, 11.

178. *MG Monthly Report*, 20 January 1946 (No. 6), 21.

179. "Report of the US Occupation of Germany, Religious Affairs Program," 23 September 1947 [Z45 F 5/337-2/6].

180. "The United States Education Mission Report," 52.

181. "*Niederschriften und Beschlüsse von der Sitzung der Arbeitsgemeinschaft für Hochschulfragen*," 24 April 1947 [Z1 999].

182. "The university may not retreat into being an island separated from responsibility," in: "Minutes of the University Committee Meeting in Bad Schwalbach."

183. "*Sitzung der Arbeitsgemeinschaft für Hochschulfragen*"; "Report of the Rector Conference of 21-22 April 1947 in Heidelberg" [Z1 999]; "Guideline for the Reform of the Higher Education Constitutions," 1947 [Z1 1019].

184. "Gegen Staatseinfluß," *Frankfurter Rundschau*, 27 March 1947 [Z1 1029]; "Report of the Rector Conference."

185. "Das Berliner Modell." *FU Nachrichten*, 4 December 1998. Details about the foundation of the university are in: James Tent, *The Free University of Berlin: A Political History* (Indianapolis: Indiana University Press, 1988).

186. Historical Division, Office of the Executive Secretary, US High Commissioner for Germany (HICOG), *The West German Education System: With Special Reference to the Policies and Programs of the Office of the U. S. High Commissioner for Germany* (1953), 100.

187. Organisation for Economic Co-operation and Development (OECD), *Reviews of National Policies for Education: Germany* (Paris: OECD, 1972), 22-23.

188. "American Education Policy: Address to German Ministries by Dr. John W. Taylor."

189. "Report of the United States Education Mission to Germany," 48.

190. "Memorandum on Postwar Education Reconstruction in Germany."

191. HICOG, *The West German Education System*, 92.

192. *Hochschultag des britischen Besatzungsgebietes und Hochschultag des amerikanischen Besatzungsgebietes Schönberg* on 18 July 1947, in Neuhaus, *Dokumente zur Hochschulreform*, 28; "Minutes of the University Committee Meeting in Bad Schwalbach"; *Rektorenkonferenz der amerikanischen Zone Heidelberg* on 25 November 1946, in: Neuhaus, *Dokumente zur Hochschulreform*, 23-24.

193. Hans Wenke, *Education in Western Germany. A Postwar Survey* (Washington DC: The Library of Congress, European Affairs Division, 1953), 70-71.

194. HICOG, *The West German Education System*, 93; Ullrich Schneider, "Hochschulreform, *Studium generale* und das *Collegium Academicum* Heidelberg 1945-1952," *Bildung und Erziehung* 36, no. 1 (1983): 55-67.

195. Jaspers translated the term "*Geisteswissenschaften*" into English as "spiritual sciences." Jaspers, "The Rededication of German Scholarship," 183.

Part III

Chapter Six

Conclusion

1. THE CAUSES OF DIFFERENCES IN MAJOR EDUCATION REFORMS

The Interplay of the Causes

As seen in the previous chapters, the education reforms in Japan and Germany resulted, for the Americans, in overall success and failure respectively. Thus far I have argued that these differences resulted from politically and culturally based conditions. Politically, apart from the different power structure of the two Occupations, the US policies for Japan and Germany were swayed by the intensity and the timing of the Cold War in East Asia and Europe. The less acute political tension in Asia permitted the United States to devote more effort to socio-cultural and educational changes in Japan than in Germany. In contrast, within the more complex political context in central Europe, the Occupation authorities gave only a minor political priority to the education reform in Germany. Culturally, the enthusiasm of the Americans for changing Japanese education can be explained by their belief that Japanese education had been not only ideologically problematic but also inferior in quality. In contrast, American respect for the educational traditions of Germany and the self-confidence of the Germans in their own traditions hampered the undertaking of far-reaching education reforms which were framed by the American model.

However, the relations involved were more complex than this. *Tensions and histories had deep roots.* From the Meiji period, Japan had developed its relationship with the United States, based on Japan's unilateral interest in, and admiration for, American ideas about society. During the Occupation, this relationship of cultural imbalance was shown particularly clearly in the reactions of Japanese leaders toward the suggestions made by the Occupation authorities. The Japanese exhibited their ambiguous ideas about indigenous socio-cultural values, ideological cleavage with the rest of the people, and relatively weak group cohesion played an important causal role in transforming the pre-1945 Japanese education system on the foreign model. This situation made a sharp contrast with the case of Germany, where the indigenous socio-cultural values had deliberately been maintained both by the people and the elite from the time of state formation and where relatively reciprocal relationship with the Americans had been developed.

Thus, among the reforms, those related to moral and religious issues, the traditional social order, and the relationship between education and the state are taken here as—potentially—very sensitive areas to show the historical and sociological conditions which shaped changes.

The Reform of Religious and Moral Education

From the preparatory phase of the Occupation, the American stance toward religious issues heavily influenced their planning and undertaking of education reforms in Japan and Germany. Starting with the purge of "unfaithful Christians" among the Japanese, American enthusiasm for remolding Japanese religion continued almost until the withdrawal of the Occupation authorities. American zeal for attacking *Shinto* was abnormally strong, as the Americans themselves have admitted. The destruction of the *Tenno* state was central to American policy for post-War Japan. Measures for the elimination of the national ideology *Kokka Shinto* went further than bans on militaristic and ultra-nationalistic cults. Further measures called for Japan's adoption of the principle of the separation of the state and religion throughout Japanese public life, including education. No significant objections were raised by Japanese leaders to this American interference in religious issues. Like *Kokka Shinto*, *Shushin* was banned by a military order within a few months after the war, despite the Americans' own investigation which had judged it generally sound. Nor did Japanese leaders raise any appeal to the Occupation authorities about this contradiction. In the post-War Japanese education system, instruction in Confucian ethics, which had been a long tradition in Japanese learning, disappeared.

In Germany, the Americans paid profound respect to German decisions on matters of religious education, even though they judged the influence of the German church in educational administration to be excessive. The Germans were also determined to retain the traditional pattern of religious education. The influence of Christianity on Nazi *Weltanschauung* was never debated. The Occupation authorities located the post-war reaffirmation of Christianity in German education against a view that there had been a German deviation from Western civilization in the Nazi period.

In Japan, these discussions on religious and moral education were extended to questioning the validity of the original educational principle of the nation—the *Kyoiku Chokugo*. Its validity was discussed partly as an issue of moral education and partly as a political problem related to the *Tenno* system. For the Americans, the *Kyoiku Chokugo* symbolized the idea of the *Tenno* system per se. Unlike the cases of other reforms, many of Japanese leaders reacted against the abolition of the *Kyoiku Chokugo*. What was crucial about Japanese reactions against the ban of the *Kyoiku Chokugo* was not the question of whether the Japanese leaders were acting as the guardian of traditional socio-cultural values. Reverence for the *Tenno* was a product of the abrupt Meiji refurbishment of the ideas of imperial divinity as the national ideology. Thus, the question was, rather, the depth to which the Japanese were indoctrinated by this political ideology. What they wished to retain was not the system of "traditional socio-cultural values" which the German leaders believed in, such as *Kultur*, German cultural identity, or traditional social order. What the Japanese adhered to was the political ideology of the *Tenno* state which had been deeply embedded in the Meiji education system.

The Reorganization of School Structure

The implementation of the 6-3-3 school system in Japan most clearly signified a historically continuing inclination of Japanese leaders toward Western ideas. In the context of the Occupation, the reform also signaled the impact of a characteristic interplay between the effects of Western ideas in the minds of Japanese leaders and the strong political power of the US Occupation authorities. The enthusiasm of the Japanese and the Americans was so strong that this ideal plan was made real.

In Germany, discussions on the introduction of a single-track system were not simply about the reorganization of the school structure or the abolition of elitism, but were about the potential destruction of traditional values in German society. The Americans' lack of understanding of this significance resulted in their failure of the reform. In fact, the partial attempt at the introduction of the *Einheitsschule* was based on long discussions by the Germans themselves from the Weimar period. Failing to gain the acceptance of their model, the Americans took more oppressive but ineffectual measures toward implementation of reform.

Discussions on the State, Society, and Education

Unlike the other difficult discussions on the reform of German education, the issues of educational decentralization were relatively simple, compared with the case of Japan. Although the OMGUS had difficulties with the various administrative organs and different educational ideas of the individual *Länder*, the Americans had to agree to retain the tradition of *Kulturhoheit* based on democratic principles. The claim by the Germans that the mistake of excessively centralized control of education, as committed by the Nazis, would not be repeated was also accepted.

In Japan, educational decentralization revealed the complex relationship between the state and the elite. University academics and prominent educators enthusiastically discussed the deconstruction or substantial reorganization of the Ministry of Education. At the school level, the introduction of the local education board was welcomed. However, at the university level, the national universities, including the Imperial Universities, rejected administration by local authorities and stuck to the principle of state control. In the face of rejection by the Japanese, American criticisms of state control over the university were toned down. The academic hierarchy of Japanese universities based on state control and protection continued to exist. Insistence on retaining their own political privileges and social prestige by the separate groups of Japanese leaders exhibited their weak group cohesion. Each group refused to be mixed up with "lower levels" in the academic hierarchy. This showed a sharp contrast to the case of Germany where the traditional equilibrium of the relationship of the state, local authorities, and the school was defended by monolithic affirmation from Germans involved in the reform debate.

Now the historical framing of these roles played by the Japanese and German leaders during the Occupation is to be revisited.

2. THE PATTERNS OF ELITE FORMATION, THE ROLE OF THE UNIVERSITY, AND STATE FORMATION

It has been the argument of this book that the complex layers of interrelationship between the patterns of state formation, elite formation, and the role of the university in the late nineteenth century created the conditions for the different reactions of the Japanese and German educational leaders to proposed reforms in the Occupation.

As investigated in chapters 2 and 3, Meiji Japan and the *Kaiserreich* started with a different core political agenda, although both states emerged as a consequence of political and military conflict with foreign countries. Both were "catching-up" states, lagging behind the leading Western powers politically and economically, though to different degrees. The Meiji government had a clear view of the role of education as a means of political consolidation and economic development of the nation. The universalization of primary education at a rapid pace showed the government's zeal for the socialization of all Japanese and the enhancement of their conformity with state policy. Heavy investment in elite institutions signaled their role in fulfilling the political agenda of state formation. These dual policies were clearly demonstrated in heavy emphasis on the ultra-nationalist ideology in the school on the one hand, and on Western learning and meritocratic principles in the university on the other. Consequently ideological divisions were created between the educated elite, inspired by Western knowledge, and the vast majority of the Japanese to whom Western ideas were foreign. The dual policies also caused ideological uncertainty within the elite: a fear and revulsion toward the Western powers and an admiration for Western ideas.

What was extraordinary about Japan as a non-Western "catching-up" state was that the equation of modernization with Westernization was not critically questioned by national leaders. In Japan, there had been no organized political and cultural movement by leaders which would arrest Westernization, as had commonly occurred in the other developing countries. In pre-industrial Russian society, for example, Russian high culture had already blossomed through the work of intellectuals from the Tsarist period. During this period, they formed a cohesive social group by cultivating indigenous culture. This group was also keen on absorbing Western knowledge and culture. But the Russian *intelligentsia* eventually started a major anti-Western movement, by viewing the cultural Westernization of Russia as excessive.[1] Their ideological uniformity, despite the difference in their political stances, ultimately halted Westernization in Russia. A similar phenomenon was witnessed in Latin America and in Islamic nations.[2] But in the context of Meiji Japan, the role of the university-educated leaders as guardians of the socio-cultural traditions was less prominent.

In addition, the university-educated elite in Japan developed a specific characteristic in the weakness of its group cohesion. Most of the early Meiji leaders, such as Fukuzawa and Mori, returned from Western countries with a strong admiration for Western ideas. As Fukuzawa noted later, the most impressive thing about Western countries, the United States in particular, was not the advance of technology, which had already been known to some Japanese from the end of the Tokugawa period, but the advance of society. The political aspirations of Meiji leaders were concentrated on modernizing Japanese society by loosening the traditional social order. The formation of a new elite through the highest level of education in the country did not permit the consolidation of the old ruling group of the ancien régime. The assumption which would unite highly educated national leaders was not nobility but meritocracy.

In Germany, the establishment of the *Kaiserreich* was the product of the long struggle of the German cultural domains to establish the political boundary of a unified Germany. This history shaped a solid framework of their identity as Germans and a sense of nationhood, before the formation of Germany as a state. The treasured notion of *Kultur* was often juxtaposed with the foreign notions of English materialistic culture and French encyclopedic civilization. At all levels of education, the sense of German cultural identity was infused.

Similarly, the group cohesion of university-educated people was also related to the pattern of state formation within which the Prussian-guided policy was legitimized. During the *Kaiserreich*, it was emphasised that the reinforcing of the traditional social order would intensify the internal order of German society and consequently strengthen the political consolidation of the German state. In addition, in its late industrialization, the German middle class developed when socialist movements were affecting Europe. An important consequence of this was the creation of a socio-political basis for the preference of the middle class for conservative policies. For its existence, the German middle class chose to adopt the political ideas and socio-cultural values of the aristocracy rather than to challenge them. At the university level as well the students of middle-class families were politically and culturally associated with those of aristocratic origin. An increasing number of middle-class students was an important component of the *Bildungsbürgertum*. Sharing an esprit de corps with the aristocracy, the *Bildungsbürgertum* gradually recognized itself as an intellectual aristocracy within German society. The rise of the economically powerful middle class as a consequence of industrialization came much later in German society. The early development of the state bureaucracy and late industrial development in Germany accentuated the high social positioning of the *Bildungsbürgertum* in German society.

Additionally, the university and university education gained more value and social prestige, as the developing state bureaucracy required bureaucrats to show intellectual capacity rather than have noble social origins. These sociological conditions generated a status group of the *Bildungsbürgertum* in the highly bureaucratized and pre-industrial German society. To highlight these characteristics of the German *Bildungsbürgertum* as a status group, which I have been trying to elucidate in this book, I would like to detour with a brief observation of social phenomena on the European continent, which are similar to the pattern of the formation of the university educated elite in Germany, for example, that in France and Russia, and which are not so explicitly analogous, for example, that in England.[3]

In France, where the state bureaucracy exerts strong political power over the university, the pattern of elite formation was and is affected by the political vision of the state. The university-educated elite is relatively uniform in character, constructed by the vision of the state. In France, as Robert Anderson notes, "the formation of a homogeneous elite was seen as essential to the unity of a modern nation-state."⁴ This state-led pattern of elite formation in France was also related to the rise of laicism in the French education system. After the formation of the Third Republic in France, the university system served the state in building moral solidarity in French society. With the departure from the authority of the Catholic Church, moral authority came to rely on the value of bourgeois high culture rather than religious authority.⁵ Like the German *Bildungsbürgertum*, a cohesive status group of the educated French bourgeoisie was the key to the underlining of the socio-cultural values of French society. Thus, the university environment served the state in forming French moral beliefs or *conscience*.⁶ These double social phenomena of the secularization of society and the development of the role of the university as a moral, spiritual, and cultural authority were prevalent in Europe.

In Russia as well, educational qualifications and a university education played a vital role in the social stratification system of pre-revolution and pre-industrial Russian society. By the early nineteenth century, an increasing number of the educated middle class had come to dominate high-ranking positions of the initially noble-dominated military and civil bureaucracy.⁷ In the relatively well-bureaucratized monarchical state, these higher-ranking bureaucrats gained political power and formed a status group.⁸ During this period, university education expanded rapidly. In this context, the Russian *intelligentsia* developed. Like the process of the development of German society, Russian industrialization and the rise of the Russian economic middle class took place much later than the formation of the *intelligentsia*.⁹ Therefore, the university-educated middle class had already established, like the German *Bildungsbürgertum*, a cohesive social group and had gained high position within Russian society before the rise of the economic middle class.¹⁰ As in the German pattern, high social position for the educated middle class vis-à-vis the economic middle class was a phenomenon specific to pre-industrial societies.¹¹ This group acted as a dynamic force for the cultural Westernization of Russia from the second half of the nineteenth century. At the same time, Russian high bourgeois culture had blossomed in the arts, such as novels and poetry, appreciated by groups of highly educated people in the Tsarist period. There developed a shared sense of esteem for the cultivation of indigenous cultural and intellectual assets. During this process of modernization and Westernization, the Russian elite directed a major cultural countermovement which was anti-Western.¹²

In contrast, in England, from the establishment of the universities at Oxford and Cambridge in the thirteenth century up until 1850, higher education was only loosely related to the economy and to occupation. Even in the middle of the nineteenth century, as Harold Perkin put it bluntly, the sudden disappearance of universities would have brought almost "no" impact on "aristocratic, conservative, and class-ridden" English society.[13] A university degree was customarily not a prerequisite for most of the liberal professions in law, medicine, and teaching and in the civil service.[14] This insignificant economic role of the English university can be related to the relatively small and weak position of the state bureaucracy in English society. Unlike the situation of Germany and France, the bureaucracy was not the most significant factor in state affairs in England, and entering it did not require any particular legal qualification from a university. Prolonged general education from the public schools and "Oxbridge" was regarded as enough to support, according to John Armstrong, "the amateur administration" in England.[15] The Report on the Organisation of the Permanent Civil Service by Northcote and Trevelyan in 1853 initiated only a slow introduction of meritocratic principles in civil-service entry toward the end of the century.[16] In England, tertiary education gradually became important for the higher social prestige of the middle class a full century later than in Germany.[17] Thus the English social positioning and occupational options rested largely on the bases of hereditary and apprenticeship job training rather than educational qualifications gained in the university. An additional English condition for the relatively insignificant role of the educated middle class and the university within social stratification was the early Industrial Revolution. In the highly industrialized English society, the social positioning of middle-class status was based on new economic power. Before the rise of the educated middle class, the economic middle class had already gained high social status in industrialized English society. The educated middle class formed no specific social stratum.[18]

In the case of Meiji Japan, all political, economic, and social transformations were the consequence of the national crisis and the key processes of state formation. The bureaucratization of state affairs, industrialization and the development of the state education system, which had occurred simultaneously, were driven by state power and control to meet core state objectives. The role of the university was thus framed by the key political agenda of the state. The university was given the task to equip the modern Japanese state with capable state bureaucrats and technical experts through imported learning. Given the political framing of state formation, the system of the Japanese university was distant from the ideal of German as well as other European universities. The university-educated elite from the Meiji period did not share many of the characteristics of German and French elites, either. Conversely, the university-educated elite in Germany deliberately attempted to retain the indigenous elements of German political thought, social values, and educational traditions. The notion of *Kultur* and class society also became important values for the German middle class. This was more pronounced in the *Kaiserreich*.

After World War Two, Japanese leaders were continuously inclined to absorb Western ideas. The belief in them was deeply rooted in the value system of Japanese elites from the period of the formation of the modern Japanese state. This phenomenon was in sharp distinction to the emphasis of the German elite on the value of *Kultur* and Christianity, as the principles for the reconstruction of the state and society. In the face of the post-war national crisis, the way in which national leaders reaffirmed indigenous socio-cultural values was a key to laying down the political and cultural direction of a new state.

3. A NEW APPROACH TO THE OCCUPATION REFORMS: A COMPARATIVE REFLECTION

This book has been looking at the role of national leaders in specific national crises under particular conditions—that of temporary American military occupation. The book has examined these roles in close relation to other major and historical processes, such as the formation of a modern state. Through these broad perspectives, the book sought a comparative understanding of the development of educational ideas and the educational system in Japan and Germany in two periods of time. The differences are dramatic.

The ideas and practices for the establishment of a state education system and the formation of a national elite in the university were shaped in Japan and Germany by the different and particular *raisons d'état* of Meiji Japan and the *Kaiserreich*, respectively.[19] The latter drew on indigenous traditions, and the former drew on exogenous influences. This was more than a literal borrowing.[20] This, as has been argued throughout the book, was not as simple as a combination of Western technology and Eastern morality—a broadly accepted view in the Western literature about the spectacularly successful Japanese pattern of modernization. The shift in domestic political power groups, the destruction and the reconstruction of the central value system of the state and the social stratification system—twice in less than a century—and changes in personal relational systems in the family, the workplace, and society as a whole brought more than a superficial metamorphosis to Japanese society.[21] In both 1868 and 1945, Japan experienced major Western influences. This should be understood also in terms of the continuing importance of beliefs about the universal value of Western ideas and practices on a world basis.[22]

As Raymond Aron has noted and as the power structure among the allied powers demonstrated, World War Two put a definitive end to the predominance of Europe in the world economy and politics.[23] This possibility had been discussed earlier by some European intellectuals, such as Nietzsche and Spengler and later Ortega. Political, economic, and military dominance gradually shifted from Europe to the United States from the late nineteenth century. So too did cultural influence. However, as Karl-Dietrich Bracher has observed, this was an extension of European influence: the "equation of European politics and world politics."[24] This extension of European ideas and its mixing with American political and military power permitted the accusation of Japan and Germany in Tokyo and Nuremberg that these societies were inherently authoritarian and lacked a notion of civil society. It is noticeable that this charge was made by England, France, and the United States—but not by nations in Asia and Europe, in particular, which had suffered from Japanese and German aggression. German society was seen through the eyes of the major victorious powers of World War Two as a deviation from the course of Western civilization in pursuit of a German *Sonderweg* [special path]. In Japan, the relationship of the Japanese to their religion was attacked strongly, given the remarkable public commitment of the Americans to Christianity.

Yet the terms "authoritarian," "totalitarian," or "non-democratic" are not fixed ones. These terms have been frequently abused and are thus elusive.[25] After the defeat of Italy, Germany, and Japan in World War Two, intellectual discussions about right-wing and fascist states centered on the underdevelopment of this concept in these countries. This academic trend was particularly strong in Europe, where massive numbers of people perished, and in the United States, which had accepted many exiles from Europe.[26] However, in the context of the growing political tensions of the Cold War, the nature of Stalinist-Communist regimes came to be the new major illustration of intellectual discourse about totalitarian and non-democratic states in social science.[27] Hostile views also gained ground in discussions of the newly independent socialist states, particularly those of so-called "Black Socialism" in Africa.[28] Yet, in the gradual decline of the political tension between the United States and the Soviet Union, the terms "totalitarianism" and "authoritarianism" became inopportune for application to the communist or socialist regimes and were redirected against particular regimes in Latin America.[29]

Thus conventional interpretations of Japan and Germany (and the reforms of education in the Occupation period) are not easily captured by simple propositions such as "Eastern morality and Western technology" or "continuity and discontinuity" or "authoritarian and democratic." The complexity of the relations—political, economic, and cultural—involved historical causes that stretch back into the period of state formation. An understanding of the relation between state and elite formation and the university cannot easily be simplified either. The concept of state formation itself is not a universal explanation. Nor is there much intellectual point in listing similarities and differences between the changes in Japanese and German education that took place against the background of a long process of political, military, economic, and cultural confrontation among many countries. It has been necessary, therefore, for this book to read the global in order to offer an understanding of these reforms.[30]

Research arising out of this book needs to continue to examine the nature of the role of education in society. An oligarchy of the state, the school and the university will not work. It is valuable to remember the maxim of Karl Jaspers who loathed narrowmindedness and always treasured self-examination of thought and action by people of intellect: "We must not shut ourselves off in the outward form of our historicity; on the contrary, a broadened understanding of ourselves is inseparable from our understanding of others."[31]

NOTES

1. Lloyd Churchward, *The Soviet Intelligentsia: An Essay on the Social Structure and Roles of Soviet intellectuals during the 1960s* (London: Routledge & Kegan Paul, 1973), 3; Richard Pipes, "The Historical Evolution of the Russian Intelligentsia," in *The Russian Intelligentsia*, ed. Richard Pipes (New York: Columbia University Press, 1961), 55.

2. Christopher Read, *Culture and Power in Revolutionary Russia: The Intelligentsia and the Transition from Tsarism to Communism* (London: Macmillan, 1990). See also: Churchward, *The Soviet Intelligentsia*; George Fischer, *Russian Liberalism: From Gentry to Intelligentsia* (Cambridge: Harvard University Press, 1958); Pipes, "The Historical Evolution"; Stuart Tompkins, *The Russian Intelligentsia: Makers of the Revolutionary State* (Norman: University of Oklahoma Press, 1957).

3. Gella, *The Intelligentsia*; Lewis Feuer, "What Is an Intellectual?," in *The Intelligentsia and the Intellectuals: Theory, Methods and Case Study*, ed. Aleksander Gella (Beverly Hills: SAGE Publications Inc., 1976), 47-58.

4. Robert Anderson, *Universities and Elites in Britain since 1800* (Basingstoke: Macmillan, 1992), 29.

5. Phyllis Stock-Morton, *Moral Education for a Secular Society: The Development of Morale Laïque in Nineteenth-Century France* (Albany: State University of New York Press, 1988), 2.

6. Ringer, *Fields of Knowledge*, 213, 237.

7. Daniel Brower, "Social Stratification in Russian Higher Education," in *The Transformation of Higher Learning 1860-1930: Expansion, Diversification, Social Opening, and Professionalization in England, Germany, Russia, and the United States*, ed. Konrad Jarausch (Chicago: University of Chicago Press, 1983), 245-46; Read, *Culture and Power*, 17.

8. Brower, "Social Stratification," 245-46.

9. Fischer, *Russian Liberalism*, 45-46.

10. Read, *Culture and Power*, 17.

11. Thomas Nipperdey, "Preußen und die Universität," in *Preußen: Seine Wirkung auf die deutsche Geschichte*, ed. Karl Erdmann (Stuttgart: Klett-Cotta, 1985), 69.

12. Fischer, *Russian Liberalism*, 16.

13. Harold Perkin, "The Pattern of Social Transformation in England," in *The Transformation of Higher Learning 1860-1930: Expansion, Diversification, Social Opening, and*

Professionalization in England, Germany, Russia, and the United States., ed. Konrad Jarausch (Chicago: University of Chicago Press, 1983), 207-9, 212.

14. Arthur Engel, "The English Universities and Professional Education," in *The Transformation of Higher Learning 1860-1930: Expansion, Diversification, Social Opening, and Professionalization in England, Germany, Russia, and the United States*, ed. Konrad H. Jarausch (Chicago: University of Chicago Press, 1983), 293-98. During this mid-Victorian period, the University of London and Durham supplied a few scientists and engineers to the new industrial society. Perkin, "The Pattern of Social Transformation," 207-8.

15. John Armstrong, *The European Administrative Elite* (Princeton: Princeton University Press, 1973), 150-51.

16. Roy Lowe, "English Elite Education in the Late Nineteenth and Early Twentieth Centuries," in *Bildungsbürgertum im 19. Jahrhundert: Bildungssystem und Professionalisierung in internationalen Vergleichen*, ed. Werner Conze and Jürgen Kocka (Stuttgart: Klett-Cotta, 1985), 150-51.

17. Kocka, "The European Pattern and the German Case," 23. Cf. Anthony Giddens and Philip Stanworth, "An Economic Elite: A demographic profile of company chairmen," in *Elites and Power in British Society*, ed. Anthony Giddens and Philip Stanworth (Cambridge: Cambridge University Press, 1974), 81-101.

18. Kocka, "The European Pattern and the German Case," 22. Certainly, people educated in the university were socially respected in British society. However, this social recognition was directly linked to their relatively high level of economic power. For instance, university academics in Britain used to be paid well by the state. Dmitri Mirsky. *The Intelligentsia of Great Britain* (London: Victor Gollancz Ltd., 1935), 10.

19. Masako Shibata, "Controlling National Identity and the Role of Education: The Vision of State Formation in Meiji Japan and the German *Kaiserreich*," *History of Education* 33, no. 1 (2004): 75-85.

20. Masako Shibata, "Educational Borrowing in Japan in the Meiji and Post-War Eras," in *Educational Borrowing: Historical Perspectives*, ed. David Phillips and Kimberly Ochs, Oxford Studies in Comparative Education (Oxford: Symposium Books, 2005b), 147-168. For a theoretical account of "borrowing," see: David Phillips, "On Comparing," in *Learning from Comparing: New Directions in Comparative Educational Research. Volume 1: Contexts, Classrooms and Outcomes*, ed. Robin Alexander, Patricia Broadfoot, and David Phillips (Oxford: Symposium Books, 1999), 15-19; Phillips, "Learning from Elsewhere in Education," 299-300; David Phillips and Ochs Kimberly, "Processes of Policy Borrowing in Education: Some Explanatory and Analytical Devices," *Comparative Education* 39, no. 4 (2003): 451-61.

21. Cowen sees this pattern of metamorphosis in the *Meiji Ishin* and the Occupation reforms as a "transitology," i.e., the almost simultaneous collapse and reconstruction of state apparatuses, economic and social stratification system, and the central value system, especially the political value system to offer a new definition of the future. Robert Cowen, "Last Past the Post: Comparative Education, Modernity and Perhaps Post-Modernity," *Comparative Education* 32, no. 2 (1996), 163-65; Robert Cowen, "Late Modernity and the Rules of Chaos: An initial note on transitologies and rims," in *Learning from Comparing: New Directions in Comparative Educational Research*, ed. Robin Alexander, Patricia Broadfoot, and David Phillips (Oxford: Symposium Books, 1999), 84-84.

22. For an interpretation of the cultural confidence about Western civilization held by Europeans from the nineteenth century, see: Coulby and Jones, *Postmodernity*, chapters 1, 2, 9.

23. Aron, *Democracy and Totalitarianism*, 202.

24. Bracher also argues that after this time, i.e., from the early twentieth century, there was "a turning point from Europe's self-glorification to its self-destruction," with World War One as its final conclusion. Bracher, *The Age of Ideologies*, 88, 97.

25. Hanna Arendt, *On Violence* (London: Allen Lane The Penguin Press, 1970); Theodor Geiger, *The Conflicted Relationship: The West and the Transformation of Asia, Africa and Latin America* (New York: McGraw-Hill Book Company, 1967); Samuel Huntington, *The Third Wave: Democratization in the Late Twentieth Century* (Norman and London: University of Oklahoma Press, 1991).

26. Adorno et al., *The Authoritarian Personality*.

27. To name only a few: Aron, *Democracy and Totalitarianism*; Karl Bracher, "Turn of the Century and Totalitarian Ideology," in *Totalitarian Democracy and After: International Colloquium in Memory of Jacob L. Talmon* (Jerusalem: The Magnes Press, 1984), 70-80; Samuel Eisenstadt, "Totalitarian Democracy: Cultural Traditions and Modernization - Introductory Remarks," in *Totalitarian Democracy and After: International Colloquium in Memory of Jacob L. Talmon* (Jerusalem: The Magnes Press, 1984), 83-85; Friedrich, *Totalitarianism*; Gino Germani, *Authoritarianism, Fascism, and National Populism* (New Brunswick: Transaction Books, 1978); John Herz, ed., *From Dictatorship to Democracy: Coping with the Legacies of Authoritarianism and Totalitarianism* (Westport: Greenwood Press, 1982); Jacob Talmon, *Political Messianism: The Romantic Phase* (London: Secker & Warburg, 1960); Jacob Talmon, *The Origins of Totalitarian Democracy* (New York: W. W. Norton & Company Inc., 1970 [1955]); Jacob Talmon, *Totalitarian Democracy and After: International Colloquium in Memory of Jacob L. Talmon* (Jerusalem: The Magnes Press, 1984).

28. Andrew Coulson, ed., *African Socialism in Practice: The Tanzanian Experience* (Nottingham: Spokesman, 1979); Robert Jackson and Carl Rosberg, *Personal Rule in Black Africa: Prince, Autocrat, Prophet, Tyrant* (Berkeley: University of California Press, 1982).

29. Guillermo O'Donnell, *Modernization and Bureaucratic-Authoritarianism: Studies in South American Politics* (Berkeley: Regents of the University of California, 1973), 87. See also: David Collier, ed., *The New Authoritarianism in Latin America* (Princeton: Princeton University Press, 1979).

30. For this approach to comparative education, see: Cowen, "Last Past the Post"; Robert Cowen, "Comparing Futures or Comparing Pasts?," *Comparative Education* 36, no. 3 (2000): 333-42. For a recent attempt of the identification of comparative methodology, see also: Kimberly Ochs and David Phillips, *Towards a Structural Typology of Cross-national Attraction in Education (A progress report)* (Lisboa: EDUCA, 2002); David Phillips, "On Comparing"; David Phillips and Ochs Kimberly, "Processes of Policy Borrowing"; Jürgen Schriewer, ed., *Discourse Formation in Comparative Education* (Frankfurt am Main: Peter Lang, 2000).

31. Karl Jaspers, *Philosophy and the World: Selected Essays and Lectures* (Chicago: Henry Regnery Company, 1963), 151.

Appendix A

The Imperial Rescript on Education [1890]

Know ye, Our subjects:

Our Imperial Ancestors have founded Our Empire on a basis broad and everlasting and have deeply and firmly implanted virtue; Our subjects ever united in loyalty and filial piety have from generation to generation illustrated the beauty thereof. This is the glory of the fundamental character of Our Empire, and herein also lies the source of Our education. Ye, Our subjects, be filial to your parents, affectionate to your brothers and sisters; as husbands and wives be harmonious, as friends true; bear yourselves in modesty and moderation; extend your benevolence to all; pursue learning and cultivate arts, and thereby develop intellectual faculties and perfect moral powers; furthermore, advance public good and promote common interests; always respect the Constitution, and observe the laws; should emergency arise, offer yourselves courageously to the State; and thus guard and maintain the prosperity of Our Imperial Throne coeval with heaven and earth. So shall ye not only be Our good and faithful subjects, but render illustrious the best traditions of your forefathers. The Way here set forth is indeed the teaching bequeathed by Our Imperial Ancestors, to be observed alike by Their Descendants and the subjects, infallible for all ages and true in all places. It is Our wish to lay it to heart in all reverence, in common with you, Our subjects, that we may all thus attain to the same virtue.

The 30th day of the 10th month of the 23rd year of Meiji [1890].
[Imperial Sign Manual. Imperial Seal.]

Appendix A

NOTE

Baron Kikuchi Dairoku claimed that this translation was the official English version of the Rescript because the Ministry of Education, Makino, decided to submit this to the *Tenno*. Kikuchi distributed this text to his audience at the inaugural address to the course of lectures on Japanese Education in University of London in 1907. Dairoku Kikuchi, "Japanese Education," *The XIX Century and After* (1907), 1013.

Appendix B

Archival Documents

NATIONAL DIET LIBRARY IN TOKYO, JAPAN

SCAPIN: SCAP Instruction for the Imperial Japanese Government
FEC: Far Eastern Commission
ERJ1: *Education Reform in Japan, 1945-1952, Part 1* (1990) eds. Sato, Suzuki, and Tsuchimochi. Washington DC: Congressional Information Service & Maruzen.
ERJ2: *Education Reform in Japan, 1945-1952, Part 2*, (1996) eds. Sato, Suzuki, and Tsuchimochi. Washington DC: Congressional Information Service & Maruzen.
ERG: *The US Occupation of Germany: Educational Reform 1945-1949* (1991) ed. Tsuchimochi. Washington DC: Congressional Information Service & Maruzen.
Notter File: Post World War II Foreign Policy Planning: State Department Records of Harley A. Notter, 1939-1945.
Trainor: Joseph Trainor Collection, Hoover Institute, Stanford University

BUNDESARCHIV BERLIN, GERMANY

NS: Einrichtungen der NSDAP
R: Zivile Behörden und Einrichtungen des Deutschen Reichs

BUNDESARCHIV KOBLENZ, GERMANY

Z: Zonenverwaltung
    Z1: Länderrat des amerikanischen Besatzungsgebietes
    Z2: Zonenbeirat der britischen Besatzungszone
    Z45 F: Office of Military Government for Germany of the United States (OMGUS)
    AGTS: Adjutant General Top Secret
    POLAD: Political Adviser's Office
    2: Control Council
    5, 44-45, 45-46: Other documents between 1944 and 1949

THE BRITISH LIBRARY AT ST. PANCREAS IN LONDON, UK

DMR: "Denazification: Monthly Report of Military Governor US Zone," Military Government of Germany. (Denazification Report)
MR: "Monthly Report of the Military Governor US Zone," Military Government of Germany. (MG Monthly Report)
The National Archives Public Record Office in Kew, UK
FO: Records of the Foreign Office of the British Government

German Glossary

Bildung: education and personal cultivation
Bildungsbürgertum: educated middle class
Chancengleichheit: equality of opportunity
Dozent(en): assistant professor(s)
Einheitsschule: comprehensive school
Fragebogen: questionnaire, in particular for screening former Nazis
Grundgesetz: basic law of the Federal Republic of Germany
Grundschule: primary school
Gymnasium: grammar school
Junker: landed aristocracy in Prussia
Kaiser: emperor
Kaiserreich: German Second Empire
Kleinbürger: petite bourgeoisie or small middle class
Kultur: culture
Kulturausschuss: committee for educational issues
Kulturhoheit: autonomy in cultural and educational matters
Kulturkampf: the political struggle over educational policy between church and state in the *Kaiserreich*
Land (pl. *Länder*): German political sub-division, state
Länderrat: council of German minister presidents
Lehrfreiheit und Lernfreiheit: freedom of teaching and freedom of learning
Nichtordinarius(-ien): non-professorial university teacher(s)
Ordinarius (-ien): tenured professor(s)
Pädagogischinstitut: normal school
Peußischen Allgemeinen Landrecht: Prussian general code
Prügelstrafe: corporal punishment

Reichstag: Imperial Diet
Staatsbürgererziehung (Staatsbürgerkunde): education for the cultivation of state citizenship
Technischhochschule(n): technical higher-education institution(s)
Umerziehung: re-education
Volksbewußtsein: folk (or racial) consciousness or confidence
Volksschule: primary school
Weltanschauung: worldview
Wirtschaftsbürgertum: economic middle class
Wissenschaft: science, knowledge, scholarship
Zucht: discipline

Japanese Glossary

Bakufu: shogunate
Bushido: warriors' ethics
Daigaku: university
Daimyo: Tokugawa feudal lord
Gakko: school
Han: Tokugawa fief
Kokka Shinto: state *Shinto*
Kokutai ideology: cardinal principles of the national entity
Koto Gakko: higher middle school
Koza: academic division of fields of study with a professorial chair
Kyoiku: education
Kyoiku Chokugo: imperial rescript on education
Meiji Ishin: Meiji Restoration
Samurai: warrior
Senmon Gakko: technical school
Shihan Gakko: normal school
Shinto: Japanese indigenous religion
Shushin: pre-1945 moral education largely based on Confucianism
Tenno: emperor
Terakoya: commoners' school in the pre-Meiji period

Bibliography

OFFICIAL PUBLICATIONS

Committee on Foreign Relations, US Senate, *Documents on Germany, 1944-1961*. Washington DC: The US Government Printing Office, 1961.

Daigaku-kijun-kyokai Junen-shi Hensan-iinkai (DJH) ed., *Daigaku-kijun-kyokai junen-shi*. Tokyo: Daigaku-kijun-kyokai, 1957.

Department of State, USA (DS USA), *Occupation of Germany: Policy and progress 1945-1946*. Washington DC: The US Government Printing Office, 1947.

Departments of State and Public, Army USFET (DSP USA), *Occupation: A Handbook for Troops Proceeding on Service in the U.S. Occupation*. Washington, 1946.

Division of Publication, Department of State, US Government (DP DS USA), *Postwar Foreign Policy Preparation 1939-1945*. Washington: The US Government Printing Office, 1949.

Division of Special Records, Foreign Office, Japanese Government (DSR FO JPN). *Documents Concerning the Allied Occupation and Control of Japan*, Tokyo: Foreign Office of Japanese Government, 1949.

General Headquarters of the Supreme Commander for the Allied Powers (GHQ SCAP), *Nihon senryo no Shimei to Seika*. Tokyo: Itagaki Shoten, 1950.

Government Section, Supreme Commander for the Allied Powers (GS SCAP), *Political Reorientation of Japan: September 1945 to September 1948*. Washington: The US Government Printing Office, 1948.

Historical Division, Office of the Executive Secretary, U.S. High Commissioner for Germany (HICOG), *The West German Education System: With Special Reference to the Policies and Programs of the Office of the U.S. High Commissioner for Germany*, 1953.

Japanese Education Reform Council, *Education Reform in Japan: The Present Status and the Problems Involved*. Tokyo: The Japanese Education Reform Council, 1950.

Ministry of Education, "Japan, Nihon ni okeru kyoiku kaikaku no shinten," *Monbu Jiho* 880 (1951).

Ministry of Education, Japan, *Education in Japan 1971: A Graphic presentation*. Tokyo: Ministry of Education, 1971.

Ministry of Education, Japan, *Waga-kuni no bunkyo seisaku: Susumu 'kyoiku kaikaku'*. Tokyo: Ministry of Education, 1999.

Office of Military Government for Germany US (OMGUS). *Textbooks in Germany*. Internal Affairs and Communications Division, Education and Religious Affairs Branch, 1946.
Organisation for Economic Co-Operation and Development (OECD), *Nihon no Kyoiku Seisaku*. Tokyo: Asahi Shimbunsha, 1971.
Organisation for Economic Co-Operation and Development (OECD), *Reviews of National Policies for Education: Germany*. Paris: OECD, 1972.
Religions and Cultural Resources Division, Civil Information & Education Section, General Headquarters of Supreme Commander for the Allied Powers (RC CI&E SCAP), *Religions in Japan: Buddhism, Shinto, Christianity*. Tokyo: SCAP, 1948. (published under the editorial direction of William Bunce in 1955).

SECONDARY SOURCES

Abe, Yoshishige. *Sengo no jijoden*. Tokyo: Shinchosha, 1959.
Adorno, Theodor W., Else Frenkel-Brunswik, Daniel J. Levinson, and R. Nevitt Sanford, *The Authoritarian Personality*. New York: Harper & Brothers, 1950.
Alexander, Thomas. *The Prussian Elementary Schools*. New York: Macmillan, 1918.
Alexander, Thomas, and Isaac Kandel. *The Reorganization of Education in Prussia*. New York: Columbia University Press, 1927.
Alexander, Thomas, and Beryl Parker. *The New Education in the German Republic*. New York: John Day, 1929.
Amano, Ikuo. "Continuity and Change in the Structure of Japanese Higher Education." Pp. 10-39 in *Changes in the Japanese University: A Comparative Perspective*, edited by William Cummings, Ikuo Amano, and Kazuyuki Kitamura. New York: Praeger, 1979.
——. *Koto-kyoiku no nihon-teki kozo*. Tokyo: Tamagawa University Press, 1986.
——. *Nihon-teki daigaku-zo wo motomete*. Tokyo: Tamagawa University Press, 1991.
——. *Gakureki no shakai-shi: Kyoiku to Nihon no kindai*. Tokyo: Shincho Sensho, 1992.
——. *Kyoiku to kindai-ka: Nihon no keiken*. Tokyo: Tamagawa University Press, 1997.
Amano, Ikuo, and William Cummings. "The Changing of the Japanese Professor." Pp. 127-48 in *Changes in the Japanese University: A Comparative Perspective*, edited by William Cummings, Ikuo Amano and Kazuyuki Kitamura. New York: Praeger, 1979.
Anderson, Perry. *Lineages of the Absolutist State*. London: Verso, 1974.
——. "The Prussia of the East?" Pp. 31-39 in *Japan in the World*, edited by Masao Miyoshi and Harry Harootunian. Durham: Duke University Press, 1993.
Anderson, Robert. *Universities and Elites in Britain since 1800*. Basingstoke: Macmillan, 1992.
Arendt, Hannah. *The Origins of Totalitarianism*. London: Allen and Unwin, 1967 [1951].
——. *On Violence*. London: Allen Lane The Penguin Press, 1970.
Arimitsu, Jiro. *Arimitsu Jiro nikki*. Tokyo: Daiichi Hoki, 1989.
Armstrong, John. *The European Administrative Elite*. Princeton: Princeton University Press, 1973.
Arnason, Johann. *Social Theory and Japanese Experience: The Dual Civilization*. London: Kegan Paul International, 1997.
Aron, Raymond. *Opium of the Intellectuals*. New York: WW Norton & Company Inc., 1962.
——. *Main Currents in Sociological Thought 2: Pareto, Weber, Durkheim*. Harmondsworth: Penguin Books Ltd., 1967.
——. *Democracy and Totalitarianism: A Theory of Political Systems*. Ann Arbor: University of Michigan Press, 1990.

———. *Memoirs: Fifty Years of Political Reflection.* New York: Holmes & Meier, 1990.
Backer, John. "From Morgenthau Plan to Marshall Plan." Pp. 155-65 in *Americans as Proconsuls: United States Military Government in Germany and Japan, 1944-1952,* edited by Robert Wolfe. Carbondale: Southern Illinois University Press, 1984.
Bailey, Paul. *Postwar Japan: 1945 to the Present.* Cambridge: Blackwell, 1996.
Ballou, Robert. *Shinto: The Unconquered Enemy: Japan's Doctrine of Racial Superiority and World Conquest.* New York: The Viking Press, 1945.
Bariety, Jacques. "Die deutsche Frage aus französischer Sicht, 1945-1955." Pp. 172-94 in *Die deutsche Frage in der Nachkriegszeit,* edited by Wilfried Loth. Berlin: Akademie Verlag, 1994.
Bark, Dennis, and David Gress. *A History of West Germany: From Shadow to Substance 1945-1963.* vol. 1 Oxford: Blackwell, 1989.
Barnett, Correlli. "The Education of Military Elites." Pp. 193-214 in *Governing Elites,* edited by Rupert Wilkinson. New York: Oxford University Press, 1969.
Barshay, Andrew. *State and Intellectual in Imperial Japan: The Public Man in Crisis.* Berkeley: University of California Press, 1988.
Bates, Peter. *Japan and the British Commonwealth Occupation Force, 1946-52.* London: Brassey's, 1993.
Bauman, Zygmunt. *Legislators and Interpreters: On Modernity, Post-Modernity, and Intellectuals.* Cambridge: Polity Press, 1987.
Beauchamp, Edward. "Educational and Social Reform in Japan: The First US Education Mission to Japan, 1946." Pp. 175-92 in *The Occupation of Japan: Educational and Social Reform,* edited by Thomas Burkman. Norfolk: The MacArthur Memorial Foundation, 1980.
Beck, Hermann. *The Origins of the Authoritarian Welfare State in Prussia: Conservatives, Bureaucracy, and the Social Question, 1815-70.* Ann Arbor: The University of Michigan Press, 1995.
Becker, Hellmut. "Retrospective View from the German Side." Pp. 268-82 in *The British in Germany: Educational Reconstruction after 1945,* edited by Arthur Hearnden. London: Hamish Hamilton, 1978.
Bellah, Robert. *Tokugawa Religion: The Values of Pre-Industrial Japan.* Glencoe: Free Press, 1957.
———. "Intellectual and Society in Japan." *Daedalus* 101, no. 2 (1972): 89-116
Ben-David, Joseph, and Awraham Zloczower "Universities and Academic Systems in Modern Societies." *European Journal of Sociology* 3 (1962): 45-85.
Bendix, Reinhard. *Max Weber: An Intellectual Portrait.* London: Methuen & Co., Ltd., 1966.
———. *Kings or People: Power and the Mandate to Rule.* Berkeley: University of California Press, 1978.
Benedict, Ruth. *The Chrysanthemum and the Sword: Patterns of Japanese Culture.* Boston: Routledge and Kegan Paul, 1946.
Bennett, John, and Anthony Nicholls. *The Semblance of Peace: The Political Settlement and the Second World War.* London: Macmillan, 1972.
Berg, Christina. ed. *Handbuch der deutschen Bildungsgeschichte: Von der Reichsgründung bis zum Ende des Ersten Weltkriegs.* vol. IV Munich: CH Beck, 1991.
Birley, Robert. "British Policy in Retrospect." Pp. 46-63 in *The British in Germany: Educational Reconstruction after 1945,* edited by Arthur Hearnden. London: Hamish Hamilton Ltd., 1978.
Bisson, Thomas. *Japan's War Economy.* New York: International secretariat, Institute of Pacific Relations, 1945.

Bix, Herbert. *Hirohito and the Making of Modern Japan*. New York: Harper Collins Publishers, 2000.

Blackbourn, David, and Geoff Eley. *The Peculiarities of German History: Bourgeois Society and Politics in Nineteenth-Century Germany*. Oxford: Oxford University Press, 1984.

Bobbio, Norberto. *On Mosca and Pareto*. Genève: Librairie Doz SA, 1972.

Bonner, Thomas. "Abraham Flexner and the German University: The Progressive as Traditionalist." *Paedagogica Historica* 33, no. 1 (1997): 99-116

Borton, Hugh. *Japan's Modern Century*. New York: The Ronald Press Company, 1955.

Bottomore, Tom. *Elites and Society*. London: C. A. Watts & Co. Ltd., 1964.

Bowen, James. *A History of Western Education: The Modern West: Europe and the New World*. vol. 3 London: Methuen & Co. Ltd., 1981.

Bödeker, Birgit. *Amerikanische Zeitschriften in Deutscher Sprache, 1945-1952*. Frankfurt am Main: Peter Lang, 1993.

Bracher, Karl. *The Age of Ideologies: A History of Political Thought in the Twentieth Century*. London: Weidenfeld and Nicolson, 1984a.

———. "Turn of the Century and Totalitarian Ideology." Pp. 70-80 in *Totalitarian Democracy and After: International Colloquium in Memory of Jacob L. Talmon*. Jerusalem: The Magnes Press, 1984b.

———. *Turning Points in Modern Times: Essays on German and European History*. Cambridge: Harvard University Press, 1995.

Braun, Birgit. *Umerziehung in der amerikanischen Besatzungszone. Die Schul- und Bildungspolitik in Württemberg-Baden von 1945 bis 1949*. Münster: LIT Verlag, 2004.

Breuilly, John. *The Formation of the First German Nation-State, 1800-1871*. London: Macmillan Press Ltd., 1996.

Brickner, Richard A. *Is Germany Incurable?* Philadelphia: J. B. Lippincott, 1943.

Brower, Daniel. "Social Stratification in Russian Higher Education." Pp. 245-60 in *The Transformation of Higher Learning 1860-1930: Expansion, Diversification, Social Opening, and Professionalization in England, Germany, Russia, and the United States*, edited by Konrad Jarausch. Chicago: University of Chicago Press, 1983.

Brown, Delmer. *Nationalism in Japan: An Introductory Historical Analysis*. Berkeley: University of California Press, 1955.

Bruch, Rüdiger vom. "A Slow Farewell to Humboldt?: Stages in the History of German Universities, 1810-1945." Pp. 3-27 in *German Universities Past and Future: Crisis or renewal?*, edited by Mitchell Ash. Oxford: Berghahn Books, 1997.

Burlingham, Charles, James Byrne, Samuel Seabury, and Henry Stimson. ed. *Heidelberg and the Universities of America*. New York: The Viking Press, 1936.

Burmeister, Werner. "Were the British Too Neutral?" *Adult Education* 51, no. 1 (1978): 98-100.

Busch, Alexander. *Die Geschichte des Privatdozenten: Eine soziologische Studie zur großbetrieblichen Entwicklung der deutschen Universitäten*. Stuttgart: Ferdinand Enke Verlag, 1959.

Cairncross, Alec. *The Price of War: British Policy on German Reparations 1941-1949*. Oxford: Blackwell, 1986.

Carr, William. *A History of Germany 1815-1945*. London: Arnold, 1969.

Chapman, John. *The Re-education of the Japanese People*, Ph.D. dissertation submitted to the University of Houston, 1954.

Cheval, René. "Die Bildungspolitik in der Französischen Besatzungszone." Pp. 190-200 in *Umerziehung und Wiederaufbau: Die Bildungspolitik der Besatzungsmächte in Deutschland und Österreich*, edited by Manfred Heinemann. Stuttgart: Klett-Cotta, 1981.

Churchward, Lloyd. *The Soviet Intelligentsia: An essay on the social structure and roles of Soviet intellectuals during the 1960s*. London: Routledge & Kegan Paul, 1973.

Clay, Lucius. *Decision in Germany*. London: William Heinemann Ltd., 1950.

———. "Proconsul of a People, by Another People, for Both Peoples." Pp. 103-13 in *Americans as Proconsuls: United States Military Government in Germany and Japan, 1944-1952*, edited by Robert Wolfe. Carbondale: Southern Illinois University Press, 1984.

Cohen, Theodore. *Remaking Japan: The American Occupation as New Deal*. New York: The Free Press, 1987.

Collier, David. ed. *The New Authoritarianism in Latin America*. Princeton: Princeton University Press, 1979.

Conze, Werner, and Jürgen Kocka. "Einleitung." Pp. 9-26 in *Bildungsbürgertum im 19. Jahrhundert: Bildungssystem und Professionalisierung in internationalen Vergleichen*, edited by Werner Conze and Jürgen Kocka. Stuttgart: Klett-Cotta, 1985.

Cornwell, John. *Hitler's Pope*. New York: Viking, 1999.

Costell, Edwin. "An American University Officer in Occupied Germany: A Personal Account 36 Years Later." Pp. 23-33 in *Hochschuloffiziere und Wiederaufbau des Hochschulwesens in Westdeutschland 1945-1952. Teil 2: Die US-Zone*, edited by Manfred Heinemann. Hildesheim: Verlag August Lax, 1990.

Coulby, David. "Educational Responses to Diversity within the State." Pp. 7-17 in *World Yearbook of Education: Intercultural Education*, edited by David Coulby, Jagdish Gundara, and Crispin Jones. London: Kogan Page, 1997.

———. *Beyond the National Curriculum: Curricular Centralism and Cultural Diversity in Europe and the USA*. London: Routledge/Falmer, 2000.

Coulby, David, and Crispin Jones. *Postmodernity and European Education Systems: Cultural Diversity and Centralist Knowledge*. Stoke-on-Trent: Trentham, 1995.

———. "Post-modernity, Education and European Identities." *Comparative Education* 32, no. 2 (1996): 171-84.

Coulson, Andrew. ed. *African Socialism in Practice: The Tanzanian Experience*. Nottingham: Spokesman, 1979.

Cowen, Robert. "Last Past the Post: Comparative Education, Modernity and Perhaps Post-Modernity." *Comparative Education* 32, no. 2 (1996): 151-70.

———. "Late Modernity and the Rules of Chaos: An initial note on transitologies and rims." Pp. 73-88 in *Learning from Comparing: New Directions in Comparative Educational Research*, edited by Robin Alexander, Patricia Broadfoot and David Phillips. Oxford: Symposium Books, 1999.

———. "Comparing Futures or Comparing Pasts?" *Comparative Education* 36, no. 3 (2000a): 333-42.

———. "Nigel Grant and Plato: A Question of Democratic Education." *Comparative Education* 36, no. 2 (2000b): 135-41.

Craig, Gordon Alexander. *Germany 1866-1945*. Oxford: Clarendon Press, 1978.

Cummings, William. "The Conservative Reform of Higher Education." *Japan Interpreter* 8, no. 4 (1974): 421-31.

Dahrendorf, Ralf. *Society and Democracy in Germany*. London: Weidenfeld and Nicolson, 1967.

Davies, Edith. "British Policy and the Schools." Pp. 95-107 in *The British in Germany: Educational Reconstruction after 1945*, edited by Arthur Hearnden. London: Hamish Hamilton Ltd., 1978.

de Bary, William, Ryusaku Tsunoda, and Donald Keene. *Sources of Japanese Tradition*. New York: Columbia University Press, 1958.

Demeter, Karl. *The German Officer-Corps in Society and State, 1650-1945*. London: Weidenfeld & Nicolson, 1965.
Dessoir, Max. *Buch der Erinnerung*. Stuttgart: Ferdinand Enke Verlag, 1947.
Dodge, Guy. ed. *Jean-Jacques Rousseau: Authoritarian Libertarian?* London: DC Heath and Company, 1971.
Dore, Ronald. *Education in Tokugawa Japan*. London: The Athlone Press Ltd., 1992 [1965].
Dower, John. *Embracing Defeat: Japan in the Wake of World War II*. New York: WW Norton & Company, 1999.
Duke, Benjamin. *Japan's Militant Teachers*. Honolulu: University Press of Hawaii, 1973.
———. ed. *Ten Great Educators of Modern Japan: A Japanese Perspective*. Tokyo: University of Tokyo Press, 1989.
Eccleston, Bernard. *State and Society in Post-War Japan*. Cambridge: Polity, 1989.
Edholm, Felicity. *Education and Repression: Chile*. London: WUS, 1982.
Eisenstadt, Samuel. *The Political Systems of Empires*. New York: The Free Press, 1963.
———. "Totalitarian Democracy: Cultural Traditions and Modernization – Introductory Remarks." Pp. 83-85 in *Totalitarian Democracy and After: International Colloquium in Memory of Jacob L. Talmon*. Jerusalem: The Magnes Press, 1984.
———. *Japanese Civilization: A Comparative View*. Chicago: University of Chicago Press, 1996a.
———. "Some Observations on the Transformation of Confucianism (and Buddhism) in Japan." Pp. 173-85 in *Confucian Traditions in East Asian Modernity*, edited by Wei-ming Tu. Cambridge: Harvard University Press, 1996b.
Eley, Geoff. *From Unification to Nazism: Reinterpreting the German Past*. Boston: Allen & Unwin, 1986.
Eliade, Mircea. ed. *The Encyclopedia of Religion*, vol. 13. New York: Macmillan Publishing Company, 1987.
Elias, Norbert. *The Civilizing Process: The History of Manners*. Oxford: Basil Blackwell, 1994 [1939].
———. *Studien über die Deutschen: Machtkämpfe und Habitusentwicklung im 19. Und 20. Jahrhundert*. Frankfurt am Main: Suhrkamp, 1998.
Enders, Ulrich. *Die Bodenreform in der amerikanischen Besatzungszone 1945-1949 unter besonderer Berücksichtung Bayerns*. Ostfildern: Scripta Mercaturae Verlag, 1982.
Engel, Arthur. "The English Universities and Professional Education." Pp. 293-305 in *The Transformation of Higher Learning 1860-1930: Expansion, Diversification, Social Opening, and Professionalization in England, Germany, Russia, and the United States*, edited by Konrad Jarausch. Chicago: University of Chicago Press, 1983.
Engelhardt, Ulrich. *Bildungsbürgertum: Begriffs- und Dogmengeschichte eines Etiketts*. Stuttgart: Klett-Cotta, 1986.
Eyerman, Ron, Lennart Svensson, and Thomas Söderqvist. ed. *Intellectuals, Universities, and the State in Western Modern Societies*. Berkeley: University of California Press, 1987.
Feuer, Lewis. "What is an intellectual?" Pp. 47-58 in *The Intelligentsia and the Intellectuals: Theory, Methods and Case Study*, edited by Aleksander Gella. Beverly Hills: SAGE Publications Inc., 1976.
Fichte, Johann. *On the Nature of the Scholar, and Its Manifestations*. London: John Chapman, 1845 [1806].
Finer, Samuel. *The Man on Horseback: The Role of the Military in Politics*. Harmondsworth: Penguin, 1976.
Fischer, George. *Russian Liberalism: From Gentry to Intelligentsia*. Cambridge: Harvard University Press, 1958.

Fitz-Gibbon, Constantine. *Denazification*. London: Michael Joseph, 1969.
Flexner, Abraham. *Universities: American, English, German*. New York: Oxford University Press, 1930.
Fretlöh-Thomas, Sigrid. "Education for Democracy: A New Analysis of an Example of Inter-Cultural Influence." *Oxford Review of Education* 24, no. 3 (1998): 379-403.
Friedrich, Carl. ed. *Totalitarianism*. Cambridge: Harvard University Press, 1954.
———. "The Failure of a One-Party System: Hitler Germany." Pp. 239-60 in *Authoritarian Politics in Modern Society: The Dynamics of Established One-Party Systems*, edited by Samuel Huntington and Clement Moore. New York: Basic Books, Inc., Publishers, 1971.
Friedrich, Carl, Michael Curtis, and Benjamin Barbar. *Totalitarianism in Perspective: Three Views*. New York: Praeger, 1969.
Fujita, Shoji. "Shushin no seiritsu katei." *The Bulletin of Tokyo University, Department of Education* 8, (1965): 191-224.
Fujita, Tomoji. "Fukuzawa Yukichi no Tenno-kan." Pp. 31-52 in *Chishikijin no Tenno-kan*, ed. Gendai Shiso Kenkyukai. Tokyo: San'itsu Shobo, 1995.
Fulcher, James. "The Bureaucratization of the State and the Rise of Japan." *British Journal of Sociology* 39, no. 2 (1988): 228-54.
Führ, Christoph. *The German Education System since 1945*. Bonn: Inter Nationes, 1997.
Gay, Peter. *Weimar Culture: The Outsider as Insider*. London: Secker & Warburg, 1968.
Geiger, Theodor. *The Conflicted Relationship: The West and the Transformation of Asia, Africa and Latin America*. New York: McGraw-Hill Book Company, 1967.
Gella, Aleksander. ed. *The Intelligentsia and the Intellectuals: Theory, Methods and Case Study*. Beverly Hills: SAGE Publications Inc., 1976.
Gellner, Ernest. *Nations and Nationalism*. Oxford: Blackwell, 1983.
Gerhardt, Uta. "The Medical Meaning of Reeducation for Germany: Contemporary Interpretation of Cultural and Institutional Change." *Paedagogica Historica* 33, no. 1 (1997): 135-55.
Germani, Gino. *Authoritarianism, Fascism, and National Populism*. New Brunswick: Transaction Books, 1978.
Gerschenkron, Alexander. *Economic Backwardness in Historical Perspective: A Book of Essays*. Cambridge: Harvard University Press, 1962.
Gerth, Hans, and C. Wright Mills. ed. *From Max Weber: Essays in Sociology*. London: Routledge & Kegan Paul Ltd., 1970 [1948].
Giddens, Anthony, and Philip Stanworth. "An Economic Elite: A Demographic Profile of Company Chairmen." Pp. 81-101 in *Elites and Power in British Society*, edited by Anthony Giddens and Philip Stanworth. Cambridge: Cambridge University Press, 1974.
Giese, Gerhardt. ed. *Quellen zur deutschen Schulgeschichte seit 1800*. vol. 15 Göttingen: Musterschmidt-Verlag, 1961.
Giles, Geoffrey. *University Government in Nazi Germany: The Example of Hamburg*. New Haven: Institution for Social and Policy Studies, Yale University, 1976.
———. *Students and National Socialism in Germany*. Princeton: Princeton University Press, 1985.
———. "Reeducation at Heidelberg University." *Paedagogica Historica* 33, no. 1 (1997): 201-19.
Gimbel, John. *The American Occupation of Germany: Politics and the Military, 1945-1949*. Stanford: Stanford University Press, 1968.
Glaser, Hermann. *Bildungsbürgertum und Nationalismus: Politik und Kultur im Wilhelminische Deutschland*. Munich: Deutscher Taschenbuch Verlag, 1993.
Gollancz, Victor. *Shall Our Children Live or Die? A Reply to Lord Vansittart on the German Problem*. London: Victor Gollancz Ltd., 1942.

———. *In Darkest Germany*. London: Gollancz, 1947.
Goodman, Roger. "Japan: Pupil Turned Teacher?" Pp. 155-73 in *Lessons of Cross-National Comparison in Education*, edited by David Phillips. Oxford: Triangle Books Ltd., 1992.
Gouldner, Alvin. *The Future of Intellectuals and the Rise of the New Class: A Frame of Reference, Theses, Conjectures, Arguments, and an Historical Perspective on the Role of Intellectuals and Intelligentsia in the International Class Contest of the Modern era*. London: Macmillan, 1979.
Gramsci, Antonio. *The Modern Prince and Other Writing*. London: Lawrence and Wishart Ltd., 1957.
Green, Andy. *Education and State Formation: The Rise of Education Systems in England, France and the USA*. London: Macmillan, 1990.
Grew, Joseph. *Ten Years in Japan: A Contemporary Record Drawn from the Diaries and Private and Official Papers of Joseph C. Grew*. New York: Simon and Schuster, 1944.
Griffith, William. *The Denazification Program in the United States Zone of Germany*, Cambridge: Harvard University, 1950.
Hall, John, and Richard Beardsley. *Twelve Doors to Japan*. New York: McGraw-Hill Inc., 1965.
Hall, Robert. ed. *Kokutai No Hongi: Cardinal Principles of the National Entity of Japan*. Cambridge: Harvard University Press, 1949a.
———. *Shushin: The Ethics of a Defeated Nation*. New York: Bureau of Publications, Teachers College, Columbia University, 1949b.
Hampe, Peter. "Sozioökonomische und psychische Hintergründe der bildungsbürgerlichen Imperialbegeisterung." Pp. 67-79 in *Das Wilhelmische Bildungsbürgertum: Zur Sozialgeschichte seiner Ideen*, edited by Klaus Vondung. Göttingen: Bandenhoeck & Ruprecht, 1976.
Hartshorne, Edward Yarnall. *The German Universities and National Socialism*. London: Allen & Unwin, 1937.
Harvard University Committee. *General Education in a Free Society: Report of the Harvard Committee*. Cambridge: Harvard University Press, 1946.
Hashimoto, Takashi. "The Idea of University and the General Education." *Education Research Magazine* 18, no. 4 (1950): .
Hata, Ikuhiko, *Kanryo no kenkyu: Fumetsuno power 1868-1983*. Tokyo: Kodansha, 1983.
Hata, Takashi. *Sengo daigaku kaikaku*. Tokyo: Tamagawa University Press, 1999.
Hayes, Carlton. *Christianity and Western Civilization*. Westport: Greenwood Press, 1954.
Henning, Uwe, and Achim Leschinsky. ed. *Enttäuschung und Widerspruch. Die konservative Position Eduard Sprangers in Naitonalsozialismus – Analysen, Texte, Dokumente*. Weinheim: Deutscher Studien Verlag, 1991.
Herz, John. "Denazification and Related Policies." Pp. 15-38 in *From Dictatorship to Democracy: Coping with the Legacies of Authoritarianism and Totalitarianism*, edited by John Herz. Westport: Greenwood Press, 1982.
———. ed. *From Dictatorship to Democracy: Coping with the Legacies of Authoritarianism and Totalitarianism*. Westport: Greenwood Press, 1982.
Heydenreuter, Reinhard. "Office of Military Government for Bavaria." Pp. 143-315 in *OMGUS-Handbuch: Die amerikanische Militärregierung in Deutschland 1945-1949*, edited by Christoph Weisz. München: R. Oldenbourg Verlag, 1994.
Hirota, Yotsuya. "Kyu-shisan-kaikyu no botsuraku." Pp. 113-52 in *Sengo Nihon: Senryo to sengo kaikaku 2*, edited by Masanori Nakamura. Tokyo: Iwanami Shoten, 1995.
Hobsbawm, Eric. *The Age of Extremes: The Short Twentieth Century 1914-1991*. London: Abacus, 1994.
Holtom, Daniel. *Modern Japan and Shinto Nationalism: A Study of Present-Day Trends in Japanese Religions*. Chicago: University of Chicago Press, 1943.

Horio, Teruhisa. *Tenno-sei kokka to kyoiku*. Tokyo: Aoki Shoten, 1987.
———. *Kyoiku wo sasaeru shiso*. Tokyo: Iwanami Shoten, 1993.
———. *Nihon no Kyoiku*. Tokyo: University of Tokyo Press, 1994.
Hudemann, Rainer, and Georges-Henri Soutou. ed. *Eliten in Deutschland und Frankreich im 19. und 20. Jahrhundert: Strukturen und Beziehungen*. vol. 2 Munich: R. Oldenbourg Verlag, 1994.
Hull, Cordell. *The Memoirs of Cordell Hull*. vol. II New York: The Macmillan Company, 1948.
Humboldt, Wilhelm von. *The Sphere and Duties of Government* (London: John Chapman, 1954 [1852]).
Hunter, Janet. *The Emergence of Modern Japan: An Introductory History since 1853*. London: Longman, 1989.
Huntington, Samuel. *The Soldier and the State: The Theory and Politics of Civil-Military Relations*. Cambridge: Belknap Press of Harvard University Press, 1957.
———. *The Third Wave: Democratization in the Late Twentieth Century*. Norman and London: University of Oklahoma Press, 1991.
Hussarek, Paul. *Hundhammer: Weg des Menschen und Staatsmannes*. München: Treuga-Verlag, 1950.
Ichikawa, Fusae. "Fujin sansei-ken." Pp. 83-96 in *Showa no sengo-shi*, edited by Saburo Ienaga. Tokyo: Yubunsha, 1976.
Ienaga, Saburo. *Daigaku no jichi*. Tokyo: Hanawa Shobo, 1962.
Iggers, Georg. "Introduction." Pp. 1-48 in *The Social History of Politics: Critical perspectives in West German historical writing since 1945*, edited by Georg Iggers. Leamington Spa: Berg Publishers Ltd., 1985.
Ince, Richard. *A Dictionary of Religion and Religions, Including Theological and Ecclesiastical Terms*. London: Arthur Barker Limited, 1935.
Inoki, Masamichi. "The Civil Bureaucracy: Japan." Pp. 283-301 in *Political Modernization in Japan and Turkey*, edited by Robert Ward and Dankwart Rustow. Princeton: Princeton University Press, 1964.
Iokibe, Makoto. *Beikoku no Nihon senryo seisaku 1*. Tokyo: Chuokoronsha, 1985.
———. "America no tai-nichi senryo kanri koso." Pp. 93-123 in *Senryo to kaikaku*, edited by Masanori Nakamura, Akira Amakawa, Konchao Yung, and Takeshi Igarashi. Tokyo: Iwanami Shoten, 1995.
Jackson, Robert, and Carl Rosberg. *Personal Rule in Black Africa: Prince, Autocrat, Prophet, Tyrant*. Berkeley: University of California Press, 1982.
James, Dorris. *The Years of MacArthur, Volume III: Triumph and Disaster 1945-1964*. Boston: Houghton Mifflin Company, 1985.
Jarausch, Konrad. *Students, Society, and Politics in Imperial Germany: The Rise of Academic Illiberalism*. Princeton: Princeton University Press, 1982.
———. "The Humboldt Syndrome: West German universities, 1945-1989: An Academic *Sonderweg?*" Pp. 33-49 in *German Universities Past and Future: Crisis or renewal?*, edited by Mitchell Ash. Providence: Berghahn Books, 1997.
Jaspers, Karl. "The Rededication of German Scholarship." *The American Scholar* 15, no. 2 (1946): 180-88.
———. *Philosophy and the World: Selected Essays and Lectures*. Chicago: Henry Regnery Company, 1963.
Jessen, Ralph. "Diktatorischen Elitenwecksel und universitäre Milieus. Hochschullehrer in der SBZ/DDR (1945-1967)." Pp. 24-54 in *Universität und Eliten im Osten nach 1945*, edited by Jürgen Kocka. Göttingen: Vandenhoeck & Ruprecht, 1998.
Jordan, Bill. *The State: Authority and Autonomy*. Oxford: Basil Blackwell, 1985.

Kaelble, Harmut. "French Bourgeoisie and German Bürgertum, 1870-1914." Pp. 273-301 in *Bourgeois Society in Nineteenth-Century Europe*, edited by Jürgen Kocka and Allen Mitchell. Oxford: Berg Publishers Limited, 1993.

Kaigo, Tokiomi, and Masao Terasaki. *Sengo Nihon no kyoiku kaikaku 9: Daigaku kyoiku*. vol. 9 Tokyo: Tokyo University Press, 1980 [1969].

Kaizuka, Shigeki. "Senryo-ki no 'Sankyoka Teishi Shirei' no seiritsu katei ni kansuru ichikosatsu." *Bulletin of Institute of Education, University of Tsukuba* 18, no. 1 (1993): 1-13.

Kant, Immanuel. *On History*. New York: The Bobbs-Merill Company, Inc., 1963.

———. *Kant on Education (Über Pädagogik)*. London: Kegan Paul, Trench, Trübner & Co. Ltd., 1992 [1899].

Kaschuba, Wolfgang. "German Bürgerlichkeit after 1800: Culture as symbolic practice." Pp. 392-422 in *Bourgeois Society in Nineteenth-Century Europe*, edited by Jürgen Kocka and Allen Mitchell. Oxford: Berg Publishers Limited, 1993.

Kato, Takashi. *Nambara Shigeru: Kindai-Nihon to chishiki-jin*. Tokyo: Iwanami Shoten, 1997.

Katsuoka, Kanji. "Trainor no shiso to sengo kyoiku kaikaku." Pp. 295-324 in *Sengo kyoiku no sogo hyoka*, edited by Gary Tsuchimochi. Tokyo: Kokusho Kankokai, 1999.

Keenleyside, Hugh, and A. Thomas. *History of Japanese Education and Present Educational System*. Tokyo: Hokuseido Press, 1937.

Kellermann, Henry. *Cultural Relations as an Instrument of U.S. Foreign Policy: The Educational Exchange Program between the United States and Germany, 1945-1954*. Washington, DC: Bureau of Educational and Cultural Affairs, US Department of State, 1978.

Kellner, Hansfried, and Hans-Georg Soeffner. "Cultural Globalization in Germany." Pp. 119-45 in *Many Globalizations: Cultural Diversity in the Contemporary World*, edited by Peter Berger and Samuel Huntington. Oxford: Oxford University Press, 2002.

Kennoki, Toshihiro. *Zoku ushi no ayumi*. Tokyo: Shogakkan, 1977.

———. "Sengo bunkyo fu'un-roku. *Bunkyo* 66 (Spring 1994a): 35-56.

———. "Sengo bunkyo fu'un-roku. *Bunkyo* 67 (Summer 1994b): 41-61.

Kerlinger, Fred. *Japanese Attitude Change from Authoritarianism to Democracy under Occupation Education Reform in Shikoku, October 1948 – November 1949*, Ph.D. dissertation submitted to the University of Michigan, 1953.

Kershaw, Ian. *The Nazi Dictatorship: Problems and Perspectives of Interpretation*. London: Edward Arnold, 1989 [1985].

Kikuchi, Dairoku, Baron. "Japanese Education." *The XIX Century and After* (1907): 1012-23.

Kindai Nihon Kyoiku-seido Shiryo Hensan-kai. ed. *Kindai Nihon Kyoiku-seido Shiryo*. vol. 19 Tokyo: Dainihon Yubenkai Kodansha, 1957.

Kittel, Manfred. *Die Legende von der "Zweiten Schuld": Vergangenheitsbewältigung in der Ära Adenauer*. Berlin: Ullstein, 1993.

Knowlton, James, and Truett Cates. ed. *Forever in the Shadow of Hitler?: The Dispute about the Germans' Understanding of History, Original Documents of the Historikerstreit, the Controversy Concerning the Singularity of the Holocaust*. Atlantic Highlands: Humanities Press, 1993.

Kocka, Jürgen. "Capitalism and Bureaucracy in German Industrialization before 1914." *The Economic History Review* 34, no. 3 (1981): 453-68.

———. *Facing Total War: German Society 1914-1918*. Leamington Spa: Berg, 1984.

———. "German History before Hitler: The debate about the German *Sonderweg*." *Journal of Contemporary History* 23 (1988): 3-16.

———. "Book Review: Eley, G. (1986). From Unification to Nazism: Reinterpreting the German Past. Boston, Allen & Unwin." *Journal of Modern History* 62, no. 1 (1990): 200-202.

———. "The European Pattern and the German Case." Pp. 3-39 in *Bourgeois Society in Nineteenth-Century Europe*, edited by Jürgen Kocka and Allen Mitchell. Oxford: Berg Publishers Limited, 1993.

Kohler, Lotte, and Hans Saner. ed. *Hannah Arendt Karl Jaspers Correspondence 1926-1969.* New York: Harcourt Brace Jovanovich, Publishers, 1992.

Kosai, Yutaka. "The Postwar Japanese Economy, 1945-1973." Pp. 494-537 in *The Cambridge History of Japan. vol. 6: The Twentieth Century*, edited by Peter Duus. Cambridge: Cambridge University Press, 1988.

Koza, Ingeborg. *Deutsch-britische Begegnungen in Unterricht, Wissenschaft und Kunst 1949-1944*. Köln: Böhlau Verlag GmbH & Cie, 1988.

Krane, Jay. "Polls, Press and Occupation Policy." *Columbia Journal of International Affairs* 2, no. 1 (1948): 71-75.

Kreiner, Josef. *Deutschland-Japan Historische Kontakte*. Bonn: Bouvier Verlag Herbert Grundmann, 1984.

Krüger-Bulcke, Ingrid. ed. *James K. Pollock: Besatzung und Staatsaufbau nach 1945 – Occupation diary and private correspondence 1945-1948*. München: R. Oldenbourg Verlag, 1994.

Kubo, Yoshizo. *Tainichi senryo seisaku to sengo kyoiku kaikaku*. Tokyo: Sanseido, 1984.

Kühnl, Reinhard. "The German *Sonderweg* Reconsidered: Continuities and Discontinuities in Modern German History." Pp. 115-58 in *Rewriting the German Past*, edited by Reinhard Alter and Peter Monteath. Atlantic Highlands: Humanities Press, 1997.

Langewiesche, Dieter. "Liberalism and the Middle Classes in Europe." Pp. 40-69 in *Bourgeois Society in Nineteenth-Century Europe*, edited by Jürgen Kocka and Allen Mitchell. Oxford: Berg Publishers Limited, 1993.

Lattimore, Owen. *The Situation in Asia*. Boston: Little Brown, 1949.

Lawson, Robert. *Reform of the West German School System, 1945-1962*. Ann Arbor: The University of Michigan, School of Education, 1965.

———. "Die Politik der Umstände: Eine Kritik der Analysen des Bildungswandels im Nachkriegsdeutschland." Pp. 23-39 in *Umerziehung und Wiederaufbau: Die Bildungspolitik der Besatzungsmächte in Deutschland und Österreich*, edited by Manfred Heinemann. Stuttgart: Klett-Cotta, 1981.

Lehmann, Bernhard. *Katholische Kirche und Besatzungsmacht in Bayern 1945-1949 im Spiegel der OMGUS-Akten*. Munich: Kommissionverlag UNI-Druck, 1994.

Lerner, Daniel, Ithiel de Sola Pool, and George Schueller. "The Nazi Elite." Pp. 194-318 in *World Revolutionary Elites: Studies in Coercive Ideological Movements*, edited by Harold Lasswell and Daniel Lerner. Cambridge: MIT Press, 1965.

Littell, Franklin. "The Protestant Churches and Totalitarianism (Germany 1933-1945)." Pp. 108-19 in *Totalitarianism*, edited by Carl Friedrich. Cambridge: Harvard University Press, 1954.

Loth, Wilfried. "Die Historiker und die Deutsche Frage: Ein Rückblick nach dem Ende des Kalten Krieges." Pp. 11-28 in *Die deutsche Frage in der Nachkriegszeit*, edited by Wilfried Loth. Berlin: Akademie Verlag, 1994.

Lowe, Roy. "English Elite Education in the Late Nineteenth and Early Twentieth Centuries." Pp. 147-62 in *Bildungsbürgertum im 19. Jahrhundert: Bildungssystem und Professionalisierung in internationalen Vergleichen*, edited by Werner Conze and Jürgen Kocka. Stuttgart: Klett-Cotta, 1985.

Lundgreen, Peter. "Zur Konstituierung des „Bildungsbürgertums": Berufs- und Bildungsauslese der Akademiker in Preußen." Pp. 79-108 in *Bildungsbürgertum im 19. Jahrhundert:*

Bildungssystem und Professionalisierung in internationalen Vergleichen, edited by Werner Conze and Jürgen Kocka. Stuttgart: Klett-Cotta, 1985.

———. "Mythos Humboldt Today: Teaching, Research, and Administration." Pp. 127-48 in *German Universities Past and Future: Crisis or Renewal?*, edited by Mitchell Ash. Oxford: Berghahn Books, 1997.

MacArthur, Douglas. *MacArthur kaisoki*. Tokyo: Asahi Shinbunsha, 1964.

Mann, Michael. *The Sources of Social Power. vol. 2: The Rise of Classes and Nation-States, 1760-1914*. Cambridge: Cambridge University Press, 1993.

Mannheim, Karl. *Ideology and Utopia: An Introduction to the Sociology of Knowledge*. London: Routledge & Kegan Paul Ltd., 1936.

Marcuse, Herbert. *Reason and Revolution: Hegel and the Rise of Social Theory*. New York: Humanity Books, 1999 [1941]).

Marshall, Byron. "Professors and Politics: The Meiji Academic Elite." *Journal of Japanese Studies* 3, (1977a): 71-97.

———. "The Tradition of Conflict in the Governance of Japan's Imperial Universities." *History of Education Quarterly* 17, no. 4 (1977b): 384-406.

———. *Learning to Be Modern: Japanese Political Discourse on Education*. Boulder: Westview Press, Inc., 1994.

Martin, Bernd. *Japan and Germany in the Modern World*. Oxford: Berghahn Books, 1995.

Maruyama, Masao, and Kanichi Fukuda. ed. *Nambara Shigeru Kaikoroku*. Tokyo: University of Tokyo Press, 1989.

Masuda, Hiroshi. "Kyoshoku-tsuiho no shogeki." Pp. 79-112 in *Senryo to Kaikaku. vol. 2, Sengo Nihon senryo to sengo kaikaku*, edited by Masanori Nakamura, Akira Amakawa, Koncha Yun, and Takeshi Igawashi. Tokyo: Iwanami Shoten, 1995.

Mayo, Marlene. "Psychological Disarmament: American Wartime Planning for the Education and Re-Education of Defeated Japan, 1943-1945." Pp. 21-128 in *The Occupation of Japan: Educational and Social Reform*, edited by Thomas Burkman. Norfolk: The MacArthur Memorial Foundation, 1980.

———. "American Wartime Planning for Occupied Japan: The Role of the Experts." Pp. 3-51 in *Americans as Proconsuls: United States Military Government in Germany and Japan, 1944-1952*, edited by Robert Wolfe. Carbondale: Southern Illinois University Press, 1984.

McClelland, Charles. *State, Society, and University in Germany 1700-1914*. Cambridge: Cambridge University Press, 1980.

McCloy, John. *The Challenge to American Foreign Policy*. Cambridge: Harvard University Press, 1953.

———. "From Military Government to Self-Government." Pp. 114-23 in *Americans as Proconsuls: United States Military Government in Germany and Japan, 1944-1952*, edited by Robert Wolfe. Carbondale: Southern Illinois University Press, 1984.

Mears, Helen. *America-jin no kagami: Nihon*. Tokyo: Ainekkusu, 1995. (The original version: *Mirror for Americans: Japanese*. Houghton Mifflin Co., 1948.)

Mehnert, Klaus, and Heinrich Schulte. ed. *Deutschland Jahrbuch 1949*. Essen: Im West-Verlag, 1949.

Meinecke, Friedrich. *Erlebtes 1862-1901*. Leipzig: Koehler & Amelang, 1941.

Meißner, Kurt. *Grundlagen der nationalen Erziehung in Japan*. Tokyo: Deutsche Gesellschaft für Natur- und Völkerkunde Ostasiens, 1934.

Menck, Clara. "The Problem of Reorientation." Pp. 281-307 in *The Struggle for Democracy in Germany*, edited by Gabriel Almond. Chapel Hill: The University of North Carolina Press, 1949.

Merritt, Anna, and Richard Merritt. *Public Opinion in Occupied Germany*. Urbana: University of Illinois Press, 1970.

Mirsky, Dmitri. *The Intelligentsia of Great Britain*. London: Victor Gollancz Ltd., 1935.

Mommsen, Wolfgang. *Imperial Germany 1867-1918: Politics, Culture, and Society in an Authoritarian State*. New York: Arnold, 1995.

Montgomery, John. *Forced to Be Free: The artificial revolution in Germany and Japan*. Chicago: The University of Chicago Press, 1957.

Moore, Barrington, Jr. *Social Origins of Dictatorship and Democracy: Lord and Peasant in the Making of the Modern World*. London: Allen Lane the Penguin Press, 1966.

Moore, Ray. "Reflections in the Occupation of Japan." *Journal of Asian Studies* 38, no. 4 (1979): 721-34.

———. "Kami no heishi: Nihon wo kirisuto-kyo-koku tosuru MacArthur no kokoromi." Pp. in *Tenno ga Bible wo yonda hi*, edited by Ray Moore. Tokyo: Kodansha, 1982.

Moore, William. "Some German Attitudes Toward U. S. Occupation." *Columbia Journal of International Affairs* 2, no. 1 (1948): 76-82.

Mosca, Gaetano. *The Ruling Class*. New York: McGraw-Hill Book Company, 1939.

Mosse, George. *The Crisis of German Ideology: Intellectual Origins of the Third Reich*. London: Weidenfeld and Nicolson, 1966.

Mosse, Werner. "Nobility and Bourgeoisie in Nineteenth-Century Europe: A Comparative View." Pp. 70-102 in *Bourgeois Society in Nineteenth-Century Europe*, edited by Jürgen Kocka and Allen Mitchell. Oxford: Berg Publishers Limited, 1993.

Murata, Noboru. *Kokka to kyoiku: Spranger seiji kyoiku shiso no kenkyu*. Kyoto: Minerva, 1969.

Müller, Sinfried. *Schulpolitik in Bayern inm Spannungsfeld von Kultusbürokratie und Besatzungsmacht 1945-1949*. Munich: R. Oldenbourg Verlag, 1995.

Nakae, Chomin. *San suijin keirin mondo*. New York: Weatherhill, 1984 [1887].

Nakamura, Masanori. "Meiji-Ishin to sengo kaikaku." Pp. 251-95 in *Sengo minshu shugi*, edited by Masanori Nakamura, Akira Amakawa, Koncha Yun, and Takeshi Igawashi. Tokyo: Iwanami Shoten, 1995.

———. *Gendai-shi wo manabu: Sengo kaikaku to gendai Nihon*. Tokyo: Yoshikawa Kobunkan, 1997.

Nakauchi, Toshio, Tsuneichi Takeuchi, Akira Nakano, and Sadahiko Fujiwara. *Nihon kyoiku no sengoshi*. Tokyo: Senseido, 1987.

Nakayama, Shigeru. *Rekishi to shite no gakumon*. Tokyo: Chuo Koronsha, 1974.

Neuhaus, Rolf. ed. *Dokumente zur Hochschulreform 1945-1959*. Wiesbaden: Franz Steiner Verlag GmbH, 1961.

Neumann, Franz. "Military Government and the Revival of Democracy in Germany." *Columbia Journal of International Affairs* 2, no. 1 (1948): 3-20.

———. ed. *The Democratic and the Authoritarian State: Essays in Political and Legal Theory*. New York: Free Press of Glencoe, 1957.

Night, Maxwell. *The Gemran Executive, 1890-1933*. Stanford: Stanford University Press, 1952.

Nihon Kindai Kyoiku Shiryo Kenkyukai (NKK). ed. *Kyoiku Sasshin Iinkai, Kyoiku Sasshin Shingikai Kaigi-roku: Sokai 1*. vol. 1 Tokyo: Iwanami Shoten, 1995.

———. ed. *Kyoiku Sasshin Iinkai, Kyoiku Sasshin Shingikai Kaigi-roku: Sokai 3*. vol. 3 Tokyo: Iwanami Shoten, 1996.

———. ed. *Kyoiku Sasshin Iinkai, Kyoiku Sasshin Shingikai Kaigi-roku: Tokubetsu Iinkai 5*. vol. 10 Tokyo: Iwanami Shoten, 1998a.

———. ed. *Kyoiku Sasshin Iinkai, Kyoiku Sasshin Shingikai Kaigi-roku: Shiryo.* vol. 13 Tokyo: Iwanami Shoten, 1998b.

Nipperdey, Thomas. "Wehlers 'Kaiserreich': Eine kritische Auseinandersetzung." *Geschichte und Gesellschaft* 1, (1975): 539-60.

———. "Preußen und die Universität." Pp. 65-85 in *Preußen: Seine Wirkung auf die deutsche Geschichte,* edited by Karl Erdmann. Stuttgart: Klett-Cotta, 1985.

———. *Deutsche Geschichte 1866-1918.* vol. 1 Munich: Verlag CH Beck, 1990.

Nishi, Toshio. *MacArthur no 'hanzai': Hiroku Nihon senryo.* vol. 1 Tokyo: Nihon Kogyo Shimbunsha, 1983.

Norman, Herbert. ed. *Origins of the Modern Japanese State: Selected writings of E. H. Norman.* New York: Pantheon Books, 1975.

Nowak, Kurt. "Protetantische Eliten. Aspekte eines Vergleichs zwischen Deutschland und Frankreich (1870/71-1918)." Pp. 156-73 in *Eliten in Deutschland und Frankreich im 19. und 20. Jahrhundert: Strukturen und Beziehungen,* edited by Rainer Hudemann and Georges-Henri Soutou. Munich: R. Oldenbourg Verlag, 1994.

Ochs, Kimberly, and David Phillips. *Towards a Structural Typology of Cross-National Attraction in Education (A progress report).* Lisboa: EDUCA, 2002.

O'Donnell, Guillermo A. *Modernization and Bureaucratic-Authoritarianism: Studies in South American Politics.* Berkeley: Regents of the University of California, 1973.

Okakura, Kazuo. *The Book of Tea.* New York: Dover Publications, Inc., 1964 [1906].

Oppen, Beate von. ed. *Documents on Germany under Occupation 1945-1954.* London: Oxford University Press, 1955.

Oppenheim, Lassa. *International Law: A Treatise.* vol. 2 London: Longmans, Green and Co., 1944.

Orr, Mark. *Education Reform Policy in Occupied Japan,* Ph.D. dissertation submitted to the University of North California, 1954.

Osaki, Hitoshi. *Daigaku Kaikaku 1945-1999.* Tokyo: Yuhikaku, 1999.

Pareto, Vilfredo. *The Mind and Society: Non-Logical Conduct.* vol. 1 London: Jonathan Cape, 1935a.

———. *The Mind and Society: Theory of Derivations.* vol. 3 London: Jonathan Cape, 1935b.

Passin, Herbert. *Society and Education in Japan.* Tokyo: Kodansha International Ltd., 1965.

———. *Encounter with Japan: The American Army Language School.* New York: Harper & Row, Publishers, Inc., 1982.

Paulsen, Friedrich. *Geschichte des Gelehrten Unterrichts: Auf den deutschen Schulen und Universitäten. Vom Ausgang des Mittelalters bis zur Gegenwart. Mit besonderer Rücksicht auf den klassischen Unterricht.* Leipzig: Verlag von Veit & Comp., 1896.

———. *Die deutschen Universitäten und das Universitätsstudium.* Berlin, 1902.

———. *The German Universities and University Study.* New York: Longmans, Green, and Co., 1906.

Perkin, Harold. "The Pattern of Social Transformation in England." Pp. 207-18 in *The Transformation of Higher Learning 1860-1930: Expansion, Diversification, Social Opening, and Professionalization in England, Germany, Russia, and the United States,* edited by Konrad Jarausch. Chicago: University of Chicago Press, 1983.

Peterson, Edward. *The American Occupation of Germany: Retreat to Victory.* Detroit: Wayne State University Press, 1977.

Phillips, David. "Lindsay and the German Universities: An Oxford Contribution to the Post-War Reform Debate." *Oxford Review of Education* 6, no. 1 (1980): 91-106.

———. ed. *German Universities after the Surrender: British Occupation Policy and the Control of Higher Education.* Oxford: University of Oxford Department of Educational Studies, 1983a.

———. *Universitätsreform in der britischen Besatzungszone 1945-1948*. Cologne: Studien und Dokumentationen zur deutschen Bildungsgeschichte, 1983b.

———. "British Educational Policy in Occupied Germany: Some problems and Paradoxes in the Control of Schools and Universities." Pp. 75-88 in *International Currents in Educational Ideas and Practices*, ed. Peter Cunningham and Colin Brock. Leicester: History of Education Society, 1988.

———. "On Comparing." Pp. 15-20 in *Learning from Comparing: New Directions in Comparative Educational Research. Volume 1: Contexts, classrooms and outcomes*, edited by Robin Alexander, Patricia Broadfoot and David Phillips. Oxford: Symposium Books, 1999.

———. "Beyond Travellers' Tales: Some Nineteenth-Century British Commentators on Education in Germany." *Oxford Review of Education* 26, no. 1 (2000a): 49-62.

———. "Learning from Elsewhere in Education: Some Perennial Problems Revisited with Reference to British Interest in Germany." *Comparative Education* 36, no. 3 (2000b): 297-307.

Phillips, David, and Ochs Kimberly. "Processes of Policy Borrowing in Education: Some Explanatory and Analytical Devices." *Comparative Education* 39, no. 4 (2003): 451-61.

Piper, Reinahrd. ed. *'Historikerstreit' Die Dokumentation der Kontroverse um die Einzigartigkeit der nationalsozialistischen Judenvernichtung*. Munich: Humanities Press, 1987.

Pipes, Richard. "The Historical Evolution of the Russian Intelligentsia." Pp. 47-62 in *The Russian Intelligentsia*, edited by Richard Pipes. New York: Columbia University Press, 1961.

Plischke, Elmer. "Denazification in Germany." Pp. 198-225 in *Americans as Proconsuls: United States Military Government in Germany and Japan, 1944-1952*, edited by Robert Wolfe. Carbondale: Southern Illinois University Press, 1984.

Pritchard, Rosalind. *The End of Elitism?: The Democratisation of the West German University System*. New York: St. Martin's Press, 1990.

———. "Academic Freedom and Autonomy in the United Kingdom and Germany." *Minerva* 36, (1998): 101-24.

Read, Christopher. *Culture and Power in Revolutionary Russia: The Intelligentsia and the Transition from Tsarism to Communism*. London: Macmillan, 1990.

Rein, Mónica. *Politics and Education in Argentina 1946-1962*. New York: M. E. Sharpe, 1998.

Reischauer, Edwin. *The Japanese*. Cambridge: Harvard University Press, 1977.

Reisner, Edward. *Nationalism and Education since 1789: A Social and Political History of Modern Education*. New York: The Macmillan Company, 1922.

Remy, Steven. *The Heidelberg Myth*. Cambridge: Harvard University Press, 2002.

Rieff, Philip. ed. *On Intellectuals: Theoretical Studies Case Studies*. Garden City: Doubleday & Company, Inc., 1969.

Rikkyo Gakuin Hayku-niju-go-nen-shi Henshu Iinkai (Rikkyo). ed. *Rikkyo Gakuin hyaku-niju-go-nen-shi*. vol. 1 Tokyo: Dainippon Insatsu, 1996.

Ringer, Fritz. *Education and Society in Modern Europe*. Bloomington: Indiana University Press, 1979.

———. *The Decline of the German Mandarins: The German Academic Community 1890-1933*. Hanover and London: University Press of New England, 1990 [1969].

———. *Fields of Knowledge: French Academic Culture in Comparative Perspective, 1890-1920*. Cambridge: Cambridge University Press, 1992.

Rosenberg, Hans. "The Pseudo-Democratisation of the Junker Class." Pp. 81-112 in *The Social History of Politics: Critical Perspectives in West German Historical Writing since 1945*, edited by Georg Iggers. Heidelberg: Berg Publishers Ltd., 1985.

Rosenzweig, Beate. *Erziehung zur Demokratie?*. Stuttgart: Franz Steiner, 1998.

Roth, Andrew. *Dilemma in Japan*. London: Civtor Gollancz, 1946.

Rubenstein, Richard. "Holocaust and Holy War." *The Annals of the American Academy of Political and Social Science* 548, (November 1996): 23-44.

Rust, Val. "The German Image of American Education through the Weimar Period." *Paedagogica Historica* 33, no. 1 (1997): 25-44.

Said, Edward. *Representations of the Intellectual: The 1993 Reith Lectures*. London: Vintage, 1995.

Samuel, Richard, and R. Hinton Thomas. *Education and Society in Modern Germany*. London: Routledge & Kegan Paul Limited, 1949.

Sato, Hideo. ed. *Rengokoku-sasikoshireikan-soshireibu Minkan-joho-kyoiku-kyoku no jinji to kiko*. Tokyo: Kokuritu Kyoiku Kenkyusho, 1984.

Schlander, Otto. "Der Einfluß von John Dewey und Hans Morgenthau auf die Formulierung der Re-educationspolitik." Pp. 40-52 in *Umerziehung und Wiederaufbau: Die Bildungspolitik der Besatzungsmächte in Deutschland und Österreich*, edited by Manfred Heinemann. Stuttgart: Klett-Cotta, 1981.

Schleunes, Karl. *Schooling and Society: The Politics of Education in Prussia and Bavaria 1750-1900*. Oxford: Berg Publishers Limited, 1989.

Schneider, Ullrich. "Hochschulreform, *Studium generale* und das *Collegium Academicum* Heidelberg 1945-1952." *Bildung und Erziehung* 36, no. 1 (1983): 55-67.

———. "The Reconstruction of the Universities in American Occupied Germany." Pp. 1-8 in *Hochschuloffiziere und Wiederaufbau der Hochschulwesens in Westdeutschland 1945-1952. Teil 2: Die US-Zone*, edited by Manfred Heinemann. Hildesheim: Verlag August lax, 1990.

Schonberger, Howard. *Aftermath of War: Americans and the Remaking of Japan, 1945-1952*. Kent: The Kent State University Press, 1989.

Schriewer, Jürgen. ed. *Discourse Formation in Comparative Education*. Frankfurt am Main: Peter Lang, 2000.

Schwantes, Robert. "Foreign Employees in the Development of Japan." Pp. in *The Modernizers: Overseas Students, Foreign Employees, and Meiji Japan*, edited by Ardath Burks. Boulder: Westview Press, 1985.

Sebald, William J. *With MacArthur in Japan*. New York: Norton and Co., 1965.

Seki, Masako. *Nihon no daigaku kyoiku kaikaku: rekishi, genjo, tembo*. Tokyo: Tamagawa University Press, 1988.

Shibata, Masako. "Controlling National Identity and the Role of Education: The Vision of State Formation in Meiji Japan and the German *Kaiserreich*." *History of Education* 33, no. 1 (2004a): 75-85.

———. "Religious Education Reform under the US Military Occupation: The Interpretation of State Shinto in Japan and Nazism in Germany." *Compare* 34, no. 4 (2004b): 423-41.

———. "Education, National Identity and Religion in Japan in an Age of Globalisation." in *World Yearbook of Education 2005: Globalisation and Nationalism in Education*, edited by David Coulby, Crispin Jones, and Evie Zambeta. London: Kogan Page, 2005a.

———. "Educational Borrowing in Japan in the Meiji and Post-War Eras." Pp. 147-68 in *Educational Borrowing: Historical Perspectives*, edited by David Phillips and Kimberly Ochs. Oxford: Symposium Books, 2005b.

Shils, Edward. "The Intellectuals and the Powers: Some Perspectives for Comparative Analysis." Pp. 25-48 in *On Intellectuals: Theoretical Studies Case Studies*, edited by Philip Rieff. Garden City: Doubleday & Company, Inc., 1969.

Shimizu, Ikutaro. "Konnichi no kyoiku tetsugaku." *Shiso* 322 (1951): 1-7.

Silberman, Bernard. "Elite Transformation in the Meiji Restoration: The Upper Civil Service 1868-1873." Pp. 233-59 in *Modern Japanese Leadership: Transition and Change*, edited by Bernd Silberman and Harry Harootunian. Tucson: The University of Arizona Press, 1966.

———. *Cages of Reason: The Rise of the Rational State in France, Japan, the United States, and Great Britain.* Chicago: The University of Chicago Press, 1993.

Skocpol, Theda. *States and Social Revolutions: A Comparative Analysis of France, Russia, and China.* Cambridge: Cambridge University Press, 1979.

Smith, Helmut. *German Nationalism and Religious Conflict: Culture, Ideology, Politics, 1870-1914.* Princeton: Princeton University Press, 1995.

Smith, Jean. ed. *The Papers of General Lucius D. Clay: Germany 1945-1949.* Bloomington: Indiana University Press, 1974.

Smith, Thomas. "Japan's Aristocratic Revolution." Pp. 135-40 in *Class, Status, and Power*, edited by Rreinhard Bendix and Seymour Lipset. London: Routledge & Kegan Paul Ltd., 1967.

Snyder, Louis. *Roots of German Nationalism.* London: Bloomington, 1978.

Speier, Hans. *Social Order and the Risks of War: Papers in Political Sociology.* Cambridge: The MIT Press, 1952.

Spinks, Charles. "Indoctrination and Re-Education of Japan's Youth." *Pacific Affairs* 17, no. 1 (1944): 56-70.

Spranger, Eduard. *Wilhelm von Humboldt und die Humanitatsidee.* Berlin: Verlag von Reuther & Reichard, 1909.

———. *Volk, Staat, Erziehung. Gesammelte Reden und Aufsätze.* Leipzig, 1932.

Stern, Fritz. *The Failure of Illiberalism.* London: George Allen & Unwin Ltd., 1972.

———. *The Politics of Cultural Despair: A Study in the Rise of German Ideology.* Berkeley: University of California Press, 1974.

Sternburg, Speck von. "American and German University Ideals; An Address at the Commencement of the University of the South." *Sewanee Review,* (July 1904): 361-67.

Stimson, Henry, and McGeorge Bundy. *On Active Service in Peace and War.* New York: Harper & Brothers, 1948.

Stock-Morton, Phyllis. *Moral Education for a Secular Society: The Development of Morale Laïque in Nineteenth Century France.* Albany: State University of New York Press, 1988.

Stolper, Gustav. *German Realities.* New York: Reynal & Hitchcock, 1948.

Struve, Walter. *Elites against Democracy: Leadership Ideals in Bourgeois Political Thought in Germany, 1890-1933.* Princeton: Princeton University Press, 1973.

Sugihara, Seishiro. *Nihon no Shinto/Bukkyo to Seikyo-bunri Soshite shukyo-kyoiku.* Tokyo: Bunka Shobo Hakubunsha, 1992.

Sugo, Hiroshi, Seiichi Miyahara, and Seiya Munakata. ed. *America kyoiku shisetudan hokokusho yokai.* Tokyo: Kokumin Tosho Kankokai, 1950.

Suzuki, Eiichi. "Haisen chokugo no Kyoiku Chokugo hihan." *Kyoiku* 396 (1981): 70-81.

———. *Nihon senryo to kyoiku kaikaku.* Tokyo: Keiso Shobo, 1983.

Takahashi, Shiro. "Shinto-shirei to Tenno-sei." Pp. 74-90 in *Sengo kyoiku kaikaku tsushi*, edited by Meisei University Sengo Kyoiku-shi Kenkyu Centre. Tokyo: Meisei University Press, 1993.

Talmon, Jacob. *Political Messianism: The Romantic Phase.* London: Secker & Warburg, 1960.

———. *The Origins of Totalitarian Democracy.* New York: WW Norton & Company Inc., 1970 [1955].

———. *Totalitarian Democracy and After: International Colloquium in Memory of Jacob L. Talmon.* Jerusalem: The Magnes Press, 1984.

———. *Myth of the Nation and Vision of Revolution: Ideological Polarization in the Twentieth Century.* New Brunswick: Transaction Publishers, 1991.

Taylor, Alan. *The Course of German History: A Survey of the Development of Germany since 1815.* London: Hamish Hamilton, 1945.

Tent, James. *Mission on the Rhine: Reeducation and Denazification in American Occupied Germany*. Chicago: University of Chicago Press, 1982.
——. *The Free University of Berlin: A Political History*. Indianapolis: Indiana University Press, 1988.
Terasaki, Masao. "Nihon no kindai kyoiku to kirisuto-kyo-shugi gakko." *Kyoshoku Kenkyu* 8, (1997).
——. *Daigaku no Jiko-henkaku to Autonomy*. Tokyo: Toshindo, 1998.
——. *Daigaku kyoiku no sozo: Rekishi, system, curriculum*. Tokyo: Toshindo, 1999.
Teschke, John. *Hitler's Legacy: West Germany Confronts the Aftermath of the Third Reich*. New York: Peter Lang, 1999.
Thwing, Charles. *The American and the German University: One Hundred Years of History*. New York: Macmillan Company, 1928.
Tilly, Charles, Louise Tilly, and Richard Tilly. *The Rebellious Century 1830-1930*. London: JM Dent & Sons Ltd., 1975.
Tompkins, Stuart. *The Russian Intelligentsia: Makers of the Revolutionary State*. Norman: University of Oklahoma Press, 1957.
Toyama, Shigeki. *Meiji Ishin*. Tokyo: Iwanami, 1951.
Trainor, Joseph. *Educational Reform in Occupied Japan: Trainor's Memoir*. Tokyo: Meiji University Press, 1983.
Trimberger, Ellen. "A Theory of Elite Revolution." *Studies in Comparative International Development* 7, (Fall 1972): 191-207.
——. *Revolution From Above: Military Bureaucrats and Development in Japan, Turkey, Egypt, and Peru*. New Brunswick: Transaction Books, 1978.
Tsuchimochi, Gary Hoichi. "Beikoku tai-nichi kyoiku shisetsudan hokokusho no seiritu jijo ni kansuru sogoteki kenkyu." *Bulletin of the Faculty of Education, Nagoya University* 31, (1984): 256-63.
——. *Senryo Doitsu no kyoiku kaikaku: America taidoku kyoiku shisetsudan to America taidoku shakai-ka iinkai*. Tokyo: Meiji University Press, 1989.
——. *6-3 sei kyoiku no tanjo: Sengo kyoiku no genten*. Tokyo: Yushisha, 1992.
——. *Education Reform in Postwar Japan: The 1946 U. S. Education Mission*. Tokyo: University of Tokyo Press, 1993a.
——. "Gakko seido kaikaku." Pp. 123-44 in *Sengo kyoiku kaikaku tsushi*, edited by Meisei University Sengo Kyoiku-shi Kenkyu Centre. Tokyo: Meisei University Press, 1993b.
Tsurumi, Shunsuke. *Senjiki Nihon no Seishin-shi*. Tokyo: Iwanami Shoten, 1982.
Turnbull, George. *The Educational Theory of J. G. Fichte: A Critical Account, together with Translations*. London: The University Press of Liverpool Limited, 1926.
Vaillant, Jérôme. "Was tun mit Deutschland?: Die französische Kulturpolitik im besetzten Deutschland von 1945 bis 1949." Pp. 201-11 in *Umerziehung und Wiederaufbau: Die Bildungspolitik der Besatzungsmächte in Deutschland und Österreich*, edited by Manfred Heinemann. Stuttgart: Klett-Cotta, 1981.
Vansittart, Robert. *Black Record: German Past and Present*. London: Hamish Hamilton, 1941.
——. *Lessons of My Life*. London: Fight for Freedom, 1942.
Vogel, Walter, and Christoph Weisz. ed. *Akten zur Vorgeschichte der Bundesrepublik Deutschland 1945-1949. Band 1. Teil 1&2*. Munich: R. Oldenbourg Verlag, 1989.
Vondung, Klaus. "Zur Lage der Gebildeten in der wilhelminischen Zeit." Pp. 20-33 in *Das wilhelmische Bildungsbürgertum: Zur Sozialgeschichte seiner Ideen*, edited by Klaus Vondung. Göttingen: Bandenhoeck & Ruprecht, 1976.
Ward, Robert. "The Legacy of the Occupation." Pp. 29-56 in *The United States and Japan*, edited by Herbert Passin. Englewood Cliffs: Prentice-Hall, Inc., 1966.

———. ed. *Political Development in Modern Japan*. Princeton: Princeton University Press, 1968.
Ward, Robert, and Dankwart Rustow, ed. *Political Modernization in Japan and Turkey*. Princeton: Princeton University Press, 1964.
Weber, Max. *Gesammelte Politische Schriften*. Tübingen: JCB Mohr (Paul Siebeck), 1958.
———. *Economy and Society: An Outline of Interpretive Sociology*. Berkeley: University of California Press, 1978.
Weegmann, Carl von. *Die vaterländische Erziehung in der japanischen Volksschule: Tokuhon und Shushinsho*. Tokyo: Deutsche Gesellschaft für Natur- und Völkerkunde Ostasiens, 1935.
Wehler, Hans-Ulrich. *The German Empire 1871-1918*. Leamington Spa: Berg Publishers, 1985.
———. *Deutsche Gesellschaftsgeschichte: Vom Feudalismus des Alten Reiches bis zur Defensiven Modernisierung der Reformära 1700-1815*. vol. 1 München: Verlag CH Beck, 1987a.
———. *Deutsche Gesellschaftsgeschichte: Von der "Deutschen Doppelrevolution" bis zum Beginn des Ersten Weltkrieges 1849-1914*. vol. 3 Munich: Verlag CH Beck, 1987b.
Weil, Hans. *Die Entstehung des deutschen Bildungsprinzips*. Bonn: Friedrich Cohen, 1930.
Weinacht, Paul-Ludwig. "Steps toward Westernization in the German Educational System 1945 and 1989." *Paedagogica Historica* 33, no. 1 (1997): 351-67.
Weisz, Christoph. ed. *OMGUS-Handbuch: Die amerikanische Militärregierung in Deutschland 1945-1949*. Munich: R. Oldenbourg Verlag, 1994.
Wenke, Hans. *Education in Western Germany. A Postwar Survey*. Washington DC: The Library of Congress, European Affairs Division, 1953.
Wildes, Harry. *Typhoon in Tokyo: The Occupation and Its Aftermath*. New York: The Macmillan Company, 1954.
Wilkinson, Rupert. "Elites and Effectiveness." Pp. 215-24 in *Governing Elites*, edited by Rupert Wilkinson. New York: Oxford University Press, 1969.
Wolfe, Robert. ed. *Americans as Proconsuls: United States Military Government in Germany and Japan, 1944-1952*. Carbondale: Southern Illinois University Press, 1984.
Woller, Hans. *Gesellschaft und Politik in der amerikanischen Besatzungszone: Die Region Ansbach und Fürth*. Munich: R. Oldenbourg Verlag, 1986.
Woodard, William. *The Allied Occupation of Japan 1945-1952 and Japanese Religions*. Leiden: E. J. Brill, 1972.
Wunderlich, Herbert. *The Japanese Textbook Problem and Solution, 1945-1946*, Ph.D. dissertation submitted to Stanford University, 1952.
Wyman, David. *The Abandonment of the Jews: America and the Holocaust, 1941-1945*. New York: Pantheon Books, 1984.
Yamamoto, Reiko. "Educational Purge (Part I): Purges by SCAP Memorandum (Memo Case)." *Research Bulletin of Educational History of the Postwar Japan* 4 (1987): 133-54.
———. "Senryo-ka ni okeru kyoshoku tsuiho kensho: CIE staff no shisaku to sono haikei." Pp. 189-216 in *Sengo kyoiku no sogo hyoka*, edited by Hoichi Tsuchimochi. Tokyo: Kokusho Kankokai, 1999.
Ziemer, G. "Our Educational Failure in Germany." *American Mercury*, (June 1946): 726-33.
Zink, Harold. *The United States in Germany: 1944-1955*. Westport: Greenwood Press, Publishers, 1957.

Index

Abe, Yoshishige, 74, 85, 98n24
ACJ. *See* Allied Council for Japan
Alexander, Thomas, 117, 131
Allied Council for Japan (ACJ), 59–60
The Allied Powers: dissension among, 59–60, 107–11, 120–21, 127, 129, 151n106; resistance in Germany against, 63–65, 136; US hegemony in Japan, 59–60
Althoff, Friedrich, 45, 52n46. *See also* The Minister/Ministry of Education, in Prussia
Amano, Teiyu, 82
The American Council on Education, 118
Anderson, Ronald, 99n32
Ariga, Tetsutaro, 83
aristocracy: in Germany, 9–10, 12, 35–37, 42–43, 48, 48n3, 116. *See also Junker*; in Japan 18–19, 28. *See also Daimyo*
Armstrong, Hamilton, 62
Auerbach, Bethold, 40
Australia, 65
Austria, 31n7, 35
authoritarianism: in Germany, 5, 38, 45, 49n7, 111, 124–25, 129, 141, 146–47n29, 170; in Japan, 5, 62, 73–74, 78, 85

Ballantine, Joseph, 98n21
Ballou, Robert, 61
Barth, Karl, 129
Bäuerle, Theodor, 120–21, 132–33. *See also* The Minister/Ministry of Education, in Württemberg-Baden
Bavaria, 39, 114, *115*, 116, 119–21, 129, 131–33, 137–39, 148n54. *See also* The Minister/Ministry of Education, in Bavaria
BCOF. *See* The British Commonwealth Occupation Force
Belgium, 70
Benedict, Ruth, 62
Benton, William, 118
The Biedermeier period, 44–45
Bildung or bilden, xii, 39–40, 42–43, 46–47, 52n50, 55–56, 121–22
Bildungsbürgertum, 8, 11, 28–29, 42–48, 166–67
Bismarck, Otto von, 35–36, 38, 41, 52n48
The Blackship Turmoil, 17
Blakeslee, George, 62, 66, 98n21
The board of trustees system: in Germany, 139–41; in Japan, 88–89, 92–93
Böhm, Franz, 132. *See also* The Minister/Ministry of Education, in Hesse

Borton, Hugh, 62, 64, 98n21, 107–8
Bosse, J. R., 45. *See also* The Minister/Ministry of Education, in Prussia
Bremen, *115*, 120, 133, 154n144. *See also* The Minister/Ministry of Education, in Bremen
The British Commonwealth Occupation Force (BCOF), 60, 96n4
Brown, Delmer, 70
Buddhism, 32n13, 81
Bureaucracy: in Germany, xii, 10, 36, 39–40, 42–47, 119–21, 166–68; in Japan, xii, 10, 18, 22–23, 27–28, 30, 40, 73–75, 78, 84–89, 95
Bushido, 32n13
Byrnes, James, 108–9, 118

CAC. *See* The Civil Administration Committee
Canada, 65
CASA. *See* The Civil Affairs Staging Area
The Casablanca Conference (1943), 107
Caselmann, Christian, 133
Catholicism: in Germany, 38, 42, 120–21, 128–29, 132–33, 152n121, 153n130, 167; in Japan, 99–100n47
CATS. *See* The Civil Affairs Training School
CC. *See* The Control Council
CCG (BE). *See* The Control Commission for Germany (British Element)
CDU. *See* The Christian Democratic Union/*Christlich-Demokratische Union*
Chamberlain, Basil, 62
Chiang, Kai-shek, 96n4
China, 24, 29, 31n7, 32n13, 97–98n18; government of, 20–59, 64–65, 96n4
The Christian Democratic Union/*Christlich-Demokratische Union* (CDU), 132, 150n72
The Christian Social Union/*Christlich-Soziale Union* (CSU), 150n72

Christianity: in Germany, 38–41, 112, 128–33, 139, 144, 162, 169; in Japan, 62, 67, 74–75, 79–80, 82–83, 90, 94, 99–100n47, 104n144, 162, 170
Churchill, Winston, 98n24
CI&E. *See* The Civil Information & Education Section
The Civil Administration Committee (CAC), 78
The Civil Affairs Staging Area (CASA), 71, 81
The Civil Affairs Training School (CATS), 71, 82
The Civil Information & Education Section (CI&E), 66–67, 70–77, 81–82, 84–86, 88–90, 93–96; staff's qualification of, 71–72, 77, 100n62, 117; The steering committee of, 76
Clay, Lucius, 60, 108, 112–19, 131, 133, 147n36, 148n44; alleged personality of, 109; authority of, 60, 96n5; sense of rivalry to MacArthur, 117–18
co-education: in Germany, 50n21; in Japan, 86, 103n123
Cohen, Theodore, 69, 71, 97n7, 98n23
The Cold War: in East Asia, 77, 95, 109, 114, 160–61, 170; in Europe, 108–9, 139, 142
colonialism, xii, 8–9, 17–19, 98n24
The Committee on Post-War Programs, 78, 111
communism: in Germany, 108–9, 142, 150n76; in Japan, 64–65, 69, 77, 85, 88, 103n116
Conant, James B., 72, 100n64
The Conant Report, 94
Confucianism, 18–22, 32n13, 74, 81, 162
The Constitution: of the Empire of Japan/The Imperial Constitution (1889), 20, 65–66; of Germany (1949). *See* The *Grundgesetz*; of Japan (1946), 65–66, 81, 84
continuity vs. discontinuity debates, 4–6, 170

Index

The Control Commission for Germany (British Element) (CCG (BE)), 111
The Control Council: Directive No. 24, 113; Directive No. 32, 126; Directive No. 38, 113; Directive No. 54, 131; Law No. 8, 148n48
Costell, Edwin, 117
Crofts, Alfred, 88
CSU. *See* The Christian Social Union/*Christlich-Soziale Union*
curriculum: in Germany, 40–41, 130, 137, 141–43; in Japan, 22, 24, 40, 78, 81–82, 85, 94

Daimyo, 17–18, 27. *See also* aristocracy, in Japan
De Gaulle, Charles, 110
democracy: in Germany, xii, 35, 109, 112–13, 117–18, 122–32, 136–40; in Japan, xii, 5–6, 62–63, 66, 71–74, 77–78, 92–94, 96n4, 97n15
denazification, 113, 119, 126–28, 136–39, 148n53, 148–49n54; classification in screening, 114–15, 127; in comparison with the purge in Japan, 68, 79–80; of school teachers, 127; in the Soviet zone, 127, 155n168; of students, 126–27, 136, 138–39; of university academics, 136–39
Dessoir, Max, 45, 52n46
Dewey, John, 5, 40, 72, 125
The Dodge Plan, 87
Donovan, Eileen, 71
Dotoku, 82. *See also* education in Japan, on moral
Dreiklassenwahlrecht, 36, 48n4
Dyke, Ken, 71, 83

E&CR. *See* The Education & Cultural Relations Division
E&RA. *See* The Education & Religious Affairs Branch
Ebbinghaus, Julius, 122, 137
Eden, Anthony, 108
The Education & Cultural Relations Division (E&CR), 116–17, 125–26
The Education & Religious Affairs Branch (E&RA), 116–17, 119–20, 130–33, 137, 149n61; staff's qualification of, 117, 123–24
education in Germany: administration of, 39–40, 44–45, 48, 119–26, 132–35, 137–42, 162–64; on citizenship, 40, 130, 142–43; equality of, 39–49, 50n21, 124, 130–34, 144, 163; high valuation by the US, 118–19, 125–26, 134–35; on moral, 40–41; on religion, 40–41, 128, 130–32, 162, 169. *See also* Christianity, in Germany; religion, in Germany
education in Japan: administration of, 22, 34n32, 72–75, 79, 84–85, 89–90, 92–93; on citizenship, 22; equality of, 21–22, 78, 85–87, 90–92, 130–33; on moral, 22–23. *See also Dotoku*; on religion, 66, 80–81
education in US: equality of, 22, 32n21, 124, 130–31
Eells, Walter, 88, 90, 104n136
Einheitsschule, 130–31, 133, 153n129, 162. *See also* school in Germany, system of multi-and single-track
The Elementary School Ordinance (1890), 21
elite: definition of, 11, 13n11, 13n12, 13–14n14; formation in Germany, 9–12, 27–31, 38, 41–38, 55–56; formation in Japan, 9–12, 18–19, 23–31, 55–56; group cohesion in Germany, 11–12, 36, 41–45, 47–48; group cohesion in Japan, 11, 28, 30–31, 42, 55–56, 144, 162, 164; in the military, 28, 36
Emperor. *See Tenno*
England, 36–37, 44, 46, 48n3, 52n40, 129, 166, 170
exiles from Germany, 111, 152n113

Falk, Adalbert, 41. *See also* The Minister/Ministry of Education, in Prussia
The Far Eastern Commission (FEC), 3, 59–60, 64–65, 99n30
FEC. *See* The Far Eastern Commission
Fendt, Franz, 120. *See also* The Minister/Ministry of Education, in Bavaria
feudalism: in Germany, 35, 43; in Japan, 5, 17, 64, 88
Fichte, Johan G., 39, 42, 46, 50n21, 111
Flexner, Abraham, 134
Flitner, Wilhelm, 143
foreign experts in Meiji Japan, 24
Fragebogen, 68, 114, 138, 143, 148n48
France, 24–25, 31n7, 36, 39, 42, 44, 46, 48n3, 80, 120–21, 127–29, 143, 145n8, 151n106, 152n121, 166–68, 170; government of, 17, 35, 65, 108–10, 112
Führerprinzip, 125
Fukuzawa, Yukichi, 22, 28–29, 34n39, 165
The Fundamental Code of Education (1872), 21
The Fundamental Law of Education (1947), 81, 84

general education in Germany. *See Studium generale*
general education in Japan, 93–94
German problem, 109–10, 143–44
Germany: government of, 112, 156n177; local government of, 107, 113–14, 116–17, 119–21, 131, 140. *See also* Bavaria; Bremen; Hesse; Württemberg–Baden
Gollancz, Victor, 110
Grace, Alonzo, 126
Grew, Joseph, 62, 64, 97–98n18
Griffith, William, 114
The *Grundgesetz*, 66, 116, 130
Gymnasium, 43, 124–25, 132

The Hague Rules on Land Warfare, 63
Hall, Robert King, 81–82
Hartshorne, Edward, 117, 137, 149n60
Henderson, Harold, 61, 97n16
Herder, Johann G., 42
The Herrenchiemsee Conference (1948), 116
Hesse, 52n40, *115*, 119–20, 130, 132, 137. *See also* The Minister/Ministry of Education, in Hesse
Heuss, Theodor, 120. *See also* The Minister/Ministry of Education, in Württemberg-Baden
HICOG. *See* The Office of the High Commissioner (US), Germany
Hipp, Otto, 120. *See also* The Minister/Ministry of Education, in Bavaria
Hitler, Adolf, 107, 129, 136
The Holocaust, 110, 128, 146–47n29, 152n113
Holtom, Daniel, 61–62
Hornbeck, Stanley, 62
Hull, Cordell, 59, 63, 65
Humboldt, Wilhelm von, 39–40, 42, 50n17, 140–41
Hundhammer, Alois, 120–22, 129–32, 150n72, 152–53n123, 153n138. *See also* The Minister/Ministry of Education, in Bavaria

IA&C. *See* The Internal Affairs & Communications Division
ICD. *See* The Information Control Division
Ichikawa, Fusae, 68
The Imperial Household, 12n3, 17–18, 20, 62, 64–65, *69*, 99n37
India, 65
industrialization: in Germany, 9–10, 31n7, 35–37, 43–48, 49n8; in Japan, 9–10, 18–20, 24, 30, 31n7
The Information Control Division (ICD), 116–17, 126

The Initial Post-Surrender Policy for
 Japan, 60, 63, 66
Inoue, Kowashi, 24, 26
The Institute on Re-Education of the
 Axis Countries, 125–26, 135
intellectuals: in Germany, 42–43, 46,
 166; identity of, 11, 13–14n14,
 14n15; in Japan, 12, 28–29; low
 valuation of US education/culture in
 Germany, 122–24, 126; in the rest of
 Europe, 29, 165–70, 172n18,
 172n22, 172n24
The Internal Affairs & Communications
 Division (IA&C), 113, 116
international law, 6, 63
Italy, 60, 95, 139
Ito, Hirobumi, 20

Japan: adoption of German models in
 the Meiji period, 2, 4, 18, 24–25,
 88–89, 94; adoption of US models in
 the Meiji period, 22, 24–25, 33n21;
 government of, 59, 64–69, 71–75,
 80–81, 87–88, 90, 99n37;
 government in the Meiji period,
 17–24, 26–31, 33n17, 172n21; local
 government of, 85, 87–88, 91
The Japanese Education Reform
 Committee (JERC), 3, 73–77, 83–95,
 101n75, 121
The Japanese Educators Committee
 (JEC), 75, 101n73
"Japanophilistics" and "Japanophobics"
 in the State Department, 62, 64,
 98n21
Jaspers, Karl, 114, 122, 127, 151n80,
 154n49, 171
JEC. *See* The Japanese Educators
 Committee
JERC. *See* The Japanese Education
 Reform Committee
The Jews: criticisms of US policies,
 128–29, 152n113, 152n114; lobbying
 activities in US, 111, 128–29,
 152n113; persecution of, 138,
 152n113, 152n114, 156n174
Judo and *Kendo*, 82
Junker, 35, 37, 47, 111, 116. *See also*
 aristocracy, in Germany

Kaigo, Tokiomi, 82
Kaiser. *See* Wilhelm I
Kant, Immanuel, 39–41, 74, 111, 122,
 125
Katayama, Tetsu, 67, 74
Kellermann, Henry, 111, 139
Kikuchi, Dairoku, 176
Kokutai ideology, 62
Korea, 29
Koto Gakko, 24, 26, 74, 87, 90–91,
 99n32
Koza system, 26, 88, 92
Kultur, 38, 40–41, 44, 46–47, 55–56,
 118–19, 123–26, 139, 163, 166,
 168–69
Kulturhoheit, 10, 44, 48, 119, 123, 131,
 133, 144, 164
Kulturkampf, 41
Kuratorium, 140–42
Kyoiku Chokugo, 23, 74–75, 83–84,
 163, 175
Kyoiku Sasshin Iinkai/Shingikai. *See*
 The Japanese Education Reform
 Committee

labor union movement in Japan, 69, 71
Ladejinsky, Wolf, 71
Länderrat, 119, 149–50n80;
 Kulturausschuss, 119
land reform: in Germany, 108, 116; in
 Japan, 68–69, 71
legitimacy of the state: in Germany,
 8–11, 35, 169; in Japan, 8–11, 18,
 30, 169
liberalism: in Germany, 35–36, 44–47;
 in Japan, 4–5, 22, 29, 61–62, 65–66,
 74–77, 84, 86–87, 93, 97n15
Lichtenburg, Bernhard, 129

Litt, Theodor, 143
The London Conference (1947), 109
The London Conference (1948), 109
The Long-Range Policy Statement for German Re-Education, 109, 111
Loon, Gerard W. van, 126

MacArthur, Douglas, 61, 72–73, 96n1, 100n64, 109, 116; alleged personality of, 97n7, 116; authority of, 59–60, 96n6; commitment to the Christianization of Japan, 67
Maeda, Tamon, 74, 79
Mann, Horace, 33n21, 39, 125
Marshall, George C., 109
Mayer, Rupert, 129
McCloy, John, 109–10
Mears, Helen, 62
Meinecke, Friedrich, 117, 122, 154n149
meritocracy: in Germany, 9–11; in Japan, 9–11, 18, 24, 27–28, 30–31, 165
middle class: in Germany, 9–12, 35–37, 42–47, 49n11, 166–67; in Japan, 28
militarism: in Germany, 108, 111, 135, 138, 143; in Japan, 27–28, 61, 64, 67–68, 82
The Minister for Ecclesiastical Affairs of the Nazis, 128
The Minister/Ministry of Education: in Bavaria, 116, 119–21, 127, 129, 132, 148n54; in Bremen, 120, 133; in Hesse, 119–20, 130, 132; in Japan, 5, 21, 68, *69*, 71, 73–79, 82, 84–87, 89–90, 92–95, 98n24, 103n123, 104n144, 164; in Prussia, 40–41, 45–46, 42n46; in Württemberg-Baden, 119–132–33
The Ministry of Finance in Japan, *69*, 86–87
The Ministry of Home Affairs in Japan, 74, *69*, 84
modernization projects: in Germany, xiii, 9–10, 35–37, 39; in Japan, xiii, 2, 8–10, 17–19, 21–31, 55, 165, 168–69

Molotov, Vyacheslav, 109
Montgomery, John, 100n49
Morgenthau, Henry, 62, 107
Mori, Arinori, 21–22, 24, 33n17, 74, 165
Morito, Tatsuo, 74
Mosca, Gaetano, 13n11, 13n12
The Moscow Conference (1943), 107

Nambara, Shigeru, 73, 75–76, 86, 89, 91–93, 103n106
The National Diet of Japan, 20, 84–85, 90, 99n32
The National Education Association, 118
national identity: in Germany, 37–42, 44, 47, 50n21, 55, 122, 150n76, 151n80, 163–66; in Japan, 19–20, 29, 163
Nazism, 49n7, 52n46, 61, 111–19, 122–29, 131–38, 142, 148n53; resistance against, 120–21, 129, 136
The Netherlands, 65
New Zealand, 65
Nietzsche, Friedrich, 52n50
Nihongawa Kyoiku-ka Iinkai. See The Japanese Educators Committee
Nugent, Donald, 71, 100n61

Oberschule, 133
Obrigkeitsstaat, 38. See also authoritarianism, in Germany
OECD, 92–93, 141
The Office of the High Commissioner (US), Germany (HICOG), 139, 142, 156n177
The Office of Military Government for Bavaria (OMGBY), 129–31
The Office of Military Government for Germany of the US (OMGUS), 3, 107–9, 112–14, 116–24, 126–34, 136, 138–42, 163–64
The Office of Military Government for Hesse (OMGHE), 132
Okakura, Kazuo, 32n16

OMGHE. *See* The Office of Military Government for Hesse
OMGUS. *See* The Office of Military Government for Germany of the US
OMGBY. *See* The Office of Military Government for Bavaria
The Ordinance of the Imperial University (1886), 23
Orr, Mark, 71–72, 84–85, 97–98n18, 100n62

Pareto, Vilfredo, 13n11, 13n12
Patterson, Robert, 118
Paulmann, Christian, 120, 133. *See also* The Minister/Ministry of Education, in Bremen
Paulsen, Friedrich, 42, 45–46, 52n50
The Philippines, 65
PH&W. *See* The Public Health & Welfare Division
Poland, 40, 48n3; government of, 108–9
The Positive Policy for the Reorientation of the Japanese, 60–61, 79
The Potsdam Agreement/Declaration: Japan's acceptance of, 59; Soviet's violation of, 108
The *Preußische Allgemeine Landrecht*, 39, 41, 44
The Public Health & Welfare Division (PH&W), 116
purge: in comparison with denazification, 68; of Japanese communists, 88; of Japanese militarists/ultra-nationalists, 68, 69, 75, 77, 79–80, 83, 87–88

re-education: of the Germans, 109–12, 116, 118, 122, 125–26, 128, 135–36, 150n77; of the Japanese, 63, 72
refugees returning to Germany, 108, 145n8
The *Reichskonkordat* (1933), 129
The *Reichstag*, 36
Reischauer, Edwin, 62, 64–65, 97n17

Reisner, Edward, 39
religion: in Germany, xii–xiii, 40–41, 45, 111–12, 125, 128–32, 162–63, 170; in Japan, xii–xiii, 19–23, 33n22, 61–62, 66–68, 74–75, 80–81, 83, 94, 162–63, 167. *See also* Christianity, in Germany; Christianity, in Japan; *Shinto*
Roosevelt, Franklin, 60–61, 96n4, 107–8, 110, 116, 134
Rousseau, J. J., 37, 40
The Royal Institute of International Affairs, 63
Russia, 17, 20, 28–29, 31n7, 165–67

Samurai, 17–18, 21–22, 27–28, 32n13
SCAP. *See* Supreme Commander for the Allied Powers
Schleiermacher, Friedrich, 46
The School Board Act (1948), 85
The School Education Law (1947), 90
school in Germany: in the Nazi period, 127; re-opening of, 127, 151n102; system of multi- and single-track, 56, 130–33, 144, 153n129, 163. *See also Einheitsschule*
school in Japan: re-opening of, 103n118; system of multi- and single-track, 4, 26, 56, 74, 85–87, 90–92, 100–101n65, 103n122
Schramm, Franz, 132. *See also* The Minister/Ministry of Education, in Hesse
Scotland, 24
Sebald, William, 60
The Second United States Education Mission to Japan (USEMJ2), 73, 92
Semmon Gakko, 26, 33n27, 90–91
Shihan Gakko, 90, 91
Shimizu, Ikutaro, 73
Shinto, 19, 20, 61, 80–81, 162; *Kokka Shinto*, 20, 22–23, 33n22, 66, 80, 162; *Kokka Shinto* in comparison with Nazism, 61, 79; *Shinto* Directive, 66, 79–81

Shusin, 22, 74, 79, 81–83, 162. *See also* education in Japan, on moral
The Situation Report – Japan, 77, 83
The Social Democratic Party/Sozialdemokratische Partei Deutschlands (SPD), 120, 132–33, 154n144
social strata in Germany, xiii, 9–11, 35–37, 41–43, 45–47, 111, 124–25, 138, 146–47n29, 166–69; in Japan, xiii, 9–11, 18–19, 21, 27–31, 88, 172n21
social studies: in Germany, 130; in Japan, 82
socialist movements in Germany, 130
Sombart, Werner, 45
The Soviet Union, 59, 64–65, 96n4, 98n24, 107–10, 112, 116, 121, 123, 127–29, 139, 141, 145n8, 150n76
SPD. *See* The Social Democratic Party/Sozialdemokratische Partei Deutschlands
Speier, Hans, 109
Spranger, Eduard, 50n17, 122, 143, 150–51n82, 154n149
Staatsbürgererziehung/Staatsbürgerkunde. *See* education in Germany, on citizenship; social studies, in Germany
Stalin, Joseph, 109
Stand/Stände. *See* status group
The State Department, 3, 62, 64, 72, 76–77, 81, 97n18, 107, 109, 111, 113–14
The State-War-Navy Coordinating Committee (CWNCC), 64–65
status group in Germany, 42–44; concept of, 11
Stein, Erwin, 120, 130, 132, 154n140. *See also* The Minister/Ministry of Education, in Hesse
Stimson, Henry, 61, 109
Stoddard, George, 72, 86
Stowe, Calvin, 39
Studium generale, 140–43

Studt, Konrad von, 40
The Stuttgart Speech (1949), 108–9
Supreme Commander for the Allied Powers (SCAP), 59–60, 63–68, 71–73, 75, 77–80, 82–87, 95–96, 96n1, 100n49, 109, 117
Switzerland, 139
SWNCC. *See* The State-War-Navy Coordinating Committee

Takahashi, Seiichiro, 74
Tanaka, Fujimaro, 22
Tanaka, Kotaro, 74, 79
Taylor, Alan J. P., 61, 97n10
Taylor, John, 111–20, 126, 136, 142
teachers' union in Japan, 76–77, 82, 85
Tenno, 32n22, 59, 74–75, 79, 84, 86, 96, 97n18, 99n32, 99n38, 162; demystification of, 61–62, 64–65, 95; prosecution for war crimes of, 63–65; SCAP's use of the authority of, 63–66, 83; as spiritual authority, 8, 20, 23, 33n22, 63, 99n32; *Terakoya*, 21
textbook revision: in Germany, 127–28, 150n75; in Japan, 79, 81–82, 85
The Tokugawa period, 17–19, 21, 22–23, 28, 30, 31n2, 32n13, 33n17, 165
Trainor, Joseph, 3, 71, 74, 76, 93
Treitschke, Heinrich von, 111
Truman, Harry, 60, 116
Turkey, 19

ultra-nationalism in Japan, 61, 64, 68, 78, 82
The United Kingdom, 24–25, 31n7, 76n4, 98n24, 150n75, 172n18; government of, 17, 59–60, 62–63, 65, 96n4, 107–12, 121, 127–29, 137, 145n8, 151n90, 152n113, 152n114
The United Nations, 61, 63
The United States Education Mission to Germany, 117, 119, 124, 128, 130, 135, 139–40, 142; reception of the

Report in Germany, 118; reception of the Report in US, 149n67
The United States Education Mission to Japan, 75, 78, 85–86, 88–90, 93, 117–18; reception of the Report in Japan, 72–73, 77
The United States Government: in Germany, 107–14, 118, 125, 139, 145n14, 152n113, 152n114, 155n169; in Japan, 17, 31n1, 59, 61–66, 71, 80–81; *See also* The Office of Military Government for Germany of the US; Supreme Commander for the Allied Powers
The United States Post-Surrender Policy, 60, 63, 66
universal suffrage of Japanese women, 68
The University Accreditation Association, 89
The University Control Law (1949), 93
University in Germany: academic autonomy of, 33–34n31, 44–47, 140–41; academic hierarchy of, 135, 141; academic interaction between England and Germany, 52n40, 155n165; academic interaction within Germany, 10, 12, 43–44, 48; academic interaction between US and Germany, 117, 134–35, 139, 145n177; academic standard of, 10, 43–44, 48; administration of, 45, 139–42; Free University in Berlin, 140–41; insularity against society, 45–46, 135–36, 139–40, 142; political compliance with the State, 45, 47, 52n48; re-opening of, 136–37, 155n162; surrender to the Nazis/Nazism, 52n46; University of Berlin/Humboldt, 33–34n31, 46, 117, 134, 141; University of Erlangen, 137–38, 155n161; University of Halle, 52–53n51, 134; University of Heidelberg, 33–34n31, 122, 134, 137–38, 143, 155n161;
University of Marburg, 121–22, 134, 137, 139, 142, 144n161; University of Munich, 134, 137–38, 155n161
University in Japan: academic autonomy of, 10, 24, 27, 33–34n31, 92–93; academic demarcation of, 10–11, 26–28, 30–31, 88; academic hierarchy of, 10–11, 27–30, 87–88; academic interaction with Japan, 10, 26, 30–31; academic standards of, 10, 26, 28; administration of, 88–90; Imperial University (in general), 22, 24, 26–29, 74, 86–93, 164; Imperial University of Kyoto, 23, 27, 74; Imperial University of Tokyo/Tokyo University, 10, 22, 23–24, 26–29, 33n27, 75, 86, 88; post-graduate courses, 91–92; The University Planning Committee (UPC), 121, 137
University in UK: University of Oxford, 155n165, 167–68
University in US: Columbia University, 71, 127, 134
UPC. *See* The University Planning Committee
USEMG. *See* The United States Education Mission to Germany
USEMJ. *See* The United States Education Mission to Japan
USEMJ2. *See* The Second United States Education Mission to Japan

values: socio-cultural in Germany, 10, 12, 35, 40–41, 43–44, 47–48, 55, 123, 139, 141, 144, 162–63, 166–69; socio-cultural in Japan, 6, 10–12, 20, 28–31, 70, 81, 95, 162–63, 172n21
Vansittart, Robert, 61, 107, 110
The Vatican, 129, 132
The Versailles Education Conference (1945), 125, 134
Vieweg, Willy, 130

Volk, 38, 122, 150–51n82
Volksschule, 40–41, 55–56, 127, 130–31

The War Department, 72, 111
Weber, Max, 11, 36, 42–43, 45, 52n48
The Weimar period, 37, 111, 118, 121, 127, 129, 131
Weltanschauung, 128–29, 162
Westernization projects, 2, 11, 17, 20–22, 24, 27–31, 31n3, 55, 165; movement against, 20, 28–29, 32n16, 128, 165, 167
Wilhelm I, 35–36, 44

Wilhelm III, Friedrich, 39
Wirtschaftsbürgertum, 43, 47
Woodard, William, 67
World War One, 63, 70, 172n24
Württemberg-Baden, *115*, 119–20, 132–33, 136–38, 140. *See also* The Minister/Ministry of Education, in Württemberg-Baden
Wunderlich, Herbert, 82, 100n62

Yoshida, Shigeru, 76, 86

Zook, George, 118, 149n65

About the Author

Masako Shibata is Lecturer in the History of Education at the International Student Center, Tsukuba University, Japan.

BRADNER LIBRARY
SCHOOLCRAFT COLLEGE
18600 HAGGERTY ROAD
LIVONIA, MICHIGAN 48152